ol Yard
ter Knapp
Aged Illustrates Revolving-Door J
Violent Crime by Young People:
Math and Reading to Inner City Pupils
e faces of Harlem
Recorded in Sch
Reading Skill Called Debatable
Houston Is Setting the Pace in Sunbelt Boo
Unreso
School Tax: Can Reform Aid Quality?
nvades the Home
e perils maternity wards
Federal Funds Pour Into Sunbelt States
Housing Scandals
ay Be Called Out of Bounds
Now migration is to the 'exurbs
Downtown Hartford Marks a Resurgenc
Cities of the North
orkers Worried About Support
Hartford Battles Suburbs for Federal Aid
Mass transit, little
mass Area Jurisdictions Plan
The Shopping Mall Moves
Sunbelt Region Leads Nation in Growt
of Population
city exodu

The Urban Prospect

BY MELVIN R. LEVIN

THE URBAN PROSPECT
Planning, Policy, and Strategies for Change

MELVIN R. LEVIN, Rutgers University

Duxbury Press, North Scituate, Massachusetts

Library of Congress Cataloging in Publication Data

Levin, Melvin R.   1924-
    The urban prospect.

    Includes index.
    1.   Cities and towns—United States.   2.   Cities and
towns—Planning—United States.   I.   Title.
HT123.L38   309.2'62'0973   77-23248
ISBN 0-87872-133-9

Duxbury Press

A Division of Wadsworth Publishing Company, Inc.

The Urban Prospect: Planning, Policy, and Strategies for Change was
edited and prepared for composition by Bea Gormley. Interior design
was provided by Kathy Nitchie and the cover was designed by Garrow
Throop.

L.C. Card No.: 77-23248
    ISBN 0-87872-133-9
    Printed in the United States of America
    1 2 3 4 5 6 7 8 9 - 81 80 79 78 77

For Barbara

CONTENTS

PREFACE

Some people think that baseball is the great American game, but Thorstein Veblen said no. It has been real estate from the beginning, he said, from the speculating colonials to the footloose pioneers to Babbittish development boosters; from George Washington to Jacob Astor and beyond. But perhaps even Veblen was wrong, and America's real avocation is gratuitous political advice. In democratic countries all are free to make useful suggestions, to complain, and very occasionally to cheer and congratulate. If one presumes to add his voice to the chorus, he must be aware of the dangers, not of being attacked but of being misconstrued, pigeonholed, or, worst of all, ignored. Moreover, in the middle of the 1970s there is a special danger in picking one's way through the minefield of domestic urban policy. There is a pervasive sense of disillusionment resulting from too many unfulfilled promises, too little realistic judgment, and far too much naive moralizing.

There is a particularly baffling problem in the cities. Urban planners know how to do some modest things reasonably well; they can identify a number of problems in need of solution, and they can do a reasonably satisfactory day's work in land use planning for untroubled communities. But consistently they are either mistrusted or bypassed. Part of the reason for uneasiness concerning the urban planning profession is clear enough; although they were more tools than villains, planners were accomplices in the destruction of poor people's housing through urban renewal and highway programs. Planners, minor bureaucrats with major pretensions, were too willing to place the tools of their trade at the service of urban developers, highway engineers, and country-club suburbs. They will be a long time living down this legacy.

By definition, a tool is an instrument, an object to be used rather than consulted. And this raises another question; Why is there room for political scientists, public administrators, economists, and lawyers, lawyers, lawyers in the inner circles of political advisors, but no room for planners?

Any number of hypotheses can be offered to explain this phenomenon, but perhaps the simplest is best. By and large, planners seem to have little to contribute to a successful political campaign for city, state, or federal office, or to helping the politician retain office when the victories are won. Land use programs, still the planner's major stock in trade, are either politically unexciting, good only for a one-shot pictorial spread, or potentially explosive. Unfortunately, these professionals who have staked out the maintenance and development of cities as their own area of expertise have been unable to convince politicians that their prescriptions work.

As is obvious in reading this book, the author is an incrementalist. However, a few of my proposals (for example, see chapter 4, "Manpower: Is Full Employment Feasible?") could be construed as moderately controversial. But, there is no point in believing that the clock stopped in 1968, and all we need to do is to rewind all the old programs that ran down when the Republicans took over the presidency in the late 1960s. What is needed now are programs which offer a maximum of political attraction and a minimum of political risk in an uncertain, crisis-ridden world. This book identifies problems and suggests programs which promise genuine relief for some of the distress of this urban nation in the mid-1970s.

The fundamental assumption of this study is that cities can be a political graveyard for liberals, particularly in the borderland where issues of race, class, land use, housing, and crime meet and intertwine in dense and thorny thickets. But in the absence of constructive, coalition-building alternatives, the field will be left open for subtle and overt demagoguery exploiting divisiveness and fear. The author assumes that liberal evasion or weak, waffling assent to backlash is as clear a road to ruin as head-on confrontations exacerbating the strong apprehensions of many Americans. Fortunately, although the problems are genuine, they are susceptible to solution.

Individual chapters of this book cover some of the major urban problem areas: population, race, crime, employment, land use, education, and urban government. Each of the chapters starts with a short overview, summarizing patterns, trends, and problems, and ends with recommendations for future action, including warnings against certain types of new programs which promise to create more problems than they would solve. Transportation and environment are discussed in the land use chapter, and health in the chapter on population. Women's liberation is not discussed at all because, in the author's opinion, it will disappear as a special social concern within a decade under the powerful pressure of highly educated women turned to careers instead of housewifery and integrated into a unisex labor force.

Overall, the organization of this book reflects a personal view of urban priorities and possibilities. Obviously entire books can be, and have been , written on topics allotted only five or ten pages here. Not wishing to prepare an exhaustive series to fill a five-foot shelf, I have opted for brevity, combined with persuasive (it is hoped) logic to suggest lines of action for the remainder of the 1970s and on into the 1980s.

One special note: the reader accustomed to lengthy, arid sections of unbroken print may be surprised by an assortment of illustrative cartoons. The author has, on occasion, been accused of undue levity, an irritating propensity to find humor in misfortune. Such is not the intent; the objective is improving the readability of the book. Serious topics need not be doused in vinegar and buried in boredom. In a world drowning in grim communications, an occasional island of merriment should be welcome.

In pursuing this delicate and elusive balance between hope and useless exhortation, I would like to thank Joseph Slavet for his advice and assistance. Larry Bennett was an invaluable research assistant. I am also deeply indebted to Mrs. Vera Lee, Mrs. Barbara Swan, and Mrs. Nancy Campbell for their patience and tireless typing of draft copy. I should also like to expres my appreciation for the painstaking and thorough editing performed by Beatrice Gormley. But the analysis, suggestions, errors, and misfires are all my own.

MRL
New Brunswick 1976

1

INTRODUCTION

In the mid-1970s sizable portions of America's largest cities show advanced deterioration. Housing is boarded over, plywood replaces windows, open spaces are junkyards. Large portions of the cities are considered unsafe by their inhabitants; the three-lock door, the terrorized old folk, the broken mailboxes, the guard dogs are surface manifestations of a breakdown in a basic sense of security. The schools contribute to the deterioration; in the worst systems students are merely passed from grade to grade for ten or twelve years. With the help of fifteen or twenty thousand dollars in public educational expenditures, they eventually emerge as embittered functional illiterates, candidates for menial labor or the penitentiary. And if the city people seem relatively unconcerned with the choking air pollution and the nerve-taxing racket, with the clogged, potholed streets and rising tax rates, it is because they have even more important worries. Prices are high and going higher, jobs for many are scarce and pay badly, and overall there is a pronounced sense of terror, of senseless violence lurking in the shadows. And the city people are thoroughly frustrated by a system that seems unable to respond to their needs.

Moreover, many suburbs begin to share urban traumas. Little pockets of poverty fester; there are crime and mini-slums and racial confrontations. Ten or twenty miles from Bedford-Stuyvesant and Chicago's South Side there are reminders that the problems of urban America do not stop at the central city frontier. Rip-offs and muggings in the suburbs are met with thinly disguised efforts to zone out the blacks and the poor like the carriers of some dreaded urban plague. There is a pervasive unease with rising taxes and prices, declining investments, and a lurking fear of an economic depression which would not spare the middle class. The suburbs rest on the foundation of regular paychecks and payment of professional fees. Liquid financial reserves are small, and converting the major investment—the house and grounds—into usable cash requires a buyer and a mortgage, not easy to find in hard times.

Disillusionment with the Great Society

While all this might strike the reader as a banal recapitulation of the eleven o'clock news, there are certain perversities worthy of note. In the late 1960s and early 1970s there was a chorus of learned persons

feeding ammunition to a Republican administration bent on demol-
ishing social programs. Critics of the Great Society were persuasive and
discouraging. They proved conclusively that historically speaking,
things used to be much worse, and that the poor and the blacks are ungrateful because their own greed, encouraged by left-wing bleeding
hearts, has caused them to forego immigrant-style gratitude and give in
to unappeasable envy of their better endowed neighbors.

Moreover, the critics said, such problems as do exist are mainly the
product of the behavior of the poor themselves. The poor are the
feckless dregs of a society replete with opportunity for anyone with
enough self-discipline to study and work. These drug addicts, thieves,
and philanderers condemn themselves, their neighbors, and their
children to poverty, prisons, and an early grave. Worst of all, they make
the cities unsafe for others and perhaps even bankrupt in the process.
Since their problems are caused by personal, moral failings and since
the poor are the generators of urban blight, it follows that government
cannot do much about most urban problems except wring its hands. The
alternative, it is claimed, is to waste vast amounts of money on useless
social programs run by incompetent bureaucrats.

While this recapitulation of a score of books and journal articles
written by conservatives and quasi-conservatives is by no means a new
departure—critics of the New Deal were much more vicious—what is
surprising is the depth of disillusionment, the sense of betrayal, and
often the outright attacks by professed liberals. Discouraged by crime
in the streets, by incompetence and pilfering in poverty programs, by a
complex of pathologies that seemed impervious to all of the hopeful, exciting initiatives of the Kennedy and Johnson years, they were inclined,
albeit reluctantly, to go along with the right-wing critics. This was the
real news—not the problems, but the strange near-consensus that the
slums and the poor, the crime, the breakdown of city services are
beyond the reach of government intervention.

To some extent the fracturing of the liberal coalition was a response
to a suicidal sectarianism of the New Left and black militants who
seemed hell-bent in the late 1960s and early 1970s on alienating most of
their erstwhile labor and liberal allies. But political romanticism, verbal
violence, and liberal repulsion were only part of the story. By the early
1970s, it seemed as if we had tried everything, and everything had failed.
There was a retreat to privatism, a feeling that perhaps time and the
arsonists should be allowed to finish razing the decaying cities, that a
young violent generation should be permitted to kill itself off (or grow

"But, Tom, if we eliminate government corruption, racial violence, and crime in the streets, I shudder to think what will move into the vacuum!"

Source: Up Three Points, Please, Cartoons from the Wall Street Journal. Copyright 1970 by Charles Preston. Reprinted by permission of Simon & Schuster, Inc.

up). Then and only then, perhaps, there could be a fresh start.

The disenchantment was confined to reform programs, not to repression. There was not much money for penal reform, but large amounts for treat-em-rough police. Racism, slightly disguised, was still alive and well. There was a blurring of the differentiating line between a black and a mugger, between a dozen blacks and a dangerous street gang. But the unease went deeper than racial prejudice. It was compounded by fear of the future of the economy and shaken faith in employment security, fear of the young and of the drug culture, and fear of the uncivil and the misbehaving. All in all, it was a lean time for the diminishing band of still-hopeful liberals.

This is a snapshot of a mood, a tableau of life at one brief moment in the mid-1970s. But America is a volatile nation. Moods change, new leadership evokes new responses even to ancient problems like racism and poverty. We have been through a bewildering onrush of events in the past generation, and if anything, the camera seems to be speeding up. This fact *guarantees* that this portrait of the mid-1970s is as impermanent, as transitory, as the earlier pictures of the mid-1960s: blacks and whites with clasped hands and misty eyes, offering a chorus of "We Shall Overcome"; excited intellectuals mapping a devastating war on poverty; mayors cutting ribbons on strikingly new, massive apartment buildings for poor people.

Perhaps less naiveté, more modesty, more incremental improvements lie ahead. But then again so do new programs, new approaches, a fresh burst of activism. But let us admit it, both the initiation of social programs and their subsequent dismantling are based more on faith than hard evidence, on feeling in heart and gut, not on cold calculation.

This book is based on one fact and one assumption. The fact is that beginning in 1968 the Republican administration abolished, dehydrated, or otherwise attacked many of the bolder social programs enacted during the Eisenhower-Kennedy-Johnson era. The assumption is that the present lack of viable domestic programs in a period of deepening uncertainty over the future prospects of the economy offers a reasonable prospect for new initiatives and new programs. Standpattism has not worked either. However, the proposals advanced must reflect the needs and anxieties of an unsatisfied urban voting constituency.

While it would be tempting to write off the Republican years as an era of blind negativism, the dismemberment of urban programs following Nixon's 1972 reelection sweep cannot be blithely dismissed as prejudice in action, as sheer callousness to the needs of the needy. Both Left and Right, who could agree on nothing else, actively united on the proposition that the liberal reformist government had failed abysmally in fulfilling its basic responsibilities.

Since the mid-1960s we have seen a growing chorus of liberals assault the persistent neglect of the crime problem, along with allegedly defective housing, poverty, and education programs that did too little for their intended beneficiaries and too much for intermediary bureaucracies and contractors. The Right has attacked the programs on similar grounds, adding excessive cost and maladministration to the indictment. And, true to historical precedent, program defenders have been reluctant to admit error, swearing, when failures are too blatant to overlook, that valuable lessons have been learned and taken to heart. In consequence, they promised, the housing or manpower or education amendments of 1966 or 1967 or 1968 or 1970 or 197 - would do the things that their less sophisticated forebears had failed to accomplish.

To listen to the critics, the entire record is one of unmitigated disaster. To them the Great Society programs demonstrated the folly of "throwing money at problems" or "flinging money at a barn door in the hope that some will get through the knothole." As the text will suggest, the past is freckled; there were substantial successes along with the collapses. But in the mid-1970s the morale of the interventionists was low. The traditional liberal coalition was in disarray, partly because of a series of scandals in housing and other programs, but also because the government's actions were subject to an unprecedented amount of skeptical analysis. One result was the partial return to favor of an earlier American formula which holds that by definition government is incompetent, and private enterprise, which must withstand the rigors of the market place, must perforce be efficient. Clearly, both notions are gross oversimplifications.

Liberals' Misconceptions

But if the 1960s were an age of misconceptions, surely it is time to clear away some of the false assumptions, mistaken analogies, and nonsensical notions which we inherited from the 1960s and are perpetuating in the 1970s. In the 1960s, for example, draftsmen of New Frontier and Great Society programs were apparently convinced of the following propositions:

1.   Circa 1960-65 there existed a sufficient body of knowledge to construct and operate successful, large-scale urban programs to turn the cities around—to wipe out poverty and eliminate slums and substandard schools. As a corollary, it was assumed that opponents and doubters were at best part of, or lent support to, dead bureaucracies, or at worst represented a wicked conspiracy to keep the blacks and the poor in their place.

2.   Following this reasoning, the chief problem was a dearth of money (not of ideas or talent). Such failures as could not be ignored were chiefly due to insufficient funding (Christianity hasn't failed—it's never been tried!). The proper response to failure in the War on Poverty,

just as to failure in the Vietnam War, was to tinker with the program, replace part of the top leadership, and pour in more resources.

3.   Such resources were indeed available. Using the space program and military analogies and adding optimistically projected national economic growth, a simple reordering of priorities away from the military (the so-called "peace dividend") would enable us to fund all of the urgently needed social programs simultaneously. That is, brutal choices between equally vital programs were unnecessary.

4.   The space program and world war mobilization indicated that difficult problems could be transformed into "objectives" which could be achieved by sufficient exercise of will, imagination, proper organization, and lots of money.

5.   The success of the Marshall Plan, an American economic aid program to European countries after World War II, proved that a "Marshall Plan for the cities" or for the poor would achieve similar successful results.

6.   As a corollary, conquest could proceed swiftly, at high cost, somewhat like the U.S. Marine practice of smashing through defensive works rapidly, accepting the necessary high casualties for the sake of quick victory.

7.   America's urban poor circa 1960 were like previous occupants of the slums, particularly the Jews and Orientals. That is, when barriers to better jobs and housing were removed, they could similarly be relied upon to climb up the proffered ladder, using previously suppressed talents. The bill drafters, unfamiliar with the complex realities of the poor, saw them as an idealized mass, half nostalgic Porgy and Bess, half ambitious Harry-Golden-Lower-East-Side.

8.   By implication, the preceding assumption led to the belief that those opposed to having the poor move into their neighborhoods, schools, or workplaces were benighted bigots in need of enlightenment and, if necessary, chastisement.

9.   The extent of crime among the poor was exaggerated and would greatly diminish when housing and job programs took hold. In general, like kindly intellectuals in other eras, they greatly underestimated the persistence of antisocial behavior (even if only a minority was involved)

and its power to generate real and perceived threats in an age of graphic mass media.

10.   Fundamental changes in the behavior of the urban poor could be effected through changes in housing. In its most simple-minded form, this approach blamed slum housing for all the social characteristics exhibited by slum residents (that is, bad surroundings stimulate bad behavior, and good housing brings more than sunshine and modern plumbing into the lives of the unfortunate).

11.   A sufficient supply of talent existed to man newly created or expanded programs, and a combination of new and existing agencies could capably handle large amounts of new money and new responsibilities. Furthermore, by sitting down and reasoning together, agency executives could achieve intergovernmental coordination at all levels. Lion and lamb, highway engineer and urban planner, Employment Service bureaucrats and Community Action manpower technicians could and would work rationally together, particularly if coordination was mandated by program guidelines.

12.   Fundamentally, urban problems were manageable, and the key to progress was specially designed programs rather than a buoyant economy. This assumption led to a habit of overlooking the benefits of a rising tide of prosperity in diminishing the number of poor and also providing the wherewithal to pursue social progress. It also reflected an anti-private sector bias which focused on the past and present evils of private enterprise rather than on its contributions.

13.   Insofar as the liberals considered the matter, the mushrooming expansion of government jobs inherent in the traditional interventionist approach posed no threat to the fiscal viability of the urban areas or the national economy. The economic and social instability of cities in which the majority of the inhabitants either work for government agencies or are on welfare was simply not part of their mental horizon.

14.   There are substantial leadership resources among the poor. Since the poor could not rely on existing governmental structures to protect their interests, honest and efficient representatives of the poor could be chosen through community elections to serve the interests of the entire population of impoverished neighborhoods.

15.   As a corollary to this projected release of poverty area energy associated with federal funding and program responsibility, it was suggested that the basic answer to poverty lay in a redistribution of power, beginning with such functions as the schools but subsequently progressing into other areas. Further, it was believed that since money in slum areas is systematically skimmed off by nonresident owners of businesses and residences, it follows that a sizable flow of funds can be diverted inward to create a new resident middle class and to upgrade local living conditions.

Conservatives' Misconceptions

Naturally a collection of delusions of this magnitude led to errors of equal size. The new programs became fair game for academic critics, conservative candidates, and the Internal Revenue Service. But were the delusions of the Right any better? Consider the following assumptions:

1.   Despite past evidence of upward mobility by their predecessors in the slums, virtually all of the people now living in poverty are inferior persons. Many of them are genetically deficient, and many are prone to animal instincts which doom them to low incomes, ill health, prison, promiscuity, and alcoholism. The improvident poor, who drink up their paychecks and fornicate carelessly and frequently, should blame themselves rather than society; they are unjustly envious of and hostile to their betters.

To a remarkable extent the belief in predestined grace of Calvinism is alive and well in the late twentieth century. Horatio Alger, too, has not died: To the really deserving, poverty is a transitory, character-building school for success. Numerous recent examples—flourishing post-1961 Cuban refugees, happy post-1956 Hungarians, learned post-1950 Chinese—are cited to prove that America still yields substantial affluence to the hard-working, sober majority and her full bounty to the hard-driving, imaginative few. This being the case, clearly the poor should blame their fate on their weak moral fiber.

2.   America is a land of marvels, of which the chief wonder is, in former President Nixon's phrase, the "mighty engine of the private enterprise system." Capitalism, American-style, has not only given us the world's highest standard of living but has gone far to eliminate

poverty among all but an unfortunate hard core. Left to work its way without interference, capitalism will do more for the poor (and for urban problems generally) than all the government's misguided poverty and housing and other reformist ventures, many of which actually make matters worse.

3. Insofar as government housing is necessary (or a necessary evil), state and local government is to be preferred because it is "closer to the people." Even better are well-managed private sector activities (private charities) for the genuine victims of misfortune. But the best choice of all is the cohesive family, making its own way, solving its own problems. It follows that one of the federal government's chief sins is the attempt to substitute for and thereby stifle family solidarity, local and personal initiatives, and charitable impulses.

4. One of the most heinous offenses of the liberals is to exaggerate the scope and severity of the problems confronting the nation. Wrenching present problems out of historical context, the reformers fail to note the enormous progress achieved in the past few decades. Moreover, by harping on remaining deficiencies and by publicizing unrealistic comparisons between the living standards of the poor and the more affluent, liberals are helping to unravel the national fabric by encouraging people's baser instincts—jealousy, spite, and criminal theft and aggression.

5. Insofar as government must indeed exist and function, the answers to its inherent gross defects can be found in the private sector, in transferring business leadership and business methods to executive agencies. (For some reason the military is exempted from these recommendations. Generals, who are not tarred with the bureaucratic brush, are believed to be moderately efficient at their job. They are certainly ideologically sound, and they are thought to be trained to take resolute, decisive action.)

6. The unfavorable, often dangerous behavioral characteristics of the nastier slum dwellers can most effectively be curbed with swift, drastic, and certain punishment. Furthermore, the police and the prisons, if not harrassed by liberal bleeding hearts over-concerned with legal niceties, can be relied upon as effective agents of law and order. (Police and prison guards also seem to be exempt from underlying prejudices concerning civil servants.) The lower-class criminal is viewed as

a person who has deliberately chosen evil intead of good and therefore deserves appropriate (harsh) punishment. Lacking a sturdy conscience, he must be taught to modify his behavior by learning that the weed of crime bears bitter fruit—certain retribution from a wronged society.

7.   Sometime in the past, probably in the first Franklin Roosevelt administration (or perhaps it was Woodrow Wilson), America took a wrong turn. Through a still inexplicable chain of circumstances, America departed from the ideas and ideals characteristic of her great past. It is believed that there was once a Golden Age, a happier time when business initiative was properly rewarded with respect and affection in addition to money. This ideal America, which was so eloquently described by Tocqueville circa 1835, was a land of paternal, familial responsibility, of vigorous small towns and unflinching patriotism. Nevertheless, much greatness remains, latent but pure as gold. One can only wonder at the intelligence or the motives of unpatriotic detractors who focus on problems instead of achievements, on the minority of poor, sick, and unemployed instead of the vast, relatively satisfied majority.

8.   On the whole, governmentally inspired change, particularly when it emanates from the federal level, represents more of a threat than a promise. This statement is of course subject to important exceptions. Rapid, often bewildering technological advances and foreign consumer importations are usually greeted by the political conservative with anticipation and pleasure; quantum advances in military technology are welcomed as vital protection against enemy miscalculation and also as a major source of business. But there is much uneasiness focused on social engineering—tinkering with poverty, race relations, housing, or the distribution of income, status, and power. There is also a generalized apprehension over the size of the government budget and its alleged (but largely mythical) "confiscatory" tax bite. And the more sophisticated stress the historic tendency of intervention to stand on its head—regulatory agencies are captured by regulatees, urban renewal destroys more slum housing than it replaces.

9.   Large cities tend to debilitate one's character. The chief target is of course wicked New York City, but there is widespread belief that all large cities are inherently unhealthful from a physical and moral standpoint. Clearly this view harkens back to a Jeffersonian contrast between the nobility of the rural environment as compared to the turbulent ur-

ban cesspools. Out of this mysterious urban miasma seep ideas and immoral life styles inconsistent with a mental portrait of America as it was and should be again, which conservatives cherish.

10.   Intellectuals as a collective entity are basically hostile to American ideals. Strains of xenophobia and antiintellectualism have simmered in this country for centuries. If anything they are far less pronounced at present, in an age of travel and almost universal post-high school education. But they remain just below the surface, bubbling up periodically with proposals to "saw off the eastern seaboard" and insulting remarks concerning "effete intellectual snobs," "pointy-headed intellectuals," etc.

11.   Fundamental problems related to poverty and slums can only be lessened, not resolved. This point is extremely significant, since it suggests that the conservatives have long since raised the white flag in confronting the nation's more serious urban problems. (In this respect they have been diametrically different from the liberal interventionists, who called for victory in the domestic war against poverty, but demanded, in opposition to conservatives, that the United States give up notions of victory in Korea and Vietnam or of a "rollback" of communism in Eastern Europe.)

The Majority Consensus

The preceding analysis has deliberately presented a simplified version of conflicting ideologies and mythologies. It has also suggested that a wide gulf separates liberals and conservatives, social interventionists and the old-line Right and Center, and deliberately ignores the complex interplay of shared beliefs and experience which points to a remarkable amount of convergence. In America the political pendulum swings from right to left and back again in a narrow arc within a prescribed, peaceful framework.

Despite the substantial divergence between liberal and conservative, there is a sufficiently broad foundation of common understandings to permit the design of an urban program which will appeal to a majority of the electorate in the late 1970s. This is not to suggest that formulating acceptable proposals is a simple task, but there do seem to be some helpful guiding principles:

(1) The objectives must be modest and achievable.

(2) By virtue of persuasive presentation and actual execution the programs must be perceived by a majority coalition as offering them genuine benefits, rather than as threats to the relatively affluent majority for the sake of appeasing the poor minority.

We should have learned enough from the past to improve our batting average. A period of marking time and reappraisal, the first half of the 1970s, in the author's opinion, has stoked the furnace for a renewed burst of government action on the urban front. Fortunately a basis for a new quasi-consensual approach appears to have emerged out of past experience. To continue our system of classification, it is possible to identify several critical areas where a sufficiently broad consensus exists to give wide, bipartisan support for appropriate new or overhauled programs. There is general agreement on the following propositions:

1.   The principal urban problems and programs must be related to people's behavior patterns and their interactions, rather than to inferior structures and technologies. The main problem is people, not land use or buildings.

2.   Urban problems are part of a broader pattern of national policy, embracing policy toward rural areas and even international policy, especially the issue of domestic vs. foreign policy priorities. The recognition of this kind of wider lens perspective offers a number of opportunities for building broad constituencies for programs affecting urban areas.

3.   Many old programs have outlived their usefulness or need a major overhaul because of serious defects. The pervasive climate of disenchantment, which underlay the post-1972 administrative reorganization and dehydration of executive agencies, can also be used to gain support for fresh approaches lacking the stigma of past failures.

4.   Many programs relating to urban government are too large, too unwieldy, and too unresponsive. There seems to be a readiness to try a variety of alternative mechanisms, ranging from a direct confrontation with municipal unions, to the appointment of ombudsmen and outside review committees, to neighborhood government (new town meetings?), to direct citizen choice via school chits or outright cash income payments.

5.   Any acceptable approach to poverty and welfare must be grounded on the traditional work-education ethic. This point is critical, since most of the potentially employable among the welfare recipients

are AFDC (Aid For Dependent Children) mothers. This implies the possibility of broad support for expensive, effective day care systems for *all* working mothers, and a job generation program to guarantee work for all.

6.   Social progress and reform programs must be grounded in self-interest. This is another traditional approach which occasionally has been neglected. It suggests continuing support for piece-of-the-action approaches to increase housing ownership and to provide a stake for many more people in other areas, on the theory that ownership, profit, and the prospect of middle-class rewards are powerful incentives in achieving upward mobility and social stability.

7.   Attempts to ensure a decrease in crimes affecting persons and property must be placed high on the political agenda. This priority receives across-the-board support, not least from the slum dwellers, who are the chief victims.

8.   One contribution to the crime problem is to redefine private practices, including vices which do not harm other people, as matters of personal life style, rather than cause for legal action. Removal of legal sanctions against gambling, pornography, abortion, and fornication by consenting adults of the hetero- and homosexual varieties and perhaps against marijuana will focus law enforcement on activities which directly threaten the well-being of other persons.

9.   Health and housing costs are exorbitant. Measures ranging from confrontations with medical guilds and construction unions to new preventive medicine and approaches to reduce housing costs would un-doubtedly receive wide public support.

10.   Radical movements, groups which see the present structure of America as beyond redemption via reform, do not constitute a serious threat. Increasingly John Birchers and other rightists and various left revolutionary groups are viewed as picturesque, irritating nuisances rather than grave menaces to the Republic. To a degree this reflects a decline in the belief that malign cabals of Left or Right seriously threaten to overthrow a relatively helpless, rule-bound majority. The implications of this change are important in several areas, not the least of which is the recognition of rationality and good faith on the part of most serious political participants, Left and Right.

11.   There is a widespread recognition that some foreign nations, for reasons not wholly understood, have managed to create more attractive, more livable urban environments than we have. Moreover, there is growing willingness to plagiarize, adopt, and revamp foreign innovations for domestic use.

12.   The time for the hard sell, for claims of instant successes, and for the accompanying inspirational rhetoric is past. The order of the day is humility and prudence, rather than big promises based on shaky premises.

13.   There seems to be growing agreement that it is unwise to overload vehicles for reform lest they topple from the weight. For example, urban schools are not effective if they are given the role of civilizing as well as educating unruly children whom their parents cannot handle; new housing projects for the poor may provide safe and sanitary housing only temporarily because in itself good housing cannot assure tolerable tenant behavior; prisons find it difficult to reform as well as punish; and the welfare system can nourish the destitute but often finds it difficult to return its clients to the gainfully employed mainstream.

14.   There is a growing realization that we have concentrated on trying to cure the rash while neglecting the syphilis. For one example, stiff penalties for drug peddlers are not the key element in reducing high crime rates that they were supposed to be. For another, teaching human relations and trying to transmit vocational skills to persons unlikely to be more than marginally employable is not a useful effort, especially in sagging labor markets. Years of struggle have been devoted to programs in which victory was absolutely certain to fall far short of promised results. Examples include the exhausting attempts to equalize public school expenditures as the sure road to equalizing educational results, or to alter suburban zoning practices in order to achieve significant migration of the very poor from slums to outlying communities. It is time to concentrate on more fruitful areas.

15.   The record suggests that new government programs, formulated in part as knee-jerk reaction against past failures, may contain the seeds of future disasters. They may themselves be even more defective than their predecessors. For example, greater community control, which has been recommended as an approach to improving schools, reducing crime rates, and diminishing alienation in big-city neigh-

borhoods, can also lead to more corruption in petty kleptocracies, to more political and social fragmentation, and to even greater interarea differentials in municipal program quality.

16.   In the late sixties and early seventies, critics charged that there was an urgent need for reform or revolution. It was claimed that people in our society were separated into the minority—the vicious and successful—and the majority—those who were too moral and (possibly) lacking the opportunity or the special talents to join the ranks of the oppressors. Sufferers were enjoined to survive as best they could, to opt out by migrating abroad or to cooperative communes, or to alter this upside-down system through prayer or the barricades. But this kind of fatalism is not consistent with the American character, which tends toward the view that the only problems that we have not yet solved are those we haven't properly worked on.

17.   Although there is a substantial consensus of dissillusionment with a number of domestic programs, it should be remembered that early on, before time and experience wore off the gilt, these now vulnerable targets were once glamorous innovations. The amazing thing about the Kennedy-Johnson programs was the rapidity of the wilting process; the gamut from conception to senility often occurred in the space of a few years.

It must also be remembered that in practice some problems were found to be easily soluble—for example, finding suitable employment for well-educated blacks who had been oppressed by discriminatory job practices. But other problems, like linking hard-core unemployed to regular jobs, proved to be infernally complicated, involving changes in motivation, work habits and training, health improvements and suburbanization of employment. Other associated problems were the unavailability of low-cost transportation, the insufficiency of low-rent housing near job centers, credentials barriers, restrictive union hiring practices, industrial skill requirements, and perhaps most of all, the state of the job market. A swarm of constantly revised special manpower training programs, employer incentives, equal employment legislation, housing acts, transportation subsidies, etc., has failed to make much of a dent in the critical problem of structural (hard-core) unemployment and underemployment. And the problems of housing abandonment in central cities, big-city public school education, and public safety in inner-city areas are equally complicated. This all underscores the key observation made earlier: construction is easy but people problems are tough.

18.   Traditionally—and paradoxically—the Left in America has taken a less tolerant view of many kinds of messiness than has the Right. Conservatives have been relatively undisturbed by the existence of pockets of poverty, by huge disparities between areas in income and quality of services, and they have tended to attribute these problems to genetic deficiency or behavioral malfunctions. Liberals, on the other hand, have been greatly troubled by these problems, and have believed implicitly in the doctrine of human perfectibility. But the gap has narrowed increasingly. The liberal also opts for insulation; like his right-leaning neighbor, he too has been exiting to the suburbs. He will contribute more for the poor as long as they stay in the slums, but draws the line at danger to personal safety and substandard schools for his children.

19.   Despite mountains of research we still know far too little concerning basic questions, such as how best to motivate children to learn and adults to work, how to reduce the crime rate and how to create healthy neighborhoods. The research agenda is enormous. Furthermore, we need much, much less theological philosophizing, opaque jargon, and moral exhortations.

20.   The nation needs fresh, exciting programs and people to replace enervated approaches run by persons with tired blood and worn-out ideas. It is now recognized that vigorous operational *talent* is as necessary as well-conceived *programs*—light now shines in the darkness.

21.   With many cities and some states in serious financial trouble to serve as horrible examples of fiscal irresponsibility, liberals as well as conservatives now experience heightened cost-consciousness, tax sensitivity, and concern with government waste.

Conclusion

Despite broad areas of agreement on general principles, most students of the urban scene would agree that no era of good feelings can be anticipated in dealing with most domestic issues. Aside from built-in racial, class, and ethnic divisions, there are two basic sources of continuing tensions. The first is what W. F. Ogburn dubbed "cultural lag," the yawning gulf between rampant technology and slow-to-change governmental and social institutions.

A roaring torrent of new inventions and consumer goods pours out of the laboratories and other corporate auxiliaries, overwhelming personal or governmental ability to cope. It may take years to gauge the impact of a single new chemical residue (or combination of residues) on water quality, the impact of a new drug on wild life, or a new communications device on travel patterns. Meanwhile regulatory devices and other efforts to adjust limp along while more innovations come in swarms, not only from America but from the foreign nations who have learned from and frequently surpassed us in inventive and sales ingenuity.

This lag would not be so disturbing were it not for the perfectly understandable tendency to cling to familiar and controllable aspects of the political environment. The persistence of obsolescent government structures, attitudes, and prejudices owes much to the fact that in a world of bewildering change it is comforting to cling like a mollusk to a few stable elements. Holding fast to local zoning power and the neighborhood school may not turn back the revolutions brewing in domestic and foreign laboratories, but it offers a tangible assurance of minimal control over one's environment.

A second principal source of unease and vexation is the unresolvable conflict between equally desirable objectives—between freedom and control, between sound budgets and the rising living standards encouraged by media promotion of goods and services, between the rights of minorities and the rights of majorities. The simultaneous and constant pressure on brake and accelerator, toward impulse and caution, are so much a part of life in the United States that we fail to notice the schizophrenia-producing barrage of conflicting signals that astounds the visitor.

To the historian, of course, this is old stuff, not the product of the 1960s or 1970s. Alexis de Tocqueville wrote in the 1830s of the staid,

careworn American, disturbed in his slumbers by thoughts of opportunities lost, mistakes made, and decisions which must be made
tomorrow and every day thereafter. In contrast, he suggested, there
was the placid calm of authoritarian society, where decisions are made
on high, and a quiet resignation or apathy prevails among the citizenry.
The apparent torpor of an autocracy may be pleasing to the refugee
from turbulence, but as Tocqueville also reminds us, anxiety is part of
the price for liberty. If there is to be another concerted effort to direct
the shape of the urban future, Americans will continue to live and die
worried people. As in the Chinese curse, we are condemned to live in interesting times. Inevitably, for us too there will be chances lost, mistakes made, and an unending series of difficult choices.

This volume appears at a time of crucial change. We have had two
such pivotal moments before in the past generation—the inauguration
of the New Deal and the decision to enter the second World War. Obviously the present, the mid-1970s, lacks the drama of world depression
and world war, but in a sense it is the direct result of these crises. Fundamentally, these were two crucial interventionist moves to use the
power of the federal government to combat depression and fascism. In
the mid-1970s there is no such clear and present danger—our problems
are a serious business recession, the deteriorating environment, decaying cities, and tense race relations. But there is no obvious indication of
a national consensus coalescing around a program, a leadership, or a
powerful thrust to meet desperate situations. And so we are left with a
collection of serious but not fatal irritations that call—but not
loudly—for action.

Perhaps the most vexing problem confronting the nation as we
lurch toward the 1980s is the prospect of enormous regional decay, as
the balance shifts toward the Southwest and against the older industrial areas in the northeast quadrant of the country. It is one thing
to write off Newark, and quite another to face the prospect of deepening
economic and urban obsolescence in all of New Jersey—and New York
and New England and, indeed, much of the Midwest. There is little hope
of a massive national effort solely to save the central cities, especially
with dubious prospects of success. But when tens of millions of voters
are involved, including legions of respectable surburban conservatives,
abandoning areas to regional decay seems less likely. Nevertheless the
prospect of a convulsive national effort to tilt substantial growth away
from the Sunbelt states is one that staggers the imagination. On the
other hand, the idea of benign neglect of a sizable chunk of the middle
class is equally frightening to the practicing politician. One can hear

faint echoes of the bitter sectionalism that almost tore the nation apart a century ago.

The analysis and the remedies offered in these chapters reflect the author's interpretation of the national mood. The Chicken Little, sky-is-falling approach won't work; the sky hasn't fallen, and persons who maintain that it will do so tomorrow are shunted aside as alarmists and cranks. This volume attempts to set forth approaches suitable for the times: they are reasonable, hopeful, and reformist, and they seem to be politically marketable.

> The fear of losing one's job, the necessity of being somebody in a crowded and clamorous world, the terror that old age will not be secured, that your children will lack opportunity—there are a thousand terrors which arise out of the unorganized and unstable economic system under which we live. These are not terrors which can be blown away by criticism; they will go only when society is intelligent enough to have made destitution impossible, when it secures opportunity to every child, when it establishes for every human being a minimum of comfort below which he cannot sink. Then a great amount of social hesitancy will disappear. Every issue will not be fought as if life depended upon it, and mankind will have emerged from a fear economy.[1]

Walter Lippmann wrote these words in 1914. We can hope that in another generation they will be historical reminiscences rather than a still timely critique of a troubled nation.

Notes

1.   Walter Lippmann, "Drift and Mastery," reprinted in Otis Pease, ed., *The Progressive Years* (New York: Braziller, 1962), p. 451.

2

POPULATION TRENDS:
Opportunities for the
1980s.

As a topic of concern, population has the rare quality of creating in most audiences a profound somnolence verging on stupefaction. Aside from the most cursory tidbits—did we gain or lose?—the recitation of population statistics, however exciting to the demographer, is regarded by most people as on a par with freight car loadings and odd lot purchases. True, the much-heralded population explosion broke the monotony for a time; there was drama in the media and elsewhere concerning America's forthcoming people squeeze. But now that the birth rate is down and that nightmare has been dissipated, population, as a topic, ranks with plumbing as something we cannot do without but are perfectly willing to leave to the overpaid expert. This discussion suggests, however, that an understanding of population trends is crucial, since it affects any number of perfectly comprehensible matters like the distribution of congressional seats, the location of retail customers and housing markets, the extent and siting of traffic congestion, and crime rates, all of which directly concern most Americans.

Future Impact of Present Trends

In the course of the next ten or twenty years profound changes in population trends are likely to have fundamental impact on significant aspects of urban development. Critically important elements of the nation's social and economic fabric will undergo important alterations as a consequence of a steep decline in birth rates, the trend toward an aging population, the population shift away from the Northeast, and rising educational and income levels. These are all part of a far-reaching process which has already had major effects on housing, land use, and job patterns and presents new problems in adjustment and new opportunities and challenges for government and the private sector.

POPULATION LEVELING OFF

A first item of business is to finish off the myth that America is going to be a national sardine can jammed border-to-border with people. This dismal prospect simply does not seem to be in the cards.

There was a time only a decade ago, back in the 1960s, when serious scholars predicted that matrimony, or more accurately its product, was about to kill off America. Television presented vivid dramas of a nation swarming with people, futilely elbowing each other for a patch of green lawn. Strangely, even after the steep unprecedented decline in birth rates in the early 1970s, the population Cassandras are still with us, warning that with the enormous increase in women of child-bearing age, the slightest tendency toward fecundity could bear out all of the gloomy prophecies of the sixties.

So far the prophets are wrong; population growth in the nation is leveling off at a rate of less than one percent a year. The Bureau of the Census's low population projection for 1990 points to a total of 239 million, only 35 million above 1970. While this is certainly a large increase over the 1970 total, it is only about half the 60 million, twenty-year gain confidently expected in the 1960s.[1]

In terms of population densities, the lower numerical increase points to a further rise above the 1970 level of 200 to 1000 people to the square mile in the urban states.[2] But as every planner and developer knows, the "average" acre is not necessarily buildable. For this reason effective population density on easily developable, available land might well rise steeply, were it not for other important demographic changes.

We should note that any prediction of this kind is necessarily hazardous. The expectation of a modest, two-decade population gain in the United States is based on a continued decline of birth rates from twenty-seven per one thousand population after World War II to perhaps the fourteen per one thousand population level by the end of the 1970s. Combined with a death rate of nine per one thousand, the birth rate may result in a natural increase rate of about 0.4 percent per year, or about 6 percent per decade.

One of the factors responsible for the decline in birth rates is the development of virtually foolproof contraceptive techniques, particularly the contraceptive pill. Nevertheless, the importance of this factor should not be overestimated. America's second lowest birth rates occurred forty years ago, in the pre-pill 1930s. But improved contraception has clearly been responsible for diminishing the odds that increased sexual activity will result in pregnancy.[3] However, even in the 1960s an estimated 20 percent of births were unwanted. (13 percent of white, 27 percent of black births).[4] It may be noted that the unwanted figure was 14 percent among "nonpoor" couples and a staggering 40 percent among poor families in the early 1960s. Thanks in part to more effective contraceptive devices and expanded family planning services, the overall birth rate declined by 20 percent between 1967 and 1974, with the largest decline occurring among poor nonwhites.[5]

For those who can't or won't use foolproof defenses, there is abortion. An average of 200,000 abortions yearly since the early 1970s has taken place among poor families; an estimated 25 percent of women of childbearing age in poverty-stricken Puerto Rico have been sterilized. These facts suggest that many poor women are well aware of the linkage between large families and a life of poverty.[6]

MIGRATION

The future of migration is probably even more difficult to predict than sharp fluctuations in the birth rate. America is a country of movers; between 1970 and 1974, 37 percent of the population changed residences. It is conceivable that internal migration rates could either rise or fall substantially, depending as much on the push out of rural areas and declining core cities generated by unfavorable living conditions as on the pull of thriving suburban and exurban communities. Most receiving urban areas have little control over what happens in the sending areas in the country or abroad, but they do have a good deal of influence over the pace and type of development that occurs within their borders. In recent years, as discussed later in this chapter, an increasing number of fast-growing communities have discarded the traditional booster ideology, which equates population growth with economic benefits, in favor of no-growth or slow-growth policies based on a fear of the social and fiscal consequences of rapid expansion.

One continuing area for concern is the trend toward population declines among middle-income families in core cities, which they perceive as undesirable places to live. (See table 2-1.) Meanwhile, poor migrants crowd into slum areas of the cities. While this trend in many cases should be considered a natural and even a desirable phenomenon, bringing population into balance with employment opportunities, substantial difficulties are generated at the destination points. Some of these are so commonplace as to deserve no more than identification; for example, the core city points of entry for the migrating rural poor are decaying slums in metropolises hard pressed to absorb new waves of restless, ill-prepared migrants. A second zone of friction is the suburban ring of communities where population growth presses hard on the ecology and the social fabric, and imposes strains on local fiscal and service capabilities. And as noted above, there is also a more subtle but serious problem which has only begun to receive serious attention.

This problem is that not very many places in the nation are popularly perceived as attractive to visit, much less to settle down in. The piling up of population in relatively few growth zones and communities

Table 2-1.   RESPONSES TO SURVEY QUESTION, "WHERE WOULD YOU PREFER TO LIVE?" — 1972

	Rural or Small Town	Small Urban	Large Urban	No Opinion
National	53%	33%	13%	1%
Residence				
Rural or small town	88	10	2	—
Small urban	39	55	6	—
Large urban	34	26	39	2
Region				
Northeast	58	28	14	—
South	57	30	12	—
North Central	46	37	17	—
West	50	38	12	—
Age				
Under 30 years	56	28	15	—
30 years and over	52	34	13	1
Color				
White	54	33	11	—
Black	33	34	33	—
Education				
Less than high school	57	30	12	1
High school complete	54	32	13	1
Some college	47	38	14	1
College complete	40	38	22	
Income				
Under $5,000	57	32	10	1
$5,000 to $9,999	53	34	12	—
$10,000 to $14,999	45	29	11	—
$15,000 or more	45	34	21	—

Note: Rural or small town includes the farm, open country, or small town responses. Small urban represents small city, or medium size city and suburb. Large urban includes the large city and its suburbs.

Source: Commission on Population Growth and the American Future, 1972, p. 605, in Stanford Research Institute, *City Size and the Quality of Life: An Analysis of the Policy Implications of Population Concentration.* Prepared for the National Science Foundation, November 1974.

offers a special cause for friction. The strenuous efforts of suburban communities to limit their growth are already fully in evidence, and there are more resistance efforts to come. Hold-the-line action is in prospect with respect not only to domestic migration but to foreign immigration as well. There may be some agitation to decrease the legal immigration which accounts for a substantial proportion of officially recorded population growth, and some action to stem the inflow of an apparently even larger number of illegal immigrants is almost a certainty. In short, immigration levels, which began to surface as a significant public policy issue in the 1973 recession, are likely to become an increasingly vexing controversy in the years ahead.

Other Recent Population Trends

It appears therefore that a host of problems, some now visible only in outline, will confront the nation in the late 1970s and 1980s. They will exert particular force on two types of areas, declining core cities and growth suburbs.

In addition to patterns and trends in population growth and distribution, this chapter considers changing sex and age ratios, various categories of urban and rural residence, and three key population characteristics: education, income, and occupation. Fundamental changes are evident in each of these areas, and most are the result of a combination of governmental policy and private decisions. The extent to which things have indeed changed has only partially been grasped, even by those who should be most aware of new trends—the officials responsible for planning future development.

AGE GROUPS AND POPULATION GROWTH

One way of examining the impact of population growth is to analyze changes by age group.[7] Over the next generation, for example, the prospects are for a general aging of the population as the birth rate declines and the waves of past enthusiasm in fertility move successively on into the upper age brackets.

Five years and under.   Children five years of age or under are the dependents whose greatest need is a good home environment with good medical care, and other services. Given continuing low birth rates, the health services. The under-five age group, which numbered 20.3 million in 1960, declined to just over 16 million in 1974. From a governmental standpoint the very young require playgrounds, preschool training, number in this age bracket may decline further over the next decades. The Census Bureau's low projection for the year 2000 is a total of just over 14 million.

Five through thirteen.   The size of the population five through thirteen years of age has large direct impact on elementary and middle schools. This group increased from 33 million in 1960 to 34 million in 1974. But a considerable falling off in numbers is in prospect for the 1980s, as the delayed impact of lower birth rates takes effect. The Census Bureau's low projection for the year 2000 is a modest 29 million.

The impact on local school budgets of these changes can be ascertained by considering that it costs over $45,000 for each new classroom to serve every twenty to thirty school children, and from $1000 to $2500 per pupil per year for school operating expenses. Judging from these facts, one would predict good news from the half-empty maternity wards—closing down of surplus public schools and some relief from the pressure of rising school budgets can be expected. On the other hand, it is entirely conceivable that closedowns and budget relief will not occur. As a precedent, the average size of public school classes in the early 1900s was more than fifty pupils, and only gradually was progress made in reducing class size to the current twenty-five to thirty-pupil level. A combination of renewed national affluence and confidence, coupled with pressure from powerful teachers' unions, could result in a further decrease to the ten to fifteen pupils per class characteristic of many good private schools. Certainly the growing use of teacher's aides and current efforts to upgrade their educational qualifications suggests that there will indeed be a trend in the direction of lower pupil-teacher ratios. If this does occur, expenditures for instruction will rise, but there may be some savings in construction for smaller numbers of pupils.

Fourteen to twenty-four.   One of the most important population groups is the fourteen to twenty-four age bracket. This high school and college age group increased substantially between 1960 and 1974, rising very sharply from 21 million to 43 million. (The year 2000 low projection by the Census Bureau predicts a total of 36 million.) As fast-growing suburban communities can testify, a rise of this magnitude has had a very large impact both on school operating expenses and school construction costs. (Secondary school costs usually run about a third higher than those for the elementary grades.[8]) The influence of this age category is felt through its link to serious social problems in the central cities. Unemployment and delinquency rates are relatively high among both white and black central city teenagers, and this age group tends to be a prime recruiting reservoir for street gangs.

Persons aged eighteen to twenty-four are the source of most of the college students. For some years institutions of higher education were hard pressed to provide enough classrooms and enough faculty to handle the increase in college age population. This problem was caused not only by the increase in absolute numbers but also by the steady rise in the proportion of persons in this age group going on to post-high school education (although the end of draft calls has helped to decrease the proportion of young men going on to college), and to such factors as higher instructional costs resulting from lighter teaching loads.[9] This does not mean that the pressures are equally distributed; community colleges and professional schools have grown rapidly while enrollment in private four-year liberal arts colleges has declined or leveled off.

Given the delayed impact of the decline in birth rates during the 1960s, the number of college freshmen is probably going to decrease beginning in the late 1970s. Thereafter, an even larger share of college enrollment is likely to be derived from continuing education—adults returning to school part-time during evenings and weekends or taking employer-subsidized evening or day courses. Career-oriented and other educational programs designed to serve this adult market should command broad political support.

Twenty-five to forty-four.   The population twenty-five to forty-four years of age is the key element in the labor force. They are also the generators of new families and new housing starts and are prime consumers of other major forms of goods and services. In 1960, 47 million people were in the twenty-five to forty-four age category. By 1974 the total rose to 52 million. There is the prospect that the proportion of total population in this career age population group will decline, although the numbers will rise. The Bureau of the Census's low projection for the year 2000 is a total of 75 million in this category. One probable result will be increasing pressure on workers to support nonworkers and much resentment on the part of the employed. The strains on the Social Security system in the mid-1970s and the backlash against welfare allocations are a warning of things to come.

Forty-five to sixty-four.   The age group forty-five to sixty-four represents, depending on individuals and personal viewpoints, either the prime of one's earning power and the acme of career status or a rapid falling off in capacity and earnings. In any event this is a transitional group, beginning as child rearers and ending as retirees. In 1960 there were 36 million people in this category; in 1974, 43 million. Some decline is anticipated by the Census Bureau by the year 2000, when the total is expected to decrease to 38 million.

Sixty-five and over.   Age sixty-five is the usual time for retirement, although there seems to be some tendency to reduce the age to sixty-two or sixty. Many of the aged suffer from inadequate incomes and serious health problems, and for this among other reasons the size of this group is important in government and private sector planning. Consequently, the fairly substantial increase in the over-sixty-five population between 1960 and 1974—up from 17 million to 22 million—deserves careful attention, partly because the numbers of aged will continue to grow rapidly for the next thirty years or so. The Census Bureau's low projection for people over sixty-five for the year 2000 is a staggering 31 million. By the turn of the century, a sixth of the total population is likely to be over age 62.

Old people tend to be poor. The mean income of household heads drops by 50 percent between ages fifty-five to sixty-four and over sixty-five. In 1973 the average annual income for households headed by elderly persons was less than $7,000. It is not surprising that older people tend to be tax-conscious, sensitive to inflation, and at odds with a society many perceive as heartless and ungrateful. This attitude is also due in part to chronic ill health; two-thirds of the aged are women, many of whom are subject to lingering but nonfatal diseases—unlike their spouses who died of heart attacks.

So far as the reservoir of potential customers for retirement communities is concerned, this money problem must be borne in mind. The minimal cost of purchasing a dwelling in such communities—over $25,000—sharply reduces the potential market. Indeed, the inability of many older homeowners to locate suitable smaller homes at a reasonable price in their own neighborhoods leads many to be overhoused, clinging to multibedroom homes for want of a suitable alternative. Government assistance in ungluing a sticky housing market by helping to recycle such housing would be much appreciated by both potential older sellers and potential young buyers.

Late forties and fifties.   In this connection, it must be remembered that a prime market target for retirement communities is not the elderly (over sixty-five), but adults in their late forties or fifties. Many of

these persons are "empty nesters," persons who own houses too large
for their needs now that their children are grown. The developer
attempts to persuade them that locations near a main highway offer
easy access to their children and grandchildren and that their accumulated equity will enable them to purchase a modest, resalable
retirement house in a highly attractive community with a mortgage
small enough to be paid off by the time the breadwinner(s) retires. To
the extent that this marketing strategy is successful, the potential
market for retirement communities is very large indeed. States and individual communities, confronted by the prospect of large-scale
developments of this character, may need to assess the potential impact
of an elderly population on such matters as public school bond issues,
nursing homes, and tax policy.

POPULATION TRENDS BY COMMUNITY CATEGORY

It is a cliché to reiterate the major urban population trend of the
past generation, the leveling off or decline of many older core cities and
the growth of low-density suburbs. Since 1970, however, growth in
many suburbs has slowed as a larger share of population movement
heads for smaller communities, away from metropolitan areas. In consequence the fast-growing outer rings of metropolitan suburbia have
been accorded a breathing space to absorb past waves of in-migration.
Within this general demographic context, however, there are important
differences and shadings which deserve careful attention. This is particularly so not only because total population size is important in com-
puting federal and state capitation grants and political representation,
but also because population characteristics are critical factors in
determining service needs.

For convenience it is useful to divide urban communities into the
following five broad groups.

Core cities.   The nation contains about one hundred and fifty
sizable (100,000 or larger) central cities as defined by the U.S. Census
Bureau. In addition there are literally hundreds of cities which do not
fit the official census definition but which exhibit many similar
characteristics—high population density, concentrations of slums and
poverty, and stable or declining populations.

The nation's central cities are characterized by population densities
ranging from a low of 5,000 persons per square mile to the most common 10,000 to 15,000 range and thence to New York City's astronomical

25,000 per square mile. In recent decades most such cities have experienced population decreases or at most minimal growth amounting
to only half or less of their natural increase (their surplus of births over
deaths), partly because people no longer care to live in big cities. Most
are short of developable, readily accessible, and reasonably priced land.
All possess obsolete or redundant public facilities such as old, undersized, half-deserted schools in slum areas as well as abandoned housing
and rundown neighborhoods. Most have serious financial problems
related to the conditions described in the following paragraphs.

1.   Low-income minority populations are rapidly growing. In 1970
the black population of the nation's central cities ranged from a low of 1
to 2 percent (Spokane, Washington; Salt Lake City, Utah; San Jose,
California) to a high of 70 percent (Washington, D.C.). To an increasing
extent, the growth of the black population is self-generating through an
increase in births over deaths rather than the product of out-of-state in-
migration. It is this relatively rapid rate of increase through births,
combined with the tendency of younger whites to exit to the suburbs,
that has resulted in an aging white population (for example, the median
1970 age of white males in Chicago was 32.5 years, compared with 21.1
years for black males) and disproportionately black school populations.
A deceleration in the growth rate of the black population is likely to be
caused by continuing decline in black birth rates—down by 25 percent
between 1967 and 1974—and a falling off in migration from the rural
South. (The nation's blacks are already urbanized. In 1970 less than 6
percent of the black population lived outside metropolitan areas.)

2.   White ethnic groups are clinging tenaciously to lower and
middle-income neighborhoods while resisting the influx of blacks.

3.   Upper- and middle-income neighborhoods are losing population.
To some extent these areas are being penetrated by more affluent
blacks, and some of the larger housing units are being converted into
apartments, group quarters such as nursing homes, funeral homes, or
offices. Most central cities are making strenuous but only modestly
successful efforts to balance their population structure by retaining or
attracting middle- and upper-income families.

It may be noted that the Supreme Court decision which prevents
state aid to parochial schools may weigh against ethnic working-class

and middle-class parents remaining in core cities. These parents regard many central city public schools as "jungles" and consider disciplined parochial schools as their only viable educational alternative. It is true that the high cost of suburban housing has made some stable core city areas more attractive to young families whose children have not yet reached school age. On balance, however, it is apparent that few central cities have successfully adjusted to the problems or exploited the development opportunities associated with declining populations and lower densities.

Stable suburbs.   While the standard image of the suburb is that of a upper-middle-income, fast-growing, single-family community, there are large numbers which do not fit this stereotype. With population densities stabilizing in the 1,500 to 4,000 persons per square mile range, there is an increasing number of suburban communities that have been growing very slowly (less than 0.5 percent per year). Numerous communities in this category are classified as suburbs simply because the central cities have been unable to extend their borders as they did in the last century. Some stable suburbs have large proportions of working-class individuals and may exhibit fairly high densities (more than 3,000 per square mile) as a result of the presence of garden apartments and (less frequently) high-rise buildings. Others are middle- and upper-income strongholds.

As compared to other types of communities, many of the stable suburbs seem to be relatively well adjusted to meeting their financial and public facility needs. This happy situation is particularly applicable to the smaller number of stable upper-income suburbs, but even some stable blue-collar suburbs are better off from a fiscal standpoint than many of their faster-growing lower-middle-income neighbors.

Fast-growing suburbs and exurbs.   This group of communities has received the bulk of population growth in the United States over the past three decades. Many doubled and trebled in size in ten or fifteen years, raising population densities from perhaps the 500 per square mile level to as much as 4,000 or more.

Although growth has slowed in the mid-1970s in most areas, many communities in this category complain strongly and frequently about the prospect of excessive population expansion of the wrong sort. By this they usually mean an influx of low-income population, particularly apartment dwellers, and most especially blacks or persons of Latin American extraction. In recent years much of this opposition has been couched in an environmental context on the grounds that sizable new construction would upset an area's fragile ecology.

In effect, with the exception of expensive homes for the affluent and a modest amount of new housing construction for the elderly, a growing number of suburbs have succeeded in placing sharp limits on population expansion. Often they are helped by the fact that their present public services, particularly sewer systems, are obviously inadequate to support much additional population. The residents of such communities are clearly anxious to preserve the low-density amenities which attracted them in the first place. Many display the "last settler" attitude: "Now that *my* family has moved in, this town is just the right size. Let's keep everyone else out."

But this is not solely a matter of pulling up the ladder after they have climbed aboard. Very small communities are quick to point out the unfairness of singling them out for new planned unit developments (PUD's, large subdivisions that contain commerce and services in addition to housing) or massive subdivisions. Such a scale of development would totally transform their existing land use and population patterns, while alleviating only slightly the enormous need for new housing in the metropolitan area. By implication they are recommending a return to the old system of piecemeal accretion around the center, adding lot to lot, small subdivision to subdivision, a process which tends to diffuse rather than concentrate new development. As noted earlier, the conflict between the freedom to preserve desirable neighborhoods and the right to move freely into communities, with or without benefit of court action or state-mandated low-income housing quotas, is one of the central issues of the coming decade.

Recreation communities.   One of the principal trends of past decades is the conversion of vacation areas which used to be characterized by seasonal peaks in population into year-round communities. Mountain villages, shore towns, and inland lake communities—and indeed the fast-growing Sun Belt reaching from California through Florida—offer graphic evidence of this phenomenon. One problem arises from the fact that much past resort construction tended to be polarized; a small amount was suitable for a small year-round population, while a good deal of the housing stock was comprised of high-density, flimsily built units served by limited public facilities (for example, septic tanks) designed for seasonal use. Some converted resort communities resemble instant slums, while others have taken and are taking costly and painful action designed to correct their deficiencies. Often it is difficult to adopt substantial corrective measures, since these entail such costly and controversial activities as clearing access to the shore by removing old bungalows.

Such programs are often open to charges of class bias and favoritism toward developers, who offer to replace a low-income beach front population occupying low-cost cottages with expensive housing for the affluent. In short, imposing high development standards in resort communities may lead to squeezing out persons of modest means. There is, in addition, an issue revolving around three conflicting rights: freedom of access of fortunate shore front landowners to beach areas, access of a local population to their principal community recreation facility—the shore front—and the right of metropolitan residents in general to enjoy shore areas.

There is the further issue of population size. Many resort communities, such as Boca Raton and Aspen, feel that further population growth would tend to degrade their community. Either overtly or through the environmental protection approach, they are attempting to set narrow limits on further expansion. This raises an extremely difficult political problem. Since there are so few attractive resort communities, attempts at safeguarding their rights and privileges could lose more votes than they would gain. The obvious answer is both to recognize the basic validity of the size argument—Aspen really could not handle 100,000 year-round residents and remain Aspen—and to create alternatives through improving neglected or rundown resort communities or by building new ones. The latter solution is not all that difficult, but it requires establishing and enforcing rigorous standards for the recreation community industry, which tends to be responsive to and (after much complaining) appreciative of quality controls.

Outlying communities.   Most towns in this category are quite small and fall into two classifications: those which remain virtually untouched by the wave of new development, and those which are experiencing a sizable growth influx though population densities are generally under 1,000 to the square mile. Towns in the high-growth classification often find themselves in serious trouble. Underserviced and understaffed, they are poorly equipped to deal on equal terms with developers or to cope with substantial amounts of mobile homes, tract subdivisions, or planned unit developments. Moreover, their willingness to maintain reasonably high standards is frequently sapped by the involvement of many townspeople of influence in real estate transactions as owners (for example, farmers), speculators, brokers, attorneys, developers, insurance brokers, bankers, or owners of construction firms. One question confronting the nation is to determine how such local communities can be helped to preserve adequate development standards without serious infringement on local government autonomy and without a resort to population exclusion. Further, there is the additional task of convincing sleepy little communities that population growth is really on the way and timely advance planning is urgently needed.

OTHER POPULATION CHARACTERISTICS

The Census Bureau includes a number of population, social, and economic characteristics in its studies in addition to migration, urbanization, age distribution, and ethnic and racial composition. Among the most important of these are education, occupation, and income.

Education. There are a number of trends in education, ranging from enrollment to curriculum and involving unresolved problems of race, tax policy, and life styles. One such long-term trend is the increase in the number of children being provided with preschool or kindergarten training. The Head Start program, which began in 1965 to give preschool education to children in poor families, further accelerated a trend which has been under way for a number of years. Between 1960 and 1970 public kindergarten enrollments in the nation increased by about 50 percent, rising from 2.1 million to over 3 million.

Another major trend is the continuing increase in the proportion of sixteen- and seventeen-year-old boys and girls remaining in school, although sixteen is the legal termination date. In past decades there has been a tremendous increase in the numbers of persons going on to post-high school education. This is not limited to persons attending four-year colleges and universities, but also includes many people who go on to training such as airline stewardess or beautician and barber schools and other forms of occupational training. In the nation as a whole over 30 percent were participating in post-high school education or training, but in some urban areas favored by expanding low-cost, state-aided colleges, the figure was approaching 70 percent of 18-24 year olds by the early 1970s.

The increase in higher education enrollment may be ascertained by considering the trend in college enrollment. The number of college students in the nation more than doubled in the single decade from 1960 to 1970, rising from 2.9 million to 7 million, while total population increased by only 13 percent. Census Bureau estimates in the late 1960s projected a total college enrollment of about 11.5 million in 1985, but by the mid-1970s there were signs of a leveling off in total enrollments at about 9 million.

The major gains at public institutions reflect the fact that rising costs at private colleges (up to $6,500 a year in tuition and dormitory fees) have resulted in contraction or stabilization in private higher education enrollments. One public policy issue is the question of whether to provide financial aid to hard-pressed private colleges; another is the danger of overbuilding at public institutions. By the mid-1970s some states were seriously considering closing down programs and branch institutions of their state systems.

One reason for the slowing of expansionary trends in college attendance is the end of the military draft, coupled with an apparent disillusionment with the characteristics of and returns from higher education. In combination these have helped to reverse a historic trend—between 1969 and 1972 the proportion of young males aged eighteen to twenty-one enrolled in college declined from just over 44 percent to just under 37 percent. (In contrast female enrollment held steady at roughly 30 percent.)[10] The longer range demographic picture points to more of the same, namely a decline in the primary college age population—eighteen to twenty-four—in the period from 1970 to 1988. There was, for example, a much smaller number of one-year-old infants in 1970 (the prime population group for the freshman class of 1988) than thirteen-year-olds; that is, the entering class of 1975.

This does not mean an across-the-board decline in prospect for higher education. The nation can expect further growth in public community colleges and increased demand for evening and late-afternoon professional-level education and continuing education for mature adults. But, as suggested, there is likely to be a leveling off in enrollment in most four-year liberal arts institutions. It is likely that they will suffer from aging faculties, attacks on the tenure system to keep schools "young," and demands for downward readjustment in educational facilities. These issues, already affecting elementary and secondary school systems, are just beginning to become significant controversies at the college level.

The expansion in the proportion of college graduates—up from 8 percent of the nation's adult population in 1960 to 11 percent in 1970—has already had a major impact on political and cultural patterns. By and large college graduates tend to demand higher quality public services and are more tolerant of certain deviant types of behavior (such as political and sexual) but less tolerant of public thievery. These differences, of course, presage significant changes in public pressure in such areas as law enforcement, urban development, and political candidacies.

The occupational ladder.   Long-term trends in occupational characteristics parallel the urbanization of the nation. During its first two centuries of settlement, America was predominantly an agricultural nation. Even as late as 1870 half the population worked in agriculture, but by 1970 only about 5 percent of the labor force was employed on farms, a smaller percentage than any other of the world's major agricultural producers.

Through the years there have been other declines in the relative importance of occupations in mining, lumbering, simple mercantile operations, and small pioneering manufacturing enterprises such as potteries, which are associated with settlements in hamlets or small towns. In contrast, impressive gains in professional occupations and white-collar industries tend to be heavily concentrated in medium-sized and larger metropolitan areas.

The ten broad categories for which data is reported by the Census Bureau are subdivided into more than 700 different occupations by the U.S. Department of Labor. The number of professional and technical positions has been increasing far more rapidly than the semiskilled and unskilled jobs. Over the long term, the proportion of the American labor force in the farming and mining area has decreased sharply, the proportion of unskilled laborers and semiskilled laborers has dropped, and in the past two decades the proportion of laborers in manufacturing industries has also declined. In contrast, employment in a whole range of occupations in public service, health, education and welfare, recreation, and most professional categories has increased sharply. Two statistics are illustrative: the proportion of the male labor force employed as factory operatives in the nation decreased from 14.8 percent in 1960 to 12.8 percent in 1970, while the proportion of professional and technical workers rose from 9.9 percent to 13.5 percent in that decade.

In most of the nation's metropolitan areas the proportion of persons employed in manufacturing industries declined sharply between 1950 and 1970, and the decline has continued. The metropolis has become an office-services world. In 1970, almost three out of every five persons employed in the nation were categorized as "white-collar" employees, while only one in four worked in a factory. But "white-collar" employment does not necessarily mean an escape from menial labor. In the white-collar industries there are many low-wage jobs which call for limited skills, particularly in service occupations—bus boys, hotel bellmen, deliverymen, hospital attendants, cleaning staff, etc.

The trends which appeared between 1950 and the late 1960s are expected to continue and in some cases to accelerate in the 1970s. Despite the recession of the mid-1970s, which had a disastrous short-term impact on employment levels among scientists and engineers, the U.S. Department of Labor still expects a substantial increase in jobs among this group, while the professional group as a whole is likely to increase about twice as fast as overall employment.

The issue confronting the nation is to develop a responsive system of occupational education. It is assumed that vocationally oriented training should not only be directed toward immediate employment—that is, the first job—but should also make an effort at continuing employability. Past training programs furnished redundant barbers, printers, cabinetmakers, and farmers, but newer problems of redundancy emerged in such unexpected fields as aerospace engineering and school teaching.

Equally important, the likelihood of a leveling off in the number of professional and managerial occupations suggests an increasing need to make the vast number of terminal, semiskilled, and skilled positions more meaningful and satisfying. Widespread job dissatisfaction seems to call for a basic job restructuring to add variety and status to a large number of jobs such as the assembly-line worker, patrolman, waitress, or hospital attendant. And as suggested in chapter 4, it may be useful to consider ways and means to reduce the number of hours required for work in dull, degrading occupations.

Rich and growing richer?   Almost from its very beginning the United States has been a relatively wealthy country. So far as can be estimated, per capita income in the United States (measured in constant dollars that make allowances for inflation) about the year 1800 was on the order of $200, which would have given the average family an income of roughly $1,000 per year. While this is only a rough approximation, it offers a useful comparison to the situation in developing nations in the mid-1970s, many of which have per capita incomes of less than $300.

In the course of the last century, per capita income in the United States has been increasing at the rate of two to three percent a year, despite serious depressions and a number of minor recessions. By the mid-1970s, per capita incomes of $4,000 to to $5,000 per year or more were common among the more affluent states.[11]

In 1969 median family income in the nation was $10,000. At the 1960 to 1973 rates of increase, the median national annual family income was projected by the Census Bureau to reach $15,000, in terms of constant 1968 dollars, by the year 1985. If true, this would have profound implications for every aspect of the nation's urban and cultural development. Adjusting our sights upward in a manner consistent with advanced educational attainment and higher incomes is one of the challenging tasks for the 1970s and 1980s. This cheerful news presumes that the Bureau of Census is accurate in its optimistic prediction for 1985: "We are heading into the era of the affluent majority . . . by the year 2,000 about 60 percent of families are expected to have incomes above $15,000 in constant dollars . . ."[12]

Population Issues in the 1980s

Land use practices have become an area of heated controversy, much more because of population issues than alternative zoning ordinances. As noted, one of the most serious issues in the 1970s and 1980s concerns a variation on the zoning theme, namely the conscious efforts of whole states (such as Oregon) and regions, as well as communities, to keep outsiders out. The fact that relatively few communities are generally considered to be particularly attractive suggests that their fortunate residents would like to keep it that way by keeping population growth very, very small. Meanwhile, an even larger proportion of the population would like to move out of their depressing urban environment to one of these happier places. The nation's relatively few oases of attractive places to live are faced with the serious dilemma of reconciling the freedom of outsiders to relocate to their community with freedom of present residents to protect and conserve their neighborhoods.

THE NATALISM ISSUE

With respect to the central issue of population policy—the birth rate—the government has taken, up to recently, an ostensibly pronatal posture. Children provide modest income tax advantages, although these amount to far less than the $75,000 cost per family of rearing a child through age twenty-two.[13] The American system of low-cost public education is also pronatal. Some middle-class English families are accustomed to laying out a third or more of their income for school fees from age eight through university. However, the incomes of American families can be drained by college costs, particularly because youngsters' school fees are not tax deductible. The fast-growing state college systems and long-term, low-interest loan programs can reduce much of the financial burden. Nevertheless, the total rearing cost, including opportunity costs—that is, income lost through the wife's inability to work—remains extremely large.

What the United States lacks is three essentials of population policy common in other nations. The first is a system of family allowances. Since World War II all Canadian families, for example, have received a cash allowance for each child.[14] In a population-conscious society, such allowances might provide substantial payments for the first two children and little for subsequent offspring.

A second government contribution to qualitative as well as quantitative aspects of population policy is comprehensive national health insurance. Aside from its economic benefits and its political merits, providing free medical care would remove another part of the burden of child rearing, along with helping to ensure a healthier population of adults as well as children.

Third, there should be a positive national policy on abortion and contraception. Although the previous policy of permitting states to restrict abortions and dissemination of contraceptive information and devices was overturned by the Supreme Court in 1973, some states are dragging their feet. Enough states have acted favorably on this issue, however, to ensure sufficient legal abortions to prevent hundreds of thousands of births annually.[15] There are now numerous local abortion clinics which remove the necessity for pregnant women to go to New York City or other permissive urban centers. But for many women, particularly among the poor, the safe abortion alternative is not readily available. It is hoped that research on contraception will pay off in a long-awaited breakthrough like a monthly, annual, or lifetime pill (or subcutaneous implantation), thereby removing the need for abortions.

The downward trend.   A number of hypotheses have been advanced to explain the sharp decline in the nation's birth rates, aside from the sheer cost of child raising in an urban society. Clearly former

Boston mayor James Michael Curley's gibe that the Boston Yankees "breed dogs" while the Irish, Jews, and Italians are having children is no longer applicable. Curley was referring to the practice of many of Boston's old Yankee families to limit themselves to one or two children and then to lavish large sums on private school education in the British fashion. In recent years, however, the heavy expense of proper child rearing has become apparent to other ethnic groups. It *is* cheaper to send a dependent pup to obedience school than a dependent child to college. With the emphasis on serious careers and personality development for women, young children have increasingly come to be regarded more as costly time-consuming hindrances rather than God-given fulfillment of nature's plan for man and womankind. There is also concern over population pressure on national and world resources, a weakening of traditional religious barriers to contraception and abortion, and the trend to later marriages or, less frequently, to no marriages.

If the downward trend in birth rates continues, by the late 1980s America is likely to be in the midst of a full-scale panic. Political orators will point with alarm to the drastic changes in America's population composition—the growing reliance on imported labor, a smaller work force supporting a larger dependent population, and a generally more conservative, aging society. And they will also raise the spectre of the swarming and impoverished Second and Third Worlds threatening to overrun the population-stable, affluent minority.

Day care.   In this context, the possibility of really heavy government subsidies for couples who prefer (or who can be coaxed to have) large families is one distinct possibility. For this reason, day care is likely to become one of the more significant issues of the coming decade. Only in this way is there a strong likelihood that motherhood may be made sufficiently less burdensome to reconcile parental freedoms with child rearing. But the obstacle is cost. The development of an attractive, comprehensive system of free (or very low-cost) day care centers covering infancy through age five is an extremely expensive proposition, probably involving costs of $3,000 per child annually.[16] (This is for quality care and learning, not simply for child storage. It also includes the amortization cost for fire-resistant, well-equipped, new or thoroughly renovated older buildings.) The teacher/child ratio must be extremely low—one to five or so.

Day care is difficult to justify on strict financial accounting. As of early 1975, a mother with two children in a day care center would have

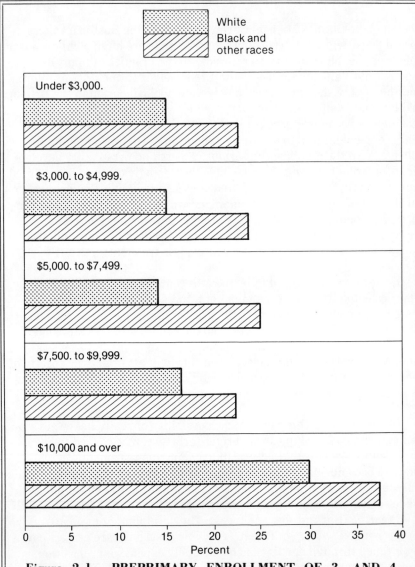

Figure 2-1. PREPRIMARY ENROLLMENT OF 3- AND 4-YEAR-OLDS, BY FAMILY INCOME AND RACE, 3-YEAR AVERAGE: 1970 - 1972

Source: The Condition of Education, National Center for Education Statistics, U.S. Department of Health, Education and Welfare. (Washington, D.C.: Government Printing Office, 1975), p. 61.

to earn $9,000 a year, if she had to pay the full tuition cost, in order to receive a modest net return for her efforts. Even women with substantial earnings might be given pause by a comparison of the costs and benefits. What is clear, however, is that the use of day care is directly correlated with income; as with many amenities and services, the poor get less. (See figure 2-1.)

Day care for older preschool children is only part of the story, however. Modern nations which make serious, uninterrupted use of female workers also attempt to provide crèches, facilities for the care of infants up to about age two. Good crèches are at least as expensive, on a per capita basis, as day care centers. (Often their attendant-child ratio runs as high as one to one.)

An alternative to providing this kind of facility is almost unavailable in the United States—the extended family with a grandmother or aunt willing to provide child care. For this reason in the absence of an infant care system most mothers are forced to withdraw from the work force for at least two years and, if there were three children spaced at two-year intervals, for a total of at least six years. The obvious implication for a career-minded young woman is that children are expensive not only in terms of money and energy, but also in terms of adverse consequences to career development.

This all suggests the need for a major national day-care effort, involving perhaps two million children from low-income families. It would require an annual direct expenditure of $6 billion a year and development of a greatly enlarged early childhood education profession, embracing a corps of 400,000 or so teachers and supporting staff. One attractive compensatory feature immediately comes to mind to practicing politicians: the institution of a large-scale day care program would create hundreds of thousands of new jobs for teachers. And to the extent that new buildings are needed, it would offer a political bonus in the form of many small construction contracts.

It is not surprising that no administration has yet seen fit to grapple with the day-care dilemma. The Nixon approach to welfare mothers illustrates this point. Recognizing that AFDC (Aid for Dependent Children) mothers were the primary labor reservoir for its sloganized approach—"workfare not welfare"—it was proposed that welfare mothers whose youngest child was six or older would be required to work. More important, perhaps, the minimum age for the youngest child was to be subsequently extended downward to age three. This might have been reasonable had there been more than the barest element of an extended day care program attached to this proposal. But there was not, and as a result, it was clear that the preschool child was to continue to rely primarily on the informal network of grandparents, aunts, and unlicensed baby-watchers. In short, there was to be more of the same evasion of responsibility and resort to baby-sitting without any pretense of educational structure or assurance of building safety, proper feeding, or sanitation.

Clearly the demand for day care is enormous and so are the potential rewards, not only in voter support but in terms of maintaining the national birth rate at a replacement level. A *serious day care program* seems to be the only way to reconcile career liberation for women, a tremendous national asset, with a sound population policy under which children are cherished as a vital national resource.

There is of course another alternative to a child-centered day care-crèche system and the present catch-as-catch-can non-system. This is an arrangement which is frankly parent-oriented; the prime goal is to keep a maximum number of women in the labor force. This would require a less expensive, semicustodial arrangement for children with minimal emphasis on child development and primary focus on providing low-cost, safe accommodation for preschoolers. This half-way house may appear to be in conflict with the cherish-the-child orientation, but it is a realistic, cost-conscious alternative to get the program started. Embellishments can be added when and if the nation feels more affluent or reorders its priorities.

THE GENERATION GAP AS A PUBLIC POLICY ISSUE

The general aging of the population presents a number of new issues. Governments dominated by old people tend to be conservative. There is the risk of political paranoia with older people consistently voting down legislative programs which they perceive as threatening; that is, leading to radical change or costing too much.

In planning terms, the 1980s may well be a period of confrontations between the elderly and the young over a wide range of issues, including housing (who gets first priority), schools (no expensive "frills"), medical policy (gerontology vs. pediatrics), recreation (shuffleboard or basketball courts), allocation of police (heavily guarded retirement areas or safe downtowns) and a host of other issues. If the aged feel particularly hard pressed, there may well be a revival of radicalism among the elderly, on the model of the 1930s Townsend movement, with old people organizing into powerful voting blocs to force priority allocations for pensions and other matters crucial to them.

As noted earlier, such a situation may require very painful political choices, particularly if there is economic stagnation or worse, a deceleration in the nation's economic growth rate. If this were the case, the nation would be confronted with what might be called Motherhood I versus Motherhood II choices. That is, do we allocate scarce resources to weary old folks who have devoted a lifetime to arduous toil, including child rearing, or do we spend money on our children, the shining hope of our future? While it is true that almost every government (and family) budget makes equally difficult choices almost every day, when resources are scarce the allocation may pose excruciating moral dilemmas as well as political nightmares.

The impact of the aged is likely to be unevenly distributed, areas which offer balmy climates expect hundreds of thousands if not millions of old folk as permanent residents. A preview of future concentrations of the elderly may be Fort Lauderdale and Miami Beach, in each of which a third of the year-round population is over age sixty.

To meet the need for safe havens, secure, almost self-contained retirement villages are springing up in a number of states. It may be that such communities will function as colonies of undemanding taxpayers, of little more import to the community than a cemetery or a nursing home. On the other hand, especially if the tax crunch is on and inflation erodes retirement incomes, the Sunshine Villages may form powerful voting blocs within little communities and even across entire states. As such instances occur, there may well be almost as much resistance on the part of demographically balanced communities to influxes of old people as there presently is to migration of the poor. The migrating flow and political impact of the elderly may well be another controversial issue of the 1980s.

The foregoing raises two possibilities for action. The first is more effort to help older people integrate with the larger community through a structure of full-time and part-time jobs to augment meager incomes and continue full participation in community, business, and political affairs. The second is a prerequisite: an improved health care system to prevent America from becoming what some physicians predict, a nation with enormous numbers of sick old people, draining its resources.

THE IMMIGRATION ISSUE

In the century between 1820 and 1920 the United States was the recipient of the most massive tide of immigration in world history. Over 40 million immigrants arrived, most of them Caucasians from Europe,

"Unfortunately there turned out to be an error in our population forecast."
Source: © 1976 Punch (Rothco).

but also millions of forcibly transported Africans and millions of Latin Americans arrived in the United States. Since a large proportion were of working age, their rearing costs having been contributed by "sending" nations, a substantial share of America's growth has been attributed to its ability to use and often exploit adult labor which it had not nurtured, fed, or educated.

Historical background.   The largest waves of immigration from abroad arrived in the sixty-five-year period from 1850 to 1914, with the greatest number disembarking during the late nineteenth and early twentieth centuries. Overall, the big year for foreign immigration into the United States was 1907, with 1.3 million; 1914 ranked second, with 1.2 million. This may be compared with a yearly average of about 300,-000 immigrants in the years since 1950. In the 1970s, with a total United States population of over 200 million, we have only one quarter of the volume of immigration annually that we had before World War I when the total population was about 80 million.

Historically, issues related to immigration have been one of the more controversial aspects of population policy. Many myths have emerged about immigration. For example, it is widely believed that most of the American population between the settlement at Jamestown in the early seventeenth century and the beginning of mass migration in the mid-nineteenth century consisted of adventurous, intelligent, and skilled emigrants escaping from Old World tyranny to religious, political, and economic freedom. In the countries from which the immigrants came, on the other hand, there grew up the belief that the departing population was little more than unstable riffraff. The people who remained were firmly of the opinion that people of substance stayed at home.

The immigration issue of the mid-1970s in some respects resembles the problems of the 1930s. During the Great Depression (as in earlier panics and recessions) there was a widespread feeling that enough was enough—a nation with 15 or 20 percent of its labor force out of work could not afford to take in needy immigrants. But to a degree the potential conflict over immigration policy was muted by the fact that during periods of depression in the United States, the rate of immigration normally declined as America began to look less inviting.

In the face of similar economic problems European nations have moved to decrease the number and proportion of legal and illegal "guest workers," while the Canadian government revised its immigration laws to stabilize intake at 200,000 annually, to shift the balance in favor of persons with a knowledge of English or French, and to establish priorities for needed skills. In combination, these moves were expected to weight the scales against nonwhite immigrants, who made up nearly 50 percent of the Canadian immigrant total in 1973.[17]

In recent years the United States has experienced a similar weighting of legal immigration patterns in favor of Latins, blacks, and Asians. In 1972, only 25 percent of total immigration was derived from Europe and Canada as compared to 70 percent in the period from 1951 to 1960.[18] It might be noted that these broad categories do not necessarily indicate race, ethnic composition, or level of job skills and education. For example, the post-Castro immigration from Cuba is a classic case of rapid, successful integration of Latins, many of whom arrived with substantial educational and skill backgrounds. On the other hand, some European migrants, particularly from southern Europe, arrive with little education and not much in readily marketable skills. In the United States, as in Canada, the level and composition of official migration represents a growing potential for controversy.

International population policy.   While friction over immigration policy may become acute during business recessions when jobs are scarce, there is a longer term issue here. If, as seems likely, the United States succeeds in achieving a no-growth population pattern before the turn of the century, the question is whether this country should continue to serve as an immigration receiving area for nations which have not made, and are not attempting to achieve, substantial progress in controlling population growth. It is true that in recent years there have been only a handful of countries which have consciously tried to increase their rate of population expansion. Argentina is trying to catch up to Brazil, Israel is attempting to counter the weight of its Arab enemies, Libya hopes to grow into its oil wealth, and Burma is trying to exert more balance against its mammoth Asian neighbors. But a number of nations in Latin America, Asia, and Africa have strongly resisted population limitations as a neocolonialist attempt to shift the focus of the developing nations away from demands for redistributing wealth and toward planned parenthood. It was only in 1975, under Indira Ghandi's dictatorship, that the largest of the Third World nations, India, seemed to move vigorously toward the adoption of a strong government policy of incentives for families with no more than two children, combined with career and other penalties for larger families.[19]

Obviously, national population goals are the province of each nation. In some cases, however, pursuit of these goals may result in overgrowth in a number of developing nations requiring free or low-cost food from developed nations to stave off famine, and perhaps also requiring developed nations to absorb part of the surplus population.

It seems likely that if present trends continue, at least one-quarter of total United States population growth will be generated by net foreign immigration over the next twenty to thirty years; most of this migration will come from rapid-growth, underdeveloped nations. Does the high-population-growth developing nation have the right to ask for, or the low-growth developed nation the obligation to supply food, credit, or a migration haven? There are many, particularly in the developing nations, whose answer is in the affirmative, partly because they blame their present plight on colonialism or more recent versions of economic exploitation. In practical terms, short of a world upheaval, the developed nations are not likely to agree with this attempt to link past oppression with current and future burdens.

If the immigration-population issue is difficult with respect to legal immigrants, the problem is explosive when illegal immigration is concerned. Estimates of the number of illegal immigrants residing in the United States range from 7 to 13 million, most of them as industrious and law abiding as legal immigrants.[20] Mexico is a prime source of such migration; a significant number also come from the Caribbean, Latin America, and Asia. Among other ramifications, the continued large-scale immigration of Latins may result in Latin Americans outnumbering black Americans by the late 1980s. There have already been interminority battles for control of model cities, inner-city schools, and antipoverty funds; more and larger scale interminority competition may lie ahead.

When times are difficult, there is an immediate temptation to round up and deport illegals as a means of opening jobs for natives, freeing housing, and reducing welfare and crime rates. As members of a nation of immigrants, most Americans have been opposed to sharp restrictions on immigration. Police roundups of honest, neighborhood-improving illegals and their families, painfully eking out a modest living in the slums, are offensive to fair play and an insult to the memory of one's ancestors who found a home and a refuge in the promised land. But unless there is a sharp reversal in the economic trends of the mid-1970s, and in particular, unless the ecological prophets who call for urgent government action in Latin America to restrict population growth to avert famine are dead wrong, there are serious questions ahead involving allocation of scarce resources. From a political and moral point of view it is reprehensible to force children to suffer for the mistakes of their government. If, however, food is scarce and jobs are limited, it would seem logical at the very least to penalize the high-growth population-exporting countries and to reward those which show genuine efforts to pursue a rational population policy.

The most urgent issue clearly involves the future relations with our southern neighbor, Mexico. The Mexican birth rate, aided by a pronatal government posture, is three times as high as the American birth rate. Despite significant economic progress and the prospect of growing industrialization of new oil discoveries, Mexico cannot provide jobs for much of its population—hence the heavy illegal migration over the northern border. At a minimum it would appear to be reasonable to confront this massive population flow to bring the problem of illegals under control and to develop a linkage between Mexican population policy and American immigration policy.

Indeed, the same principle of linkage should be extended to other nations in the Caribbean, Latin America, and elsewhere that export population surpluses to the United States. Surely the biblical injunction concerning one's responsibility as one's brother's keeper also extends to urging an end to suicidal action. The creation of incentives and disincentives to effect changes in population policy would permit the United States to continue to admit substantial numbers of immigrants, rather than to adopt the alternative; that is, a severely restrictive policy, as is the case in Sweden.

In the 1960s the Swedes provided jobs for tens of thousands of foreigners, including many Finns and Yugoslavs. But urged by its powerful trade unions, the nation revised immigration laws in 1971 to place severe limits on importation of foreign labor. Since illegal immigration is difficult in a small, highly bureaucratized nation with a unique language and no large foreign ghettos to shelter illegals, the revised laws have indeed protected Swedish labor by eliminating one of the immigration refuges for population-surplus nations. There is absolutely no question that America will experience pressures to follow suit. Even a resumption of substantial employment growth won't help much. Given the potential size of the immigration reservoir in developing nations, such a respite is likely to be temporary; this issue simply will not go away.

POPULATION CHANGES AND LAND DEVELOPMENT

Fundamental population changes are part and parcel of equally profound alterations in social trends which are reflected in, among other areas, land values and dwelling construction. Consider the trends toward late marriages or no marriages and toward smaller families, combined with rising levels of education and income. The initial effects of this combination of factors are already apparent.

Apartment buildings.   One effect is an enlarged market for high-rise and low-rise apartment buildings catering to singles, small families, retired couples, and various types of nontraditional sexual and fraternal unions. The obverse side of the coin is a decline, preceded by a leveling off, in the demand for the traditional single-family, freestanding dwelling. As noted in chapter 3, the housing market is already reflecting this trend.

Socially, there is likely to be a population with much less emphasis on sinking roots and participating in such civic activities as the PTA and Garden Club, and much more on personal leisure activities and facilities. There already exist outcroppings of this type of development, such as singles apartments outside of Washington, D.C., Los Angeles, and New York. The prospect is a growing market for intensive development clustered around clubhouses and swimming pools with adult-oriented activities provided by the management. As suggested earlier, there will be less room for the small-scale builder and more for the corporation, with substantial resources capable of providing attractive minicommunities with built-in recreation activities which will increasingly tend to resemble resort hotels. Well-educated and well-paid adult residents will be able to afford fairly expensive facilities, partly because in such a personalized society there are few children to drain away combined husband-wife incomes.

There are likely to be a number of interesting political ramifications associated with this trend. First, new, unorthodox voting groups will emerge. A classic example is the Gay Liberation movement, which represents a sizable, organized group of voters in some communities. But overall there is likely to be less active community involvement on the part of a volatile, mobile population more interested in personal development and particular issues of direct interest than in such community concerns as the local school system. It may be recalled that during the nineteenth and early twentieth centuries there was a large, permanent class of boarders, single working people living in respectable or not-so-respectable rooming houses for long periods. Then came the 1940s and 1950s and nearly everyone got married and had families. But now, in a new form, we have a revival of long-term abstention from marriage.[21]

It will be interesting to see just how volatile this new group, without the ballast of three or four children, will be. Two and three generations back it was this class that provided the excitable human raw material for gold rushes and land rushes, for instant recruiting in wars, and in fact for all sorts of activities which promised excitement, ranging from lynching parties and riots to sporting crowds and sporting houses. At this point all that can be said is that no one quite knows what voting predilections or long-term social behavior to predict for this new breed of singles and pairs.

Climate-controlled environment.   As suggested in chapter 3, the special needs of the new population can be accommodated in an enlarged, climate-controlled environment using the proven technology and marketability of the regional shopping mall. Simply by extending covered street corridors, different units such as apartment complexes, recreational centers, and various public facilities like schools, as well as research and light industry, can be joined together to form a single community. Avoiding excessive heat, cold, rain and snow should be a particularly attractive prospect for the aged, mothers of small children, single people and, indeed, for most people in northern states. It is possible to conceive of sizable developments of this type which include such lavish recreational facilities that the distinction between climate-controlled resort communities and suburban communities will become blurred. If this supposition is correct, retirement to Mediterranean-climate communities and even some forms of resort travel may decline in popularity.

The special design characteristics of a climate-controlled community offer two additional advantages to their residents. First, 100 percent lighted areas, combined with controlled ingress and egress, offer an environment which should be as close to eliminating street crime as any which we can conceivably devise. Second, the unified energy system, as well as its compactness, should provide very large savings in time, cost, electricity, and vehicular traffic. In an age of rising prices and scarcity, this is not to be easily discounted. It suggests that from a governmental point of view, such development should be strongly encouraged. It is also possible that some of the residents will work in the attached offices and shops and that most will shop at the mall and make use of ancillary services, all of which would greatly diminish the time and cost of travel.

Nodal population growth.   The prospect of revived nodal population growth, a modernized version of the development which once clustered around suburban railroad stations, raises new possibilities for land use and transportation planning. If, as suggested, a substantial amount of new suburban population will be concentrated instead of widely dispersed, there will be increased possibilities for viable public transportation. Express buses and/or transit can pick up new customers—but only to the extent that radial movement to central city jobs continues.

TOWARD A HEALTHIER POPULATION
From time to time physicians have offered optimistic judgments on the state of health care in the United States. For years the standard claim was that it was the finest in the world because, in the words of one conservative practitioner, "The rich can afford to buy the best and

the poor get it for nothing in free clinics. I spend a day a week in a clinic myself . . ."

An event that triggered much apoplectic editorializing was the proposed inauguration of health insurance plans and various group practice arrangements in the 1930s and 1940s, both of which were subsequently adopted and coopted by the physicians. (For example, there is strong evidence that the Blue Cross and Blue Shield corporations serve as a supine third-party collection instrument for the medical hospital establishment.)[22] The second trauma was the enactment of socialized medicine in Britain in 1946. With the help of plentiful propaganda ammunition from old-line English doctors bemoaning the mad rush to procure badly needed false teeth and eyeglasses and the alleged loss of personal ties between doctor and patient because of the huge number of patients arbitrarily assigned to participating physicians, the American medical establishment has so far avoided their colleagues' fate.[23]

By the mid-1970s much of the ideological storm had abated. For one thing, Britain's health had indisputably improved, and most of its physicians have adjusted successfully to the new conditions. It is true that by the mid-1970s the British medical system was encountering serious problems. Younger physicians were restive, feeling overworked, underpaid, and badly in need of modern facilities to treat their patients in a more humane and efficient manner. There was also a widespread agreement that without some limits to comprehensive medical care provided at no direct cost to patients, the costs are insupportable, particularly by a financially shaky country like Britain. There was a growing consensus (embracing many doctors) that America could do a lot better with health care. In the mid-1970s there is fairly general agreement that other nations are ahead of the United States in such areas as infant mortality rates, delivery of services with emphasis on preventive medicine, and control of medical costs.[24]

By the mid-1970s alternative national health insurance proposals were offered for congressional consideration, with the modest American Medical Association program calling for a federal expenditure of $32 billion annually. A more comprehensive bill called for $100 billion in federal spending. The larger scale, comprehensive proposal was to make use of federal withholding taxes on the Social Security model.[25]

All of the recent proposals for improvement of health care systems reflect what has been rightly called the "politicization" of the system.[26] Overburdened medical consumers and their political representatives are casting about for some way of making the system work better at manageable cost.[27]

The details of the protracted wrangling over alternatives and fine points is of no interest to a population demanding results—speedy adoption of a workable system. (By 1975 the average four-person American family was spending over $2,000 annually in health care.) Certainly in a period of slowing population growth it makes sense to nurture and cherish the nation's population, devising approaches that reflect the lessons of past experience at home and abroad.

A reasonable program for medical care might be based on the following criteria:

1.   Adequate *advance preparation* for the backlog of cases arising from past neglect. We will not be as inundated by neglected patients as were the British in the late 1940s, after a generation of depression, war, and persistent malnourishment and inadequate treatment. But we can expect a sizable backlog of health care needs that the present incomplete and distorted system has not confronted.

2.   Adequate provision for *comprehensiveness*. This should include dental care, eyeglasses, prosthetic equipment, care for catastrophic illnesses, and other medical drains on income. *This does not mean completely "free" medical care.* Medical experience in other countries indicates that, strange as it may seem, some patients, particularly lonely middle-aged and older women, nourish their hypochondria and request continuing treatment, including surgery, as a means of combatting loneliness and neglect.[28] A combination of at least minimal patient charges and psychological-social counseling is recommended rather than either gruffly dismissing such malingerers or else permitting inordinate amounts of high-paid, scarce medical talent to be absorbed by persons whose primary needs are for affection and attention.

3.   Adequate provisions for *prevention of disease* include periodic examinations, establishment and enforcement of effective occupational safety regulations, adequate pretesting of new products before approval for sale, and establishment and enforcement of environmental and occupational health protection standards. Much of the gap between the poor and others can be closed with nonmedical care; for instance, much more needs to be done in nutrition, particularly in regulating food quality and nutritional value. (This also means more action to limit intake of

hazardous substances such as tobacco and excessive amounts of alcohol.)

4.   Assurance that the *planning and administration* of an expanded health program will not be permitted to be totally captured by the medical establishment — that all the new money will not be alloted to those who were getting the old money. This, in part, is a matter of controlling costs, attempting to avoid the cozy, in-house rationalizations and misjudgments that result in construction of unneeded hospitals and overconcentration on cures and equipment rather than on prevention. In addition, there is evidence to suggest that the medical profession is reaping undue rewards from its quasi-monopoly position. Early action aimed at restructuring the medical care system by making more effective use of nurses and paraprofessionals is needed. There must also be professional medical care ombudsmen to improve weak medical policy review procedures and an infusion of outside planners, administrators, and evaluators to monitor and evaluate medical care systems.

5.   Improved *delivery of services*. This includes action to improve medical care to the inner-city poor and to persons living in rural or outlying areas. The imbalance in per capita distribution of medical facilities can be corrected in part by making more effective use of communications (for example, two-way television and computer systems), by use of financial incentives to encourage decentralizing care facilities and programmed staff and by using paramedical personnel effectively. Medical systems offer a promising area for program evaluation. Statistics are generally comprehensive and accurate and permit close, accurate international comparisons to chart progress in such critical fields as infant mortality and communicable diseases, among other indicators.[29]

WHO GETS THE MONEY? INCOME ISSUES FOR THE 1980S

Most people are aware that America is a remarkably stable country. Two hundred years with one constitution and one system of government, interrupted by only one serious attempt at disruption—the Civil War—is a record almost unique among nations. This history of political stability in the midst of sweeping and rapid demographic, economic, and technological change is at least partly due to one constant factor, spectacular economic growth. For generations there was the western frontier to absorb restless energies and ambitions, serving as a safety valve for the discontented. And before and after the closing of the frontier in the 1890s there was a general trend in the direction of economic expansion, which promised upward mobility to all the deserving. Moreover, this trend actually delivered enough success stories to make Horatio Alger heroes a credible possibility. Almost everyone had a rich and distant relative or a wealthy ex-friend.

Economic failures.   In the midst of this enthusiasm there was a darker side to life in America—pioneers "busted" before they reached Pike's Peak, hard-scrabble farmers, factory workers, exploited miners, sharecroppers, loggers, seamen. Jack London, Upton Sinclair, and others have portrayed the miseries of the poor around the turn of the century. The Wobblies (members of the Industrial Workers of the World), the anarchists, the Grangers (an association of farmers that fought the railroads), the bloody mine wars in the coal fields, and the Eugene Debs Socialists offered evidence that many at the bottom despaired of achieving a better life through pluck and luck and turned to trade unions and radical politics.

Over and above the proletarian despair there was a recurrent theme which middle-class Americans found especially poignant. This is the family that has known better days and manfully keeps up a brave front as its folk slide down and down into genteel shabbiness. Booth Tarkington (*Alice Adams* and the *Magnificent Ambersons*), Tennessee Williams (*The Glass Menagerie*), and William Faulkner (in the Yoknapatawpha novels) have all depicted distressed gentlefolk, unsuccessful middle-class or upper-class strivers or nouveau-outsiders who lost hold of the brass ring. Just as most American families have a moderately wealthy relative or two (usually distant relatives), they also have living examples of failure: soured investments, forced sales, bankruptcies.

Social peace in prosperity.   But on balance, it seems that the reality of the slim chances of achieving substantial wealth or even the pervasive possibility of disaster was less important than the fact that things were indeed getting better. After each bout of gloom the radical prophets of disaster were again confounded as incomes rose and automobiles, surburban houses, expensive appliances, and all sorts of once-luxuries became commonplace.

In this context, radicals in America have found small audiences for their calls to share the wealth, seize the means of production, expropriate the riches, destroy the system. Throughout most of American history it was in fact possible to avoid direct, bitter confrontation with the facts of inequality and poverty in two ways. First, an increasing proportion of the population was enabled to become relatively conservative persons of property. They did so through a combination of their own efforts and such government programs as the 1862 Homestead Act and later the federal mortgage insurance programs of the 1930s, which helped to transform much of America into landowners and homeowners.

Second, it was government policy to try to relate wealth to public usefulness. The government enriched canal companies, housing and land developers, railroad builders, and oil and utility corporations for performing work and producing products useful to the population. If this sounds pollyannish, this long-standing American policy can be compared to the approach adopted by some other nations, in which wealth was conferred on persons who spent all or most of it on military adventures, or gambling, or lavish display. Under such systems elites could permit the national agriculture, factories, and railroads to obsolesce, or they could simply decamp with the money to invest it or spend it elsewhere. Robber barons, price fixers, and stock manipulators or not, America received a better return for enriching its rich than is the case in many other nations. During much of American history there is surprisingly little hatred of rich people, no real lower-class revolt, no wide social and political gulf between entrenched privilege and chronically seething, disaffected, revolutionary masses.

To a great degree America owes its social peace to growth; with the pie constantly becoming larger, demands for fair shares were muted. Given a reasonable expectation of improvement and opportunity, there was patching rather than demolition; modest, incremental reforms rather than revolution. Some of the worst corporate abuses were curbed, housing and health were improved and regulated, unionization was protected, but on the whole the property system was not fundamentally altered. Its chief beneficiaries were permitted to manipulate the tax structure and generally to exercise an inordinate amount of political and economic power.

As long as the system delivers, or promises to deliver, there is some grumbling but probably more admiration for the achievers, and little resentment of America's equivalent of the nobility, old inherited wealth. There was—and is—a recognition that the key element in social and economic progress has been a broad, sustained economic expansion which created millionaires as well as high-wage factory and service jobs. In contrast, the specialized ameliorative programs designed to help

the poor, the distressed areas, or other needy targets have made a
relatively minor contribution to solving the problems of poverty and unemployment.

LESS LAISSEZ-FAIRE?

From time to time when beset by periodic business panics, recessions, and depressions which seemed to foretell the end of generations
of expansion, there have been largely unheeded calls for a reshuffling of
the deck. When it appeared from time to time that the pie was no longer
growing, that there was no longer the prospect of bigger slices for all, it
was said that the answer to redress of grievances was redistribution
rather than the traditional reliance on sheer growth.

Clearly the past quarter century has been a period of substantial
gains in real (uninflated) income for most Americans. Real national income more than doubled between 1950 and 1974; the proportion of white
families receiving less than $7,000 per year decreased from almost half
in 1950 to a fifth in 1974. (The corresponding percentages for blacks and
other nonwhites went from 85 percent in 1950 down to just over half in
1974—roughly where whites were twenty-four years earlier.)

True, not much income redistribution occurred. In 1974 as in 1950,
the poorest fifth of American families received about 5 percent of
aggregate family income, while the richest fifth received 15 percent of
the total. In point of fact, a slight redistribution did occur: the share of
the lowest fifth rose by .3 percent in twenty-four years, while the share
of the highest fifth fell by 2 percent.[30] And this substantial improvement took place from Truman through Nixon, hardly an era of political
revolution.

One of the central questions confronting the nation in the mid-1970s
is to determine whether the recession of 1973 - 77 represents a pause or
a turning point, a brief breather before another economic takeoff or an
entrance into a new era of slow growth and austerity. Many economists
and businessmen believe in the pause hypothesis.[31] If they are correct,
the high unemployment rates, the high interest rates and the cost increases in energy, food, and industrial raw materials of the mid-1970s
are passing phenomena. As in the past, problems will yield to political
decisions, technological breakthroughs, and economic readjustments.
We have passed this way before, we are reminded, and fabled American
ingenuity and American luck will see us through once again. A rebloom-
ing of that shy, sensitive flower, "business confidence," or a technological fix like cheap fusion power have been suggested as possible
avenues to regain the economic momentum of the 1960s.

It is conceivable that one of these alternatives will work and all will be as once it was: prosperity, plenty of jobs, a rising stock market, thriving housing and automobile industries—more and bigger every year. Certainly the business recovery of 1976 gives some reasons for optimism. But if we are, nevertheless, due for an era of slowing growth, the political implications are staggering. When the revolution of rising expectations meets the nation of austerity, when have-nots can no longer be soothed by realistic hope for a better life, we are in for an age of demands for painful reallocations.

One special economic issue which has simmered underneath the surface for many years is likely to reemerge if growth really slows. This is inequality in assets, the yawning gulf between practically everybody and the nation's top wealth holders. The really big money, persons with assets of $1 million or more, are a relative handful, about 200,000 people in a nation of over 200 million.[32] About a third of personal wealth is in relatively illiquid real estate holdings.[33] The fairness or unfairness of permitting this kind of concentrated wealth is at issue rather than any modest, temporary gain from a shareout. On the other hand, the real issues are the concentration of economic power and the immorality of providing a massive head start to a handful of heirs in a society that attempts to approximate a meritocracy.

Democratic nations, including England, have had their capital levies on the rich. They have gone through or are in expanded versions of the welfare state, are subject to more vigorous centralized planning to allocate resources, and have remained democratic. America has avoided centralized planning, with its inevitable confrontation and conflict, by virtue of the demonstrated results of its growth ideology. Without the reality or prospect of expansion, poverty begins to look permanent, conspicuous consumption obscene, laissez-faire cowardly. In short, a sharp slowdown in the rate of economic growth cuts deeply enough into middle-class and upper-level working-class prospects. If the base of dissatisfaction widens, we will see a modified replay of the New Deal of the 1930s. Once again income redistribution, central planning, and resource allocation will be transformed from the academic to the real, a crucial issue in the America of the late 1970s and 1980s.

Conclusion

The preceding text has sketched briefly some of the nation's important population patterns and trends and has offered a number of speculations concerning the implications and issues confronting the nation in the coming decade. It is obvious that population patterns, trends, and characteristics are related to most of the critical developmental problems in land use, housing, transportation, and education, even unto such specialist concerns as the need for dormitory construction at state colleges.

Government policy, through the medium of urban development, transportation, taxes, and environmental programs, can play a major role in affecting population (and income) growth and distribution. This chapter has identified critical changes that appear to be on the horizon. It has indicated that a number of these trends offer significant opportunities for the nation. In particular they point to a thrust in the direction of quality—on upgrading, protecting, and nurturing human as well as natural resources. With the dangers of being overwhelmed by an irresistible tide of growth receding, the nation can catch its breath and plan more prudently for the future than it has in the past. It remains to be seen if the will and capability exist to take full advantage of trends which are so deep and fundamental as to deserve to be called a second chance for urban America.

Summary

Present trends in population in the United States offer both opportunities and dangers for the future. The most important of these trends are the steep decline in birth rates, the trend toward an aging population, and rising educational and income levels. If the birth rate is to be maintained at replacement level, the government will have to provide such incentives for parents as a federally funded day care system. The trend toward a better-educated public will probably result in more pressure on government for higher quality services, such as a national health care plan. At the same time, the rising number of elderly persons in the population will mean a more conservative public, although such a population would presumably be in favor of national health care and other programs relevant to older persons.

Another significant trend which has a direct bearing on urban problems is that low-income people, including a large proportion of troubled, unstable persons, are concentrating in the core cities, while middle-class and upper working-class people are migrating to the suburbs. (A reverse movement of the middle- and upper-income persons into attractive central city housing remains small but seems to be growing.) Many suburbs, however, are attempting to limit expansion, raising the question of whether the right to preserve desirable neighborhoods prevails over an individual's right to move freely into communities. The pressure on the suburbs to admit more moderate-income residents will probably continue to build.

In recent years the occupational shift has been away from factory and agricultural work and toward professional and white-collar industry. Many menial jobs are performed by immigrants, legal or illegal, who are used as cheap labor in prosperity but are unwelcome during hard times.

Among the effects of population changes on land development will be the increasing popularity of retirement communities, a larger market for apartments for a less rooted population, higher density population growth—apartments and town houses—around transportation nodes, and a growing appeal of climate-controlled communities. The latter will probably be residential and service additions to regional shopping malls.

Recommendations

- Provide national comprehensive health insurance.

- Provide family allowances so as to encourage families of one to three children to maintain population stability.

- Establish a federally funded system of day care-nursery centers.

- Establish an immigration policy favoring those sender nations which are attempting to limit their own population growth.

- Establish a positive national policy on abortion and contraception.

- Set up careful monitoring, research, and preparation of alternatives on the following concerns:

    a.   Immigration, legal and illegal.

    b.   The national and localized implications of very large increases in the aged population.

    c.   The national and localized implications of a large population of single persons.

    d.   The problem of reconciling preservation of high-quality areas with the freedom to relocate.

    e.   Trends in the growth and distribution of income.

Notes

1.   U.S. Department of Commerce, *Statistical Abstract of the United States,* 1973 (Washington, D.C.: Government Printing Office, 1973), p. 6. Examples of the continuing dread of a new burst of population growth surface from time to time. *The New York Sunday Times* of 17 March, 1975 carried a review story entitled "In 1974 the Birth Rate Moved Up," detailing not an increase in birth *rate,* but in the total *number* of births. Between 1973 and 1980 the number of women of childbearing age may rise by 14 percent, and even a further slight decrease in birth rates could be more than overbalanced by the larger pool of potential mothers.

2.   U.S. Department of Commerce, *Statistical Abstract of the United States,* 1973, p. 15.

3.   Charles F. Westoff, "The Populations of the Developed Countries," *Scientific American* 231, no. 3 (July 1974), p. 114.

4.   Table 78, "Unwanted Fertility," *Statistical Abstract of the United States,* 1970, p. 57.

5.   U.S. Bureau of the Census, "Prospects for American Fertility: June, 1974," in *Current Population Reports,* series P-20, no. 269 (Washington, D.C.: Government Printing Office, 1974), p. 4.

6.   "Puerto Rico Aims to Cut Birth Rate," *New York Times,* 4 November 1974, p. 19.

7.   The age groupings discussed in this section correspond with Census Bureau breakdowns.

8.   Robert D. Reischauer and Robert W. Hartman, *Reforming School Finance* (Washington, D.C.: The Brookings Institution, 1973), p. 63.

9.   U.S. Department of Commerce, *Statistical Abstract of the United States*, 1973, p. 130.

10.   U.S. Bureau of the Census, "Social and Economic Characteristics of Students: October, 1972" in *Current Population Reports*, series P-20, no. 260 (Washington, D.C.: Government Printing Office, 1974), p. 4.

11.   U.S. Department of Commerce, *Statistical Abstract of the United States*, 1973, p. 326.

12.   Statement of George Hay Brown, Director, Bureau of the Census, *Statements at Public Hearings of the Commission on Population Future*, Seven (Washington, D.C.: Government Printing Office, 1972), p. 36.
It should be noted that "remembered" or "forgotten" minor or irregular sources of income, to use the Census Bureau's terms, and the fact that others undoubtedly fear that naive candor risks disclosure to the Internal Revenue Service affect the accuracy of income data. As a result, there may be much underreporting of incomes in the census, especially on the part of the self-employed and persons who enjoy receipts in cash (e.g., waiters) and persons with irregular or shady sources of income. Bookmakers, prostitutes, bootleggers, and others in illegal occupations are not specifically included in census listings, nor are they likely to report all of their earnings. Moreover, income is a rather tenuous concept. To cite one major omission, neither the Bureau of the Census nor the Office of Business Economics of the Department of Commerce includes such items as the cash value of a housewife's labor, although income estimates do include the cash value of produce grown and consumed by farm families.

13.   "Foster Care Cost Shown in Survey," *New York Times*, 4 February 1972, p. 28.

14.   Daniel P. Moynihan, *The Politics of a Guaranteed Income* (New York: Random House, 1973), pp. 48 - 49.

15.   See "Abortion: What Happens Now?" *Newsweek*, 5 February 1973, pp. 66, 69.

16.   See Margaret O'Brien Steinfels, *Who's Minding the Children?* (New York: Simon and Schuster, 1973), pp. 209, 215.

17.   "Canada Tightens Immigration Laws," *New York Times*, 23 October 1974, pp. 1, 14.

18.   U.S. Department of Commerce, *Statistics of the United States*, 1973, p. 96.

19.   *The Asian Student*, 27 March 1976, p. 1.

20.   "Saxbe Urges $50 Million for Guards to Halt Aliens," *New York Times*, 31 October 1974, p. 24.

21.   U.S. Bureau of the Census, "Marital Status and Living Arrangements: March,

1974," in *Current Population Reports,* series P-20, no. 271 (Washington, D.C.: Government Printing Office, 1974), pp. 1 - 2.

22.   For an extensive discussion of this issue, see Sylvia A. Law and the Health Law Project, *Blue Cross: What Went Wrong?* (New Haven: Yale University Press, 1974).

23.   Godfrey Hodgson, "The Politics of American Health Care," *The Atlantic Monthly,* October 1973, p. 50. The AMA considered the threat serious enough in 1950 to assess its members $25 to finance the fight against "enslavement of the medical profession."

24.   Statistical Office of the United Nations, *Demographic Yearbook, 1970* (New York: The United Nations, 1971), pp. 646, 650. See also Edward M. Kennedy, *In Critical Condition: The Crisis in America's Health Care* (New York: Simon and Schuster, 1972), pp. 219, 233.

25.   Richard D. Lyons, "U.S. Health Insurance," *New York Times,* 27 August 1974, p. 20.

26.   See *"Symposium on the Crisis in Health Care,"* *Public Administration Review* 31, no. 5 (September/October 1971).

27.   Ibid.

28.   Almont Lindsey, *Socialized Medicine in England and Wales* (Chapel Hill: University of North Carolina Press, 1962), pp. 218, 224.

29.   These recommendations follow closely those presented in *Toward a National Health Program,* The 1971 Health Conference of the New York Academy of Medicine, and *Building a National Health-Care System,* Committee for Economic Development, April 1973.

30.   Data from Tables 631 and 636, U.S. Department of Commerce, *Statistical Abstract of The United States,* 1975, pp. 890, 892.

31.   For instance, see "Economists Predict Recovery Next Summer," *Business Week,* 21 December 1974, pp. 49 - 52.

32.   Tables 669 and 670, U.S. Department of Commerce, *Statistical Abstract of the United States,* 1975, p. 408.

33.   Ibid.

3

LAND USES:
Room for Improvement

In academe the discussion is of the "physical structure of urban America"—that is, land, particularly developable land, and housing and the necessary appurtenances that transform raw acreage into residential subdivisions, tracts into neighborhoods, and collections of neighborhoods into communities. Matters are simpler and more glamorous in the real estate world. When they discuss land, realtors mean money—site costs and housing construction, sale costs and community development, salability and net profit. The emphasis on the commercial connection is said to be a requisite for clear thinking, particularly because the growth and settlement of America are virtually synonymous with housing and related real estate development. Certainly the intense interest in land use of the public which buys, rents, sells, and relocates is not from the viewpoint of measuring use compatibility or emission controls related to traffic generation, but from the very practical standpoint of balancing livability with price in money and time. That is, the prospective buyer or renter wants to know, is the housing attractive and adequate, the neighborhood as good as can be afforded, and is there adequate access to jobs, services, and stores?

It might be inferred that in the broad sense, protecting real estate values is a primary motivation for the two-thirds of American families who own their homes. If the word "values" is expanded to include not only home and land—or apartment—but also the quality of the community and neighborhood, the centrality of the issue becomes apparent. Bound up in the complex of problems, opportunities, profits, and losses linked to land use are the problems bedeviling the nation: class and race, schools and crime, the struggle for amenities.

Perhaps the most vexing land use issue is the fear that the home and neighborhood won through prolonged effort will be threatened by invasion or degradation. The area of primary concern to the electorate, the gut issue, is along the borderland where social problems confront the physical setting. In plain terms, the main worries for most Americans involve the presence or intrusion of lower-class persons who are perceived as threats to the public safety, to the quality of the schools, and accordingly to property values. Attempts to use or reuse land in middle- or upper-class cities, neighborhoods, or suburban communities for the purpose of constructing housing for low-income people are not merely land use conflicts. They are also bitter struggles over America's unresolved attitude toward class and racial intermingling. Similarly, concern over environmental protection and the preservation of housing values is often a surrogate for the prime concern with the shortage of good neighborhoods and the threat to neighborhood preservation. Furthermore, when asked to define neighborhood quality, most respondents reply in terms of the characteristics of neighbors and only secondarily in terms of physical amenities.[1]

The recognition that here, as in other urban concerns, we have to consider people problems first and resist the temptation to embark on more easily resolved physical challenges creates considerable difficulties in fashioning a viable political program. But a fixation on tangibles like housing construction, environmental problems, or new town construction, to the exclusion of the social concerns troubling the nation, can lead only to an attraction of a very substantial part of the electorate to demagogues playing on fears and insecurities. Political realism demands that the social anxieties linked to land use be confronted; an urban development posture based on promises of more suburban housing for low-income families, more parks, and more financing for new towns evades the most troubling issues. Such evasion may well be a prescription for political disaster.

The Major Issues

The major concerns over land use in the mid-1970s are the scramble for developable land, the decay of the central cities, and a new public interest in aesthetics in land development.

THE EMPTY ACRES

There are a number of remarkable observations about land use in the United States, but perhaps the strangest, in view of all of the intense bidding for prime urban sites, is the sheer lack of development. While most people might not be very much surprised that less than 3 percent of the continental United States is urbanized—97 percent remains undeveloped—they might be amazed to learn that after 300 years of settlement, metropolitan Boston is only about one-third developed. Over 50 percent of the 2,000-square-mile area—a surface larger than the state of Rhode Island—is scrub forest, wasteland, or meadow.[2] This situation is far from unique. For all the talk of the imminent running out of developable land, one planner has calculated that

all of the foreseeable need for new urban sites could be satisfied by
developing land located within fifteen miles of the heart of our central
cities.[3] Thus, for all the 500,000 acres or so we have converted from open
land into urban land each year since the 1940s, there is not much
likelihood of exhausting potential developable, close-in sites.

   Developable land.   The operative words are "developable" and
"ripe." As any real estate developer can testify, it is not enough for land
to be open; it must be "ripe," or capable of being developed and mar-
keted at reasonable cost. This means that land must be well located
with respect to transportation, employment, and private and public
facilities and services, and properly zoned or susceptible to requisite
zoning alterations. Viewed from this perspective, the prime land—well-
located, properly zoned, reasonably priced and in "good" neighborhoods—is extremely limited; hence its high cost. There are, of course,
trade-offs; some sites may be suitable for industrial or commercial use
but less attractive for residences; and cost is a variable, not a constant.
A small, expensive site may be extremely tempting for high-rise, quality development, but it may go begging in the middle of an inflationary
surge in construction costs and interest rates. Sites in a once-repellent
neighborhood can suddenly become fashionable and expensive as
affluent persons buy up brownstones and town houses, despite the fact
that most of the factors responsible for past repulsion have apparently
remained unchanged—the crime rate may still be extremely high and
the schools remain jungles.
   Two more facts: first, to qualify for development, land need not be
dry or level. Realtors suggest that three rules are vital in buying a
house or land: (1) location, (2) location, (3) location. Swampy sites, steep
sites, underwater sites in many coastal cities, sites full of rocky ledge
and sites plagued with peat, subterranean stream, or nonexistent
bedrock have all been successfully developed, when other factors compensated for the high cost of construction. Chicago developed a whole
school of building engineering focused on adaptation to muck by erect-
ing buildings on adjustable pilings; much of our land in coastal cities
was created by filling off-shore sites.
   Secondly, there is a myth concerning "cheap" sites which should be
dispelled. Land located in communities distant from developed areas
and their amenities is low in price only because it requires the developers and zoners to pay compensatory costs in terms of providing the
missing amenities, or the buyers to pay the costs of making longer

journeys to work, shops, or services. Therefore, while it may be possible to put together large tracts of relatively low-cost land in outlying areas, there are very substantial expenses involved in installing the water and sewage facilities, schools, streets, libraries, parks, etc., and for the residents, after development, in long-range commuting. This is one rationale for concentrating more public programs on stimulating development of in-town and close-in apartment-townhouse complexes. The infrastructure is already in place, and prospective buyers and renters are often willing to pay more for convenient location. There are also energy and material-saving features in this type of compact development which clearly deserve special consideration in the mid-1970s and beyond as compared to the emphasis on low-density, single-family housing of the 1950s and 1960s.

The effects of accretion.   The tendency of most urban development to grow by accretion (add-ons) has had a number of striking effects. One is the process of the amoebic tentacles of strip developments spreading out along highways and gradually filling in the open space between. Aerial photographs taken in a decade-to-decade series in metropolitan areas show new subdivisions creeping out over the landscape. Here and there the observer can note low-density gaps as development leapfrogs over an affluent community with stubborn large-lot zoning to a more vulnerable community five or ten miles farther out.

And if the observer could have a time series of earth satellite photographs, he might note a strange phenomenon in a booming century—the abandonment of large portions of the American interior, consisting of farms, farm trade centers, and mining villages. Over half the counties in the United States actually lost population in the course of the 1960s. There are large empty spaces in the vastness of the United States, and despite a modest trend toward population growth in the open country and in small rural towns, there is likely to be a further decanting of people from most rural counties as the facts of life catch up to the nation's remaining million and a half marginal farms and the small trading centers that serve them.

Even a trained aerial observer would be hard put to discover and locate the more subtle thinning out in core-city housing. New York's Lower East Side and hundreds of other big-city neighborhoods were once invariably described as "teeming," but now, while the buildings still stand, there are many abandonments, vacancies, or conversions to commercial use. Moreover, the decline in residential density has been accompanied by something invisible to the aerial cartographer. This is a decay in spirit, or perhaps more accurately a reversion to the criminal Bohemias, the hopeless "wild" neighborhoods characteristic of many cities throughout the world during much of recorded history.

The central dilemmas of the 1970s and 1980s revolve around these two major declining areas, although the decrease in farm area population is viewed as a lesser problem than the decline of the core cities. Here we have a paradox—rising agricultural productivity means a need for fewer farm workers and the consequent conversion of American (and immigrating Latin) rural poor into urban slum poor. Meanwhile, in the slums, housing abandonment associated with various social evils seems to be spreading and accelerating. In Newark, one percent of the total housing stock has been abandoned each year since 1965.[4]

While only a minority of the nation's population lives in this kind of unraveled urban area, the social costs in the form of high crime and welfare rates, serious public school problems, and a general malady compounded of despair, resentment, and frustration are a serious drain on the nation's resources and a threat and warning to neighborhoods as yet untouched. One result has been a settled resolution on the part of residents of stable, less troubled communities to avert disaster by not permitting their land to be used for housing for "them," the groups stigmatized as slum-generators.

CONTROLS AND PLANNING

The present pattern of land control is a system combining private ownership and exploitation with municipal controls which tend to be feeble, incoherent, and continually overtaken by events. The cities and towns, legally responsible for most of the land use regulation in America, are confronted with powerful extramunicipal controlling factors. General economic conditions (including interest rates, unemployment rates, and housing costs), most highway decisions, and the location of federal and state improvements are out of their area of influence. Where the municipality does have a choice, its decisions are strongly influenced by the competition for new tax bases and for avoiding social and physical ills. This all places a premium on competing with other communities to insure that land is used for clean, nonpolluting industry, and to palm off such unwanted developments as housing for low-income families, regional sewage treatment plants, half-way houses for rehabilitating drug addicts or criminals, and incinerators on someone else. In most instances the community and its officials tend to be market responsive and passive. When confronted with proposals to construct more of the same type of development they already have the tendency, over time, to say yes.

Private control. It is true that practically all communities have adopted master plans to guide land use and housing development, but except in affluent towns which have adopted an exclusionary reflex, a rigid "keep-em-out" posture, zoning controls tend to be nibbled away bit by bit through a multitude of variances. Doctor's offices in homes become doctor's office buildings, white elephant mansions become funeral homes or apartments, parks get chewed up for parking lots, and apartments spring up in single-family zones.

One trend related to growing affluence has been an acceleration toward privatism—private swimming pools, backyard playgrounds, subdivision miniparks, and condominium clubhouses. Americans, it seems, almost routinely take public inadequacy or mediocrity for granted. Rather than submit to higher taxes to be expended by mistrusted public officials, they do their best, income permitting, to secede from the public sector.[5]

This tendency toward opting out has its dangers. There is, for example, a pervasive trend toward subverting public into private ownership. Many of the nation's beaches are rendered virtually inaccessible to the general public because they are privately owned. If municipally owned, they often require high entrance and parking fees from outsiders. Moreover, in most areas most open land is privately owned. The unwary traveler who sets foot on forest or other open land within an easy ride from most metropolitan areas is likely to find the trees festooned with "no trespassing" signs.

Toward government control. Reversing this process—converting private domains into public lands—is a slow, controversial, and costly process. But high costs can be countered by a process known as land banking. It has been recommended that metropolitan area government agencies require title to the bulk of the remaining open land surrounding the city as the only sure way to control development patterns.[6] Certainly this is an expensive proposition, but there is a strong likelihood that government could recapture its investment through subsequent land sales while retaining ample forest and park land. A century ago Henry George, the advocate of a single taxation based on real estate,

pointed out the inconsistency between public creation of land values
through the building of costly highways and other public investments,
and the private landowner's harvest of the lion's share of subsequent increase in higher land values.[7]

Under present circumstances, proposals based on government acquisition of most of the chips and counters in the Great American Game
might be a hazardous political undertaking, particularly because logic
and justice demand government compensation for landowners who can
demonstrate that government action has had an adverse effect on their
property.[8] With an increasing proportion of suburban growth nodal
(concentrated) in character, if the limited, high-density development
were to be clustered in public land banks, all of the speculators thus
deprived of private buyers could ask legal remedy for loss of value of
their property.

Unfortunately, it is doubtful whether the United States is ready to
intervene in this way, to alter abruptly the very nature of the real estate business. For this reason, although a substantial acquisition
program and other stronger efforts to guide land use policy are
recommended, a variety of other recommendations are based on the
supposition that private ownership and entrepreneurship will continue
to serve as the mainsprings of urban development.

One alternative to outright acquisition is a technique known as
Transfer of Development Rights (TDR). Although it is still in its experimental stages, a number of communities and the states of New
Jersey and Connecticut are considering adopting it. In essence, TDR involves public purchase of the "development rights" for tracts of open
land (usually farmland). Developers must purchase a given amount of
such rights before proceeding with construction. This provides all land
owners, not just a lucky few, with some of the economic benefits of
development while permitting most land to remain open or to remain
farmland.

A number of trends may make the achievement of a better planned
land use-community pattern a more achievable goal than might have
been the case in the mid-1940s through the mid-1960s. Some of these
trends have been mentioned in chapter 2: family units are smaller, population growth has slowed, and there seems to be a shift toward higher
density, multifamily dwellings. As noted, this changing pattern offers
the opportunity to demand higher standards from large-scale developers, to concentrate development, and to focus it at key points along
public transportation routes, thereby allowing for large numbers of

close-in parks and other open space. This opportunity can be exploited and expanded by discouraging construction of detached single-family dwellings as much too costly to the public in terms of land and resource costs. Not much additional pressure may be needed; rising site and construction costs and higher interest rates in the mid-1970s, combined with demographic changes, are shifting the housing pattern sharply away from large single-family homes toward much smaller high-density units.[9]

ATTITUDES AND PERCEPTIONS

Another key trend is a change in attitudes toward cities. There was a time when a status hierarchy of cities was recognized and accepted in a system analogous to baseball's class A, B, and C leagues. For example, a young, creative advertising man who showed his mettle in Kansas City might be picked up by talent scouts from Chicago. If he showed class in Chicago, he moved on up to the big league in New York. The assumption in each case was that everything grew better and more exciting more or less in relation to the size of the city. A world of glamor, recognition, achievement, and the big money were there in the big cities for the successful.

The extent to which the dream has gone sour is reflected in the movement away from large cities on the part of numerous firms and in the amount of "combat pay" needed to entice reluctant executives (and professors) and their wives to move to New York, Chicago, or other large cities. Conditioned by the horror stories about the crime, poor schools, pollution, and balky transportation systems that are alleged to bedevil the big-city residents even in reasonably prestigious neighborhoods, they are reluctant to relocate. Often the lure is repackaged; now, it is argued, only the husband must spend time in the big city (commuting up to two hours or more per day) while the family lives in the distant, affluent suburb.

This is all part and parcel of a postindustrial society's concern for livability and meaning, a search which appears to be increasingly carried on in the suburbs by those who can arrange a tolerable relocation. Secondarily, there also seems to be a rediscovery of the smaller metropolitan areas, particularly those like Madison, Wisconsin; Austin, Texas; or Ann Arbor, Michigan, each of which contains a major university offering a strong cultural flavor. In the early 1970s there was also an unexpected trend toward growth in small towns in largely rural areas.

The feeling of being somehow a deprived provincial if one does not live in one of the metropolitan giants is obviously growing weaker. Fears of being spied on or frustrated by narrow, bigoted neighbors in Winesburg, Main Street, or Spoon River have not been entirely dispelled, but life in smaller cities is no longer all that different from life in the big cities—except that smaller cities are viewed as safer, cleaner, and greener. This realization increases the possibility of replanning urban patterns in the direction of smaller, lower-density, more manageable cities.

Public aesthetics.   Traditionally, a concern for architectural quality, parks, and aesthetics in general has been relegated in the United States to the affluent, especially leisured females. This seems to be a legacy of the frontier and the immigrant ship, a bequest from a population of workers and farmers who had no time, money, or patience for beauty. Environmental aesthetics was something one visited in the decadent nations, the European museum pieces, where hierarchical authority had constructed the monumental cathedrals and plazas.

It is difficult to determine when this patronizing attitude began to change. Certainly the enforced travel associated with World War II had its effect. In the decades following, there was also increased affluence, more use of higher education, the influence of the media, and travel, much more travel. Moreover, there was the discovery that beauty is money. Cities like San Francisco, Boston, New Orleans, and Atlanta were able to capitalize on their distinctive physical attractions, not only to expand the tourist industry, but, in an age of foot-loose economic development, to attract and retain a disproportionate share of the nation's leading firms and talented people. Livability has become something of a code word betokening an absence of crime and slums, but it also refers to physical attractiveness. Such communities brag about their charms, reflecting a growing interest in aesthetics and a care for preserving their reputation, their real estate values, and their future.

Does this make urban beauty a campaign issue? In some places it does. Voters in San Francisco and New Orleans were able to paralyze freeways which threatened the unique attractions of a waterfront view and the French Quarter. Here and there, historic landmarks have been preserved from destruction and parks have been saved. Local incumbent politicians have used as one plank in their platform development proposals illustrated by artistic views of a new park, the new down-

town, or the new housing project. Their campaign speeches do not
neglect to point out that the new waterfront or the salvaged historic
area mean new construction, larger payrolls, and business expansion.

A constituency for urban aesthetics.   There is in fact a sizable latent constituency, or more accurately, constituencies, for an urban
aesthetics program. At a mundane level, there are the tourist-minded
businessmen convinced that an attractive community is food for sales.
There are the equally work-a-day chambers of commerce who have been
(or can be) easily convinced that ugliness is driving new industry to
more attractive localities. And there is a sizable group of middle- and
upper-class voters who have traveled and compared their neighborhoods, notably with Europe, but also with the best of New England, the
Northwest, and California. True, the comparison is often slanted; on
vacation one often seeks an exchange between accustomed ugliness and
rare beauty. But a nagging resentment and disquiet is there, dry tinder
waiting for the kindling.

There is also scale to consider. New towns, planned unit developments, and large and small subdivisions built from 1976 to 1999 may
conceivably house only a quarter of the nation's population, and the
remaining three quarters will be living in older housing in older neighborhoods, many of which are dingy, shabby, or dull. And most of their
inhabitants are aware that their housing is not beautiful.

Costs.   One point must be made clear. *Urban reconstruction is not
necessarily a big-money program.* Remarkable results can be obtained
for very little, as in the case of closing off streets, creating small parks,
providing imaginative painting for buildings, and devising new street
furniture and signs. New subdivisions can be required to place their
phone and power lines underground, and the expense of undergrounding
older lines is not staggering. Much of the latter cost can be balanced off
against the high cost of repairs after windstorms or ice storms.
Moreover, historic preservation and renovation can often be made a
self-sustaining, paying business as in the case of Providence's Benefit
Street, Washington's Georgetown and Capitol areas, and New York's
Brownstone Revival areas like Park Slope and Cobble Hill. Good older
houses, like antiques, are a scarce commodity, attractive as long-term
investments.

Perhaps the most difficult problems arise in the case of the city
mess, the jungles of debris and jumbles of signs and wires, and the

wastelands of decaying buildings. Solving these problems will be difficult and costly. The obvious answer is to leave them for last, waiting until the neighborhood is abandoned or the population has changed. It is more rewarding to invest in areas which do not suffer from the difficult people problems that make investment in hard-care slums a hazardous proposition. Politically, covert or outright abandonment is a platform only for conservatives angling for the middle-class suburban vote and sincerely convinced that expenditures for new buildings and renovation in the slums are pouring money down a rathole because the local vandals make slums faster than they can be rebuilt.

A change in population.   Despite the manifold risks, we must try to do something about housing and neighborhoods in the barren slum areas. Part of the answer obviously lies in dealing with social problems through a comprehensive manpower program and improved police protection; experience suggests that ignoring the social problems dooms efforts at neighborhood reconstruction. One approach is to identify and work with latent strengths in the core cities. Middle-aged, upper-income people may take a chance on old neighborhoods for the sake of cheap brownstones, and young married couples or people in the arts may risk in-town housing for the sake of low rents and good location, particularly as suburban housing becomes increasingly costly. The particulars of the case vary from city to city, but a combination of morality and solid political support point in the direction of risk-taking for new building and reconstruction.

It is clear that if development in relatively open territory is a difficult business, redeveloping built-up cities is many times harder. The slum dwellers must be rehoused and, on occasion, replaced or balanced with middle- and upper-income people. This is by no means an inexpensive process. Acquisition of 100 acres of decaying slum property in a large city could involve an expenditure of $50 to $100 million, with the likelihood that an additional amount of equal size would be needed for demolition and the construction of new or renovated utilities and service facilities. And after this huge investment in infrastructure comes the cost of actual building.

It is not surprising that under present conditions, urban regeneration which involves substantial acquisition and demolition usually results in the construction of office towers or luxury apartments. Moreover, extensive structural rehabilitation for housing purposes is generally associated with a change in ownership, with middle- and upper-income families taking over and investing heavily in basically attractive but presently rundown neighborhoods.[10] Less drastic approaches, such as modest rehabilitation efforts to ensure compliance with housing codes, can also lead to a changeover in ownership and tenancy simply because slum property rented to low-income families is usually profitable only when building maintenance is cut back to a minimum.

These high costs lead to a desperate alternative: let the slums alone until they are thoroughly thinned out, burnt out, or abandoned. Then, when land and buildings become cheap and little relocation is entailed in acquisition, it once again becomes economically feasible to acquire and redevelop slum property.[11] On a limited scale, this process seems to be underway in the Woodlawn area of Chicago, where a slum adjoining the University of Chicago is slowly being redeveloped for middle-income apartments.

But as a policy, relying on this kind of natural process seems heartless. Unfortunately no one seems to have the answer to the problems and destructiveness of the hardcore underclass linked to the hardcore slum. Although guaranteed jobs and better services would be helpful, it seems likely that the best that can be reasonably hoped for in many cities is the creation and stabilization of urban enclaves, possibly with locally controlled schools. Such distinct urban areas could compensate in charm, ethnic ties, and convenience for the fact that such neighborhoods are less safe, and may be more highly taxed, than similar neighborhoods in older suburbs.

Alternative solutions. And there is a final alternative, or more accurately a final solution, for older cities—depopulation, shrinkage of functions, and eventual abandonment of core cities as America, unlike Western Europe, creates a new low-density suburban civilization without cities. Some observers see the processes of dispersion and the problems of the underclass inhabiting the central cities as so deep-rooted that nothing short of an unanticipated revolution in federal policy would suffice to turn the situation around.[12] In the author's opinion things are not that bad—serious, yes; fatal, no.

The need, and the opportunity, for reconstructing urban areas goes well beyond the dismal slum districts. A large proportion of the land area of many cities is in need of a major overhaul. For example, from a functional point of view most large cities work badly in terms of accommodating traffic and in offering adequate amenities. They are ugly, and quite often they even smell bad. Tackling even minor issues such as the removal of visual blight in the form of strip development and the proliferation of billboards, signs, and utility wires is a tiring, slow, and costly proposition. Furthermore, attempts to open up municipal waterfront areas to new public and private use by buying out and clearing up the industrial and commercial development that now preempts many such areas usually requires enormous sums.

But the primary difference between guiding development in open areas and reconstructing built-up urban areas is not simply a matter of expenditures. The difference is that heavy investment in suburban and outlying areas is much more certain and predictable. In consequence, government's role becomes a task of managing and directing a stream of urban growth which would occur in any case. In contrast, it is not at all certain that areas located outside the central business district of central cities will be the beneficiaries of a similar stream of large-scale private investment. Thus, government action in most built-up areas presupposes large-scale government expenditures. It is not surprising that when construction costs for public housing run to $45,000 per apartment and suburban homes can be built for $40,000, questions are raised concerning the rationality of building more high-rise dwellings for low-income families within the cities.[13]

For this reason the prospect of a substantial change in the composition of central city population must be accepted if these core areas are not to be written off. There is ample room for stable working-class neighborhoods and for the lower middle class, for luxury apartments and renovating Brownstoners and participants in the Victorian revival. The basic question is how to preserve a tolerable environment for these kinds of people when they must coexist with a shattered and dangerous underclass. Noise, potholes, congestion, and taxes are supportable. Neighborhood wreckers are not.

Land Use: Policies for the Future

It is clear that in the past good land use policy was usually the result of a combination of happy accident, good local leadership, and receptive developers. We cannot plan for accidental factors, but we can

ensure at least minimal quality of product on the one hand, while encouraging superior communities and neighborhoods to preserve and
strengthen their attractiveness.

GUIDELINES FOR LAND USE CONTROL

The land use problem and opportunity can be conveniently divided
into two segments. The new development, possibly twenty to thirty
million new housing units to be constructed between 1975 and 2000 (not
the fifty million target implied by the Douglas Commission) should be
by far the easier to deal with.[14] The money will be spent in any
event—the task is to channel this enormous tide of investment. It can be
directed to produce attractive communities rather than formless
checkerboard subdivisions connected by rows of billboards and festooned with telephone wires, or new towns with lost opportunities, most
of which are not much more than expanded traditional suburbs, "super-
suburbs," as one author puts it.[15]

As a preliminary step in achieving minimal levels of livability, it is
essential to curb architectural purists. Eloquent aesthetic arguments
and insults over architectural copycatting, derivations, lack of innovation, and timid aping of inappropriate models have been a source of confusion and delay. For a while, perhaps a long while, we can applaud
good plagiarism, admire honest effort. As minimal standards, a kind of
suburban Bill of Rights, we might accept as a starting point the giant
advances made in Radburn, New Jersey's new community—built in
1928. Radburn was the better mousetrap that attracted few emulators.
Fifty years ago it offered a standard of greenery, pedestrian walks safe
from automobiles, and overall neighborhood quality that remain all too
rare in America, although the approach was widely copied in England
and Scandinavia.

We can assume that it will be difficult to pry loose the primary
responsibility for land use control from the municipalities. But since
municipalities are responsible for permitting the creation of the mess
we now live in, the answer must be to escalate the right of review and
approval to a higher level of government—state government. This must
be done despite charges of dictatorship, opposition to loss of vital home
rule, and the accusation that higher standards result in higher costs and
less housing for the poor, less profit for developers, and less work for
the construction trades. There are numerous exceptions, but it is an unfortunate fact that home rule in this area has not worked well enough to
be continued in its present form. Approval of new towns and new sub-

divisions by localities should be subject to guidance, review, and approval by a strong state land use agency.[16] Approvals should be made contingent on providing, *at a minimum:*

1.   *An adequate walkway system* separated from motor traffic, particularly necessary to school children. Safe walkways leading to schools and play areas could drastically reduce slaughter on the streets and highways.

2.   A similar, allied *bike path system* (same comment applies).

3.   *A defined urban center;* the New England common, the southern courthouse square, or any of a dozen foreign variations will do as potential models.

4.   *Undergrounding of telephone and electric power* distribution lines. This is already a feature of many new subdivisions. It should be mandatory for all. Higher density development might explore the Disneyland approach, which combines utilities in service tunnels to provide easy repair and protection from the elements and vehicles. No more "Dig We Must" signs indicating street mining for utility repair or expansion.

5.   A system of *small- to medium-sized, accessible, and imaginative parks.* There are numerous models suitable for copying.

6.   *Adequate provision for retaining trees.* Developers prone to silvacide should be severely punished along with those municipal jurisdictions that still permit indiscriminate tree removal.

7.   *Conservation of open spaces* by stressing zoning for town houses, garden apartments, and an occasional high-rise apartment building. Where single-family units are permitted, cluster zoning should be the rule, not the exception. Clustering can also result in enormous savings in cost of land, materials, labor, and energy.[17]

8.   *A buffer zone of trees and/or shrubs* between developments and major thoroughfares to provide a modicum of privacy and to cut out the grossest levels of noise and visual pollution, including billboards and signs.

9. *A genuine architect.* For at least a generation architects have complained bitterly that 90 percent of the construction in the United States was built without their aid, inspiration, and fees. In the case of residential construction, the usual practice is for the builder to dust off a set of familiar plans a generation removed from plans appearing in home-builders' journals. The result is everywhere apparent, even in expensive homes: debased colonial, degenerate salt box, inappropriate mansard roofs, fake pillars. While there are numerous instances where good architecture has been built without architects, present circumstances dictate heavy odds against it. There are obviously enormous differences in tastes, needs, and outlook among clients and architects so that any attempt to dictate style is likely to be counterproductive. But there is no reason at all for not trying. All construction should at least bear the stamp of a practicing architect. There can be ways to weed out the venal, marginal practitioner whose stamp (and meager talents) is no guarantee of even an attempt at adequate design. And care can be taken to avoid impractical, costly ego-trippers out to build monuments at someone else's expense.

10. A genuine effort to *take environmental impact into account.* We have already come some distance in this direction, especially in such states as California, Hawaii, and Vermont.[18] Almost everywhere, however, building goes on in flood plains, on wetlands, on mountain ridges, and on hurricane-prone beaches. Only after development is in place come the costly programs to undo the damage—expensive dams, civil defense, disaster relief. Prevention is cheaper than picking up the pieces.

11. No more sheltering of exclusionary, country-club suburbs behind barriers of zoning, high prices, and court protection. Increasingly suburbs must recognize an obligation to remove obstacles to housing construction for their elderly, their young, their town employees, and, if applicable, for persons who work in local industries. In practice, cost realities suggest that this does *not* mean a welfare family on every block as one's fair share. Rather, it means a percentage of housing suitable for families in the $8,000 to $15,000 annual income bracket, equal to perhaps 20 percent to 30 percent of the total housing stock in the community.[19]

BILL OF RIGHTS FOR THE CITIES

A similar set of general criteria can be laid down for in-town redevelopment. It can be argued, in fact, that since most Americans live in settled neighborhoods, the reconstruction of existing urban development is even more crucial and difficult than building on open land. These principles should include:

1.   Primary attention to *conserving existing viable neighborhoods.* Abrupt, major change in land use based on ethnic or racial composition should be avoided in such neighborhoods. Strenuous efforts should be made to preserve, conserve, and if necessary, to recycle stable neighborhoods and old and middle-aged buildings. In most cases this recycling entails finding new people to invest themselves and their money in older structures, although in some instances it may mean converting old buildings to new uses. In recent years, the American propensity to bulldoze, destroy, and blight existing structures for the sake of new development has weakened. High interest rates and rising construction costs for new building have helped to slow the once-enthusiastic redevelopers and to accelerate already strong tendencies in the direction of retaining the best of existing patterns. Planners have already begun to learn to pay more attention to the possibility of keeping the old in combination with a minimum of the new, to fit new bathrooms and kitchens behind historic facades, to provide old neighborhoods with a modern civic infrastructure of modern transportation and services (such as police and schools), to retain and build on their attractive qualities.

Overall, despite the possibility of incurring higher costs, structural rehabilitation rather than clearing for new construction should be the rule in all such areas, not simply those designated for historic preservation.[20] Experience seems to prove that human scale, diversity, the organic resonance that comes with generations of active use should be preserved, even if initial costs are higher than those of the bulldoze-and-build-from-scratch alternative.

2.   *Taming the automobile.* This long overdue action should include maximum reliance on modernized public transportation, selective street closings to autos to create malls or play streets, and introduction of suitable street furniture and small parks.

3.   Exploration of the possibility of *stimulating more mixed land uses.* This might include use of a major neglected area such as apartment house roofs for recreation and commercial establishments. In addition, adoption of the commercial offices combined with residential

floors now found in American luxury apartment buildings, and adaptation of the community centers built into Russian apartment structures might be appropriate to make many apartment buildings more livable.

4.   *Attention to safety* as a key design criterion in new construction and rehabilitation. Advanced lighting and surveillance techniques, controlled egress and ingress, and resident safety systems should be a critical consideration in the urban design.

5.   *Exploiting neglected land use opportunities.* Most cities contain great opportunities for development and creation of new open space in rundown port and riverside areas and in excess railroad yards. Streets, sidewalks, and roofs can, with relatively little investment, be converted into protected walkways, bikeways, green play areas, or dining and loafing areas comparable to the European examples that impress American visitors. Imagination and will power are the critical ingredients— conversion for livability is not all that expensive.

6.   Development of an *improved population balance* might be a principal objective. Large cities might well be made smaller through lower densities, and efforts should be made to correct the typical imbalance of heavy concentrations of minority and poor persons along with a small number of luxury apartments. A primary goal should be the development of use and design policies (combined with corrective action in schools and public safety) to retain and attract middle-income families with school-age children. Various avenues to achieve this objective might be explored, including the creation of semiautonomous new communities within the city (that is, with control over local schools) and of decentralized, mixed, new towns (new communities within the city) and reconstructed neighborhoods.

It is assumed that unlike the action recommended for *suburban* land use, where state coordination and leadership is essential, the primary thrust in *municipal land use* should come from the cities themselves, backed up when necessary by the state land use agency. On the other hand, there is no reason to be dogmatic about it; depending on local circumstances, states may play a more dominant role in some cities than others at some times and on some issues. Some cities are so far gone in incompetence and corruption that they are incapable of building an honest sidewalk. Others are eminently qualified to do a first-rate planning job. A little pragmatic untidiness is all to the good; what counts is results.

TOWARD A STATE AND NATIONAL LAND USE POLICY

At the present time the most surprising thing for the reformer about land use development is that nobody is really in charge. Responsibility is so diffused and control so fragmented that for all practical purposes it is impossible to identify one official, one agency, or even the developer as the culprit in the land use mess. This poses the first challenge—the creation of focal points of land use power and accountability on a state basis. As noted above, this involves a transfer, or more accurately a recapture, of some of the power over land use abdicated by the states.

The new-model land use agencies should be strong and well led, able to weather charges of sterility, brutality, lack of creativity, adoption of canned, inappropriate solutions, tendencies to act too slowly or to act precipitately without adequate preparation. In the headlong rush toward sprawl and degradation of the countryside and in the face of a deepening depression, achieving a modest, even minimal goal would be an enormous improvement. The ideal can wait. It is critical to take control, to grasp the whole and make a real beginning in laying out desirable regional land use patterns and well-designed communities.

Opposition arguments.   Opponents can argue that strong state land use agencies are unnecessary because: (1) things aren't so bad, or (2) the alternative—centralized land use power—would be worse. On the first score we have the visual and olfactory evidence to the contrary. On the second, we have tangible evidence that some foreign countries are doing a better job than we. There seems to be no earthly reason why we cannot improve our standards.

The point has been made earlier that upgrading hardware and design is much easier than changing the behavior patterns and other fundamental causative elements of our principal urban problems. *We do know how to design good buildings. We do not know how to stop street crime.* But knowledge is only the beginning. There is an enormous amount of inertia, a galaxy of special interests opposed to a centralized control mechanism at the state level with power to establish and enforce adequate standards, although such control is the only measure which stands a reasonable chance of guaranteeing a satisfactory quality of design.

Some of the opposition is reasonable enough. Thorough analysis is slow and painstaking. Construction may be delayed indefinitely by an exhaustive examination of alternatives and all types of possible en-

vironmental impact, weighing tradeoffs between projected market demand and installation of infrastructure (for example, if sales hold up,
larger diameter sewer pipe should be installed; if sales slow down,
smaller pipe will do). There are intricate problems involved in meshing
new subdivisions with old communities within a regional framework of
highways, transit lines, and public utilities and facilities.

In this connection, large-scale suburban development like planned
unit developments (PUD's) has definite advantages. Although the
problems of external interfaces with other parts of the region remain
difficult, at least there is not the need for mosaic fitting to adjust a
thousand niggling details which is required to place new development
into an existing neighborhood and existing political, social, and physical
patterns, as is the case in new-towns-in-town.

Large developers. Requiring much more of developers in the way
of improved design is clearly a move to accelerate the trend toward
greater scale, since only the big boys have the resources to go through
the process of passing all of the new checkpoints. Smaller operators
tend to lack both the patient money (investors who can afford a long
wait for their returns) and the technical expertise necessary to produce
convincing statements respecting potential impact on water tables, traffic patterns, air pollution, etc.

All this points to the fact that it is a logical next move to escalate
the development process to a higher level of government to deal with
large-scale developers. In terms of opening up new possibilities for doing a better job, the trend is all to the good. Hard bargaining between
qualified agency staff and large developers increases the odds in favor
of better quality urban development as compared to piecemeal
negotiations with shoestring builders for very small numbers of units.
However, individual units could be fitted into new towns once the basic
system of controls and amenities has been worked out and there is ample assurance that an effective, continuing system of planning and
monitoring has been established. The present loose home-rule system
purports to do this, but in many if not most communities it is obviously
deficient in the critical areas of planning, control, and imposition of
quality standards, although it manages to impose minimal requirements for health and safety. Alternatively, a number of small
developers could form consortiums which, under effective leadership
and proper safeguards, could combine scale at the delivery end with internal flexibility for participating members.

Several points should be clarified at this stage. The first is that as noted previously, there should be no endless squabbles over architectural refinements. The results will be far more substantial if we are content with achieving substantial improvement rather than nit-picking about refinements. Second, there should be no attempt at imposed uniform solutions, no single-style architectural dictatorship. The guideline approach, requiring reasonably harmonious and consistent development with ample amenities, should be sufficient.

Finally, it should be assumed that the objective is to achieve greater livability within American life patterns. Creative plagiarism, borrowing the best from the rest of the world, is certainly the way to begin, but adaptions to a distinctive American situation are called for. It is likely, for example, that in American cities tougher, vandal-resistant artifacts will be needed. Special attention to American preferences in sports, shopping, and dining habits are obviously required.

Need for state control.   The recommendation that the suburbs yield final control over land use, including new town developments and design standards of PUD's and large subdivisions, would have seemed unthinkably revolutionary a few years back. But by the mid-1970s, with a dozen states exercising substantial control over various aspects of municipal land regulation, the suggestion is hardly startling.[21] Clearly there is a great distance to cover in persuading all states to adopt appropriate laws, in translating legislation into accepted day-to-day practice, in educating the electorate to demand higher standards. We also have a long way to go in training developers and other elements of the construction industry to operate in an environment in which quality is the norm, not an unreasonable imposition to be fought inch-by-inch through the courts and Congress.

The need for *prestigious*, well-staffed state regulatory land use agencies is clear. Nevertheless, there are major organizational alternatives. Such agencies could be expanded versions of present state planning agencies, relatively weak bodies which have great difficulty in shaping important decisions of powerful sibling functional agencies like the highway department. Discarding this approach as more of the same misguided effort responsible for the existing mess, we are left with the choice of a land use agency working out of the governor's office or a kind of supragovernmental land use supreme court. As noted elsewhere, the advantages seem to lie with the second of these two approaches, although the returns are not yet in from activist states like Vermont and California which have adopted the first alternative.[22] We have already discovered, however, that (1) formulating enforceable, flexible guidelines is extremely difficult and complex and (2) the possibilities of legal, environmental, and economic arguments, causing expense and delay, are infinite. In short, laissez-faire is intolerable, but correction is costly and unproven.

HOUSING—MORE THAN SHELTER

During the first four years of the Nixon administration, the Johnson programs expanded in what everyone had expected would be a hostile environment. Under programs inherited from the Democrats, subsidized housing starts escalated to over one-fourth of total production, and in less than four years equalled the aggregated record of the previous thirty-two years. By his second term, President Nixon had second thoughts about this achievement, partly because his administration labelled some of these successful efforts as miserable failures. Anthony Downs, an authority on real estate and urban development, documents the success of some of the programs implemented under the Housing Act of 1968, which helped to generate millions of new units for low- and moderate-income families.[23]

Unfortunately the hostility toward the urban programs developed by previous Democratic administrations, characteristic of so much of the Nixon administration's domestic policy, led in 1973 to the adoption of a moratorium on funding for federal housing programs. This paralysis was supposed to be temporary, replaced by a fresh new approach through new legislation, but the trauma of Watergate absorbed the administration's energies until Nixon's resignation in August 1974. By the end of the year the old programs, viable and shaky alike, emerged revised and resurrected in the 1974 Housing and Community Development Act. While this act represents a response to some criticism, it is a holding device rather than an adequate program. It was clear in the mid-1970s that new and enlarged housing communities legislation was a good prospect for the late 1970s.

How large is the need for new housing? A study of housing in Kansas City and Boston in 1973, undertaken by the Harvard-MIT Joint Center for Urban Studies, sketches in quick strokes a four-category pattern of housing ownership. (See table 3 - 1.) Since the study estimates that only 5 or 6 percent of the population of the nation's metropolitan areas lives in hardcore slum housing, the nation's priority "need" total is less than four million dwelling units. This amounts to roughly 20 percent of the housing stock. But this is only part of the

Table 3-1.   HOUSING AND SOCIOECONOMIC GROUPS

	I Upper Status	II Middle Class	III Working Class	IV Lower Class
Percentage of Urban Families	12.5%	32.5%	37.5%	17.5%
Income Level	$20,000+	$12,000 - $19,900	$9,000 - $11,900	$3,300 - $8,900
Occupations	Business Owners, Executives, Managers, Professionals	Clerical, Sales Workers, Technicians, Small Business Proprietors	Construction Crafts, Policemen, Firemen, Service Workers, Factory Workers, Sales Clerks	Unskilled Workers, Semiskilled Workers, Unemployed Persons
Housing Type	Very Good to Prestige	Pleasantly Good	Standard Comfortable	Substandard to Standard Marginal
Single Family	$35,000+	$25,000 - $34,000	$13,000 - $24,000	$10,000 - $17,900
Monthly Rental	$400+	$250 - $350	$150 - $240	Up to $140

Source: *America's Housing Needs: 1970 to 1980.* Harvard-M.I.T. Joint Center for Urban Studies (Cambridge, Mass.: December 1973) pp. D-5-10. (Dollar figures updated to early 1975.)

story. The Joint Center Study also suggests that a large percentage of
middle-income families who still live in older central city areas or industrial satellite neighborhoods are dissatisfied with their housing or
their neighborhoods and want to move to more modern housing in
greener suburbs. The point is that the market for housing programs is
based less on criteria of physical deprivation than on perceptions of
need or personal and family goals.

Perceived *neighborhood* quality is more important than purely objective calculations of square footage, number of bedrooms, and
appliances. People tend to view housing as a symbol as well as a reality;
it is a code word denoting a decent life in a decent neighborhood rather
than simply a dwelling with an extra half bath and a family room.
Housing is people and politics, neighborhoods and interactions, not just
a matter of heating, plumbing, and repairs. Programs have to be designed for a real world in which government programs designed for the
poor have proved disappointing, and most progress has been achieved
through government efforts for people with middle or higher incomes.
(Furthermore, partly because of rising educational levels there has been
a kind of consensual advance in standards and expectations.) The
Federal Housing Administration (FHA) has worked; urban renewal and
public housing have, by and large, been disappointments.

Where Do We Go From Here?

Among questions that come to mind in assessing possible alternatives, the first is simple: Why discontinue those housing programs that
have worked? Specifically the hundreds of thousands of acceptable units
constructed each year under Section 236 of the 1970 Housing Act
logically point to retention of the program rather than scrapping it.[24]
The faults identified in Great Society housing programs—the creaming
off of profits by contractors and other intermediaries, the maladministration and outright corruption in FHA offices working in collu-
sion with favored realtors, the shoddy construction and rehabilitation
work done on some units—can lead to one of two conclusions.[25] To many
conservatives, these deficiencies are grounds for abandonment. For
liberals, the more logical choice would seem to be to revive Section 236,

modify it, and monitor it more effectively. And when assessing the value of government intervention, continue the mortgage subsidy programs which have been highly successful as vehicles for converting most of the middle and upper class, and much of the working class, into homeowners. Efforts to expand the home ownership alternative downward into the working class deserve support, partly because ownership of housing equity appears to be an important factor in neighborhood stability.

One immediate problem in the mid-1970s was the sharp decline in housing starts during the severe business recession that began in late 1973. By early 1975 the annual rate of new construction had fallen to under one million compared to the rate of more than two million of much of the 1950s and 1960s. (An upturn in construction during the first half of 1976 was still below the pace of the early 1970s.) No similar figures are available to gauge the impact of the recession on housing maintenance and renovation. The evidence seems contradictory: some families, unable to purchase new housing, have invested substantial sums in their present units. Others, particularly the less affluent, have been forced to postpone needed repairs. In any event, whatever shape a housing program for the late 1970s takes, it is clear that a major expansion—or more accurately, recovery—from the low levels of 1971 - 75 will be needed.

OBJECTIVES AND PRIORITIES

Although the full impact of the profound changes in the housing market in progress may not be felt for some years, one major effect is already apparent—a new conflict over housing objectives and priorities.

On-site labor, the ten-dollars-an-hour carpenters and other craftsmen, represents only 10 percent of the cost of building a house. While labor provides a handy target for criticism, a very sharp reduction in on-site labor—say 20 percent—would only diminish overall costs by about 2 percent. Site costs, the amount required to purchase a lot, are more significant, representing 20 percent to 25 percent of the total for a single-family detached dwelling.[26]

High interest rates.   The impetus to find some way of reducing housing prices gained in momentum in the mid-1970s as inflation increased site and construction costs and raised mortgage interest rates to forty-year peak levels. This latter point is crucial. While an improved technology could conceivably cut housing costs by 10 percent, a reduction in interest charges on home mortgages from the 1975 level of 8.5 percent to 9.5 percent to the mid-1960s level of 5 percent to 6 percent could result in a 20 percent reduction in monthly mortgage payments.[27]

For a house selling at $40,000 (the average sales price in the United States in 1975), assuming a $10,000 down payment, a 5 percent mortgage requires a monthly debt service charge of $125 to $150. At 1975 rates of 9 percent, the monthly charge is well over $200. The difference in annual income required to pay the higher interest rates is about $3,000. Considering other increases for taxes, site, and building materials (about a third of the total), it is not surprising to find most potential homeowners priced out of the market. While it was quite possible to be optimistic concerning the great strides in eliminating slums and closing the gap between median family incomes and median housing prices that occurred in the 1960 - 1970 decade, the inflation squeeze of 1972 - 75 halted or reversed the steady improvement.

The problems were not insurmountable for those who had purchased homes in the sixties or earlier. Their homes had, in many cases, appreciated by 50 to 100 percent in five or ten years, and a swap in the $30,0000 or higher price range was not out of reach. But the first-home purchaser faced very stiff interest charges, if indeed he could find a bank willing to lend him money at 8 to 10 percent. It was not surprising, under these circumstances, that annual housing starts decreased from almost 2.5 million in 1970 to less than half that figure in 1975.

More apartments and condominiums.   Faced with mounting costs, one response of the building industry was to diminish the product and increase the sales pressure. For example, one pragmatic answer to the pressures imposed by rising materials, labor, and site costs was the construction of two-bedroom condominium units of 800 to 1,000 square feet instead of four-bedroom, single-family detached housing of almost 1600 square feet. With a sales price of roughly $30,000 and a down payment of about $1,500, these back-to-the-1950s units required monthly carrying charges of approximately $300 at the prevailing 8¾ percent to 9¼ percent interest rates of 1974 - 75. Three-bedroom units called for a slightly larger down payment—$1,750 to $2,000 for a sale price in the $33,000 to $35,000 range, along with monthly charges (for a thirty-year mortgage) of about $350. (These monthly charges include principal, interest, taxes, a condominium fee, and a small payment for mortgage insurance.) Many of these units offered clubhouses, tennis courts, and swimming pools.

As in the case of traditional single-family detached units, prospective buyers were tempted by federal tax legislation giving tax advantages for local property taxes and interest payments. Apartment dwellers usually enjoy no such benefits. This is one reason for the trend toward condominium ownership. It was suggested that $60 to $70 per month in tax savings would be derived from the purchase of a condominium apartment or town house unit, over and above the equity built up in the principal payments and possible gains accruing from future inflationary increases in the cost of housing. On the other hand, these potential benefits were offset by the maintenance and heating costs normally included in apartment rentals which may not be wholly passed on to renters, and by the risks entailed by ownership of some flimsily constructed, poorly located condominium units. Nevertheless, in a period of roaring inflation this low down payment brought housing costs down to the small family with $17,000 in annual income and to a slightly larger family with incomes in the $19,000 to $20,000 bracket.

Social effects of high costs.   It is obvious that most American families would be disqualified by this standard. But if the growing admissibility to banks of the practice of including the wife's income is taken into account, the situation changes drastically; the majority of two-income families would meet the test.

These economic facts of life lead to a simple conclusion: a working wife (or some other partnership arrangement) is becoming a necessary prerequisite for purchase or rental of housing of even moderate quality. The result is likely to be a further disincentive to have children, or to have more than one or two children. Many young couples experience with the birth of their first child the sickening sensation of a 40 percent drop in income combined with substantial increase in costs. If the nation is interested in maintaining even a zero population growth birth rate—that is, an average of slightly more than two children per family—some means must be found to compensate for this equation. Some possibilities are cheaper, heavily subsidized housing for families with two or more children, a significant family allowance system, and a good, subsidized day-care system.

The alternative to compensatory federal intervention is to rely on some sort of unforeseen and probably forlorn hope for reducing housing costs, on a basic alteration in attitudes toward children that will make large families in small units tolerable, or on some massive increase in national income to outpace inflation. These alternatives, singly or in combination, seem unlikely. More realistic is the probability that the United States will have to develop an appropriate housing policy.

In the midst of the recession and mounting inflation of the mid-1970s, the response to housing problems was complex and personal. There was much grumbling, much postponement of home purchases in favor of continued rentals, a shift toward apartment construction and purchase of mobile homes, and some trends toward discovery of salvageable big-city neighborhoods.

Short of a major federal program to reduce interest rates, a housing squeeze affecting at least half the population seems likely to continue. And if interest rates were reduced but other components of housing cost such as developable sites and materials remained expensive, the likelihood is a continued sluggish pace of construction and an acceleration of the trend toward construction and purchase of condominiums, town houses, or apartment units, which provide the buyer less square footage but offer the tax advantages formerly available only to single-family homeowners.

DIRECTION FOR POLICY

This brief review of housing development patterns and programs leads to four conclusions:

1.   The federal government should widen housing options for working-class people. However, attempts at legislating federal programs aimed at forcing the pace of income group, racial, and class dispersion are politically dangerous and likely to yield minimal results in the face of determined suburban opposition. We are due for a generation of intricate technical and legal arguments concerning elusive concepts like balance, regional fair shares, environmental protection, and neighborhood preservation—problems with no clear, consensual solutions. This does not mean that efforts to remove economic or racial barriers to freer working-class migration to the suburbs (for example, eliminating suburban racial covenants or large-lot zoning) should cease. It does mean recognizing the risk of programs subsidizing large numbers of very poor people to move to suburbs unwilling to receive them and lacking requisite services and transportation for them.

2.   Government policy should be directed toward ensuring and stimulating high-quality, high-density suburban development—hous-

"Oh, jeez! Now we'll have to move back to the city!"

Source: Editorial cartoon by Pat Oliphant. Copyright © 1976, *Washington Star.*
Reprinted with permission, Los Angeles Times Syndicate.

ing, employment, services—around public transportation nodes. Many
suburbs don't want this type of development on the grounds that it is
too much like the city, but this is a fight that must be undertaken and
won, despite the risks.

3. Home ownership should be encouraged. Housing programs in-
terface with other program areas, particularly employment, land use,
environmental protection, and transportation. In particular, there is a
basic need for an integrated housing-land use-transportation policy
emphasizing high-quality, compact urbanization maximizing use of
public transportation.

The basic policy of encouraging home ownership through liberal
mortgage subsidies should be maintained, and the ownership option
should be extended to all working families. It must also be recognized
that new, inexperienced homeowners may need technical aid through
some sort of extension service to provide guidance on housing
maintenance and renovation and to resist the lures of marginal home
improvements that they cannot afford.

4. In the long run, after restoring Section 236 for a stipulated period, serious consideration should be given to abandoning large-scale housing programs for the poor in favor of a full employment strategy. There would remain a need for small, special housing programs for the unemployable poor such as elderly, handicapped persons.

NATIONAL LAND USE POLICY AND THE STATES

In a nation in which most fortunes have been made in land speculation and land development, it would be natural to expect the central government to play a significant role in the process. And thus since the pre-Colonial era it has been national governmental policy to dredge harbors, to subsidize roads, canals, and railroads, to clear off Indians with embarrassing prior claims, and to offer potential farms for homesteaders. More recently the federal government has provided FHA mortgages and helped build highways and mass transit systems. Embedded in American tradition is the concept of a vast wilderness awaiting development in which the federal government must provide stimuli and infrastructure for the purpose of "improving" barren land. In practice, this concept has meant public subsidization for private profit derived from meritorious construction. The result is a unique schizophrenia which welcomes some types of government intervention in the form of *subsidization* as a normal supplement to free enterprise (particularly businesses in trouble) and fears centralized (nonlocal) government intervention in the form of *planning* as a tyrannical, costly interference with constitutional freedoms.

As noted elsewhere in this work, resistance to central planning falters during periods of stress. The first abortive efforts at national land use planning flourished briefly, during the Great Depression. They were stimulated by concern over erosion, notably in the Dust Bowl, and other examples of the consequences of unchecked exploitation. But the flowering of national planning was brief, and by the end of the Second World War it was all over. As soon as business confidence returned, national economic planning and the first faint attempts at developing comprehensive national land use policies were jettisoned. But functional planning, in the form of agricultural policy, federally subsidized mortgage financing, and federally aided highways, has had a profound influence on land use.

The main thrust in urban land use was in the direction of suburbanization to the point of sprawl. The detached single-family dwelling, the highway-oriented residential-shopping-industrial development pattern, and to a considerable extent the decline of the central cities were by-products of the diffusion and dispersion, which were assisted by the twin efforts to house and service America in the suburb and to provide automobiles and highways to serve a scattered population. Conversely, national policies which permitted public transportation systems to go into bankruptcy, and central city housing and services to decay, were powerful added incentives for core city decline and suburban growth.

The battle for legislation.   Given the reality of extremely limited federal intervention, why then was there such effective opposition to the rather innocuous national land use legislation proposed by Senator Henry Jackson and consistently endorsed (and tepidly supported) by President Nixon? (In his 1974 State of the Union message the president averred that he was assigning this legislation "highest priority." He did not do so.) The failure to enact a bill which merely provided minimal amounts for the states to actually *do* the land use planning is particularly surprising because other, more stringent measures were already very much in evidence. California, Hawaii, Vermont, and other states have already adopted tough land use statutes.

It can be argued that this was what made developers and the building industry generally fearful. They believed they would face much more rigorous standards if, with federal incentives, all of the states were Californianized—much as California had already led the way on air pollution controls on automobile emissions. Clearly, the wrangling over the effect on urban development of environmental impact regulations promulgated by the Environmental Protection Agency frightened developers. It requires no great exercise of the imagination to visualize an across-the-board application of stiff land use criteria for most types of development evolving out of an apparently innocuous national land use bill. Some laggard states could be coerced into an activist role, while states of interventionist persuasion might be stimulated into ventures in new areas, which would further complicate life for the building industry.

As the 1973 - 75 recession deepened, the Ford administration found a new reason for opposing a national land use bill—it would cost too much. By mid-1975 the new version of the Jackson-Udall bill had been retailored for Republican and administration support. At a maximum first-year cost of $50 million and an average of $83 million for the next five years, the legislation would create a new office of land use in the

Department of the Interior. This office would be empowered to make grants to the states, to conduct research, to call on the states to designate critical areas such as wetlands and historic zones, and to urge the development of state and national land use policies to protect prime agricultural land with these changes. The bill won tentative support from hitherto hostile farm organizations while retaining support from planning and conservationist groups, but it was nevertheless moved to a back burner until after the 1976 election.

Need for strong leaders.   Realistically, passage of national land use legislation represents a preliminary step in the direction of controlling regional and national development patterns. Although much depends on the quality, good judgment, and vigor of top agency leadership, the extent and depth of continuing presidential and congressional support are also critical factors in translating laudable general objectives into specific, implementable programs. Everyone is aware that the battle really begins *after* the legislation goes into effect. Ahead is the absolute certainty of lawsuits, complex argumentation among different experts, ambiguous research, and enormous complexities in coordinating key federal, state, and local agencies and elements in the private sector that play vital parts in development. In this respect the leadership role of the Department of Interior is weakened by the fact that it must somehow bring into line programs administered by its sibling agencies, particularly the Department of Housing and Urban Development (HUD), the Environmental Protection Administration (EPA), the Department of Transportation (DOT), and the Department of Agriculture. As if this were not a sufficiently difficult task, there is the further problem of working with a wide variety of actors and levels of competence in the states and in the localities.

As is the case with the municipal programs requiring extensive discussions and specific approvals of program content and staffing from neighborhood groups, the proliferation of actors endowed with power to veto or delay inevitably tends to retard forward movement. In the public relations phrase, each point of contact offers an opportunity for friction. Indeed, there are already so many checks and balances in so many governmental areas that it is not surprising that a genuine mover and shaker like New York's Robert Moses is usually treasured, whatever his shortcomings. Unless and until the process of national and state land use planning can be institutionalized and made routine, there will be a great need for shrewd, manipulative, ruthless leadership.

The Urban Environment

This section of chapter 3 deals with two important physical aspects of the urban environment—pollution and transportation. A sober observer considering these urban problems is struck by the fact that these issues offer very little political sex appeal in most areas and with most social classes. True, there is surface commitment to environmental programs, grumbling over traffic congestion, and deteriorating, costly public transportation. Some cities have a serious problem of air pollution, and others are surrounded by polluted waterways, but by and large, particularly during business recessions, such matters are viewed as frills, postponable problems as compared to the vital gut issues of jobs, crime, schools, and taxes

PRESENT APATHY TOWARD POLLUTION

While it is true that a few senators have effectively exploited the environment issue, it is still doubtful if a majority of the population can be carried, particularly when painful choices (such as between conservation and jobs) seem to be unavoidable. On the surface environment is a motherhood issue—who is actually, overtly *for* filthy water or pro-smog?—but underneath the veneer of consensus, there are enough doubts to permit polluters and prospective developers to mount a serious counterattack.

It has been said that the working class and the poor tend to regard environmental hoopla as a convenient copout for the affluent, an excuse for spending more on water pollution and less on low-income housing, as well as a useful ploy for keeping low-income housing out of the suburbs. But most polls rank environmental issues low, not only for the poor but for much of the middle class.[28] It is true that middle-income people provide more verbal support, but their priorities are really not very different. Big-city worries over crime and bad schools are nowhere near as urgent in the suburbs, but even then, except for the really affluent, taxes, inflation, and threats to family income are the critical matters for concern, not air or water quality. Since a proenvironment politician runs the risk of bumping into issues of economic development and jobs, the environment issue has been a card played best in places and at times where the economy is flourishing. This fact imposes serious limitations on its use.

The first reason for the prevailing apathy has already been mentioned: there are other more pressing concerns, compared to which clean air and water rank as frivolous diversions suitable for the rich. There is also widespread suspicion that environmental concern is, like urban aesthetics, an effeminate preoccupation appropriate only for garden clubs, nature nuts, and antiquarians. In addition, there seems to be a habituation factor, a callousing of visual and nasal acuity which blanks out the everyday journey through the industrial smoke and past the polluted river. And not least, there is a mildly paranoid attitude equating environmental quality with higher costs. Sanitation engineers angling for big contracts and landscape architects calling for open competitions are often viewed as self-serving, special interests waxing fat at the expense of the hard-pressed taxpayer. Competition requires time, causing delays and higher project costs during periods of inflation, and competition losers often charge that the winners were selected on the basis of flashy design rather than on low-cost, utilitarian simplicity.

The foregoing summary would seem to suggest that in most parts of the nation the intelligent politician should shun this area like the plague, conserving his efforts for topics more productive of votes. This attitude, in the author's opinion, would not only be contrary to the public interest but would also overlook productive possibilities. While the urban environment is not a burning issue, it is a potential vote-getter, needing only careful development.

POLLUTION: PERCEPTIONS, TOLERATIONS, AND ISSUES

Problems of the environment can be measured in both real and imaginary terms. It is real when poorly operated rubbish collection systems breed rats and other pest colonies. It is real when intense air pollution causes a senior citizen difficulty in breathing. On the other hand, it is somewhat artificial to announce that an environmental crisis exists when a river has been polluted for a hundred years or more. To be sure, it may be an offense against nature, but it is one which has resulted in a decreased public awareness, and become a tolerated nuisance rather than a source of rage at the continued degradation of the environment.

As a result of these differing perceptions, environmental action has traditionally been considered an expendable item in most municipal and corporate budgets, the first to get the axe at annual budget-cutting ceremonies. One reason for such vulnerability is that money spent for environmental protection often produces no immediate benefits, certainly none that could be placed on a balance sheet. It has only been within the past decade or so that a change of attitudes has occurred in the United States. Conservation of the environment became a popular public issue only in the 1960s.

Current concern about environment.   If it is possible to name one event which can be said to have generated the current emphasis on environmental quality, it is most probably the publication of Rachel Carson's *Silent Spring* in 1962. Carson, concentrating on the present and possible future effects of DDT, combined cold scientific fact with emotionalism to produce a potent mixture and a best-selling book.

Silent Spring's greatest contribution was that it altered the nation to the potential negative impact of existing and emerging technology. Potent insecticides, automobiles, chemical products, and nuclear power plants, all hailed as outstanding technological achievements of great benefit to modern man, were suddenly viewed more critically as potential instruments of disease and perhaps even of human extinction.

The growing public awareness of pollution problems stimulated the production of numerous scare books in the 1960s which confidently predicted doom within a few years or a few decades because of people's lack of concern about the deadly injuries being done to their environment. By the late 1960s, responsible scientists were beginning to compile data which reliably pointed out that human pollution was indeed a serious health and survival issue. Some, like Paul Ehrlich and Barry Commoner, wrote and talked convincingly of present dangers and future disasters.[29] Now, although the general public, government, and industry are more prepared than they have ever been to face up to the problems of pollution, it is also a fact that the environmental issue has perhaps caused wider disagreement over needed action than almost any other urban problem.

There is much disagreement, to begin with, over the dimensions and nature of environmental problems. There are a small number of pollyannas who claim that the dangers are much overdrawn—that population growth has fallen off without the need for strong government action, that there are ample, untold, untapped resources in the oceans, and that nature is forgiving.[30] Even with modest antipollution programs, the Hudson and Thames are habitable for fish once again, and the air over New York and London is far cleaner now than in years past.

Others of the Paul Ehrlich persuasion see the clock hands pointing to midnight or even a little beyond. They see an age of famine, frail oceans poisoned by oil spills and sludge, uncontrolled technology promising new disasters in rampant radioactivity, cancer, heavy metal poisoning, and synergistic monstrosities. The last phrase requires some explanation. Synergism in this instance refers to the fact that the properties of various residual wastes (effluents) combined with other factors are unknown. They may be different and perhaps more dangerous than one of these factors in isolation. Half a dozen chemicals given off as air or water wastes in the same area may create in combination much more hazardous conditions than one of them alone. Unfortunately, far too little is known of many of these interactions. In any event, the fact that there are reputable researchers who maintain that environmental problems are exaggerated and that we need more research before adopting preventive legislation helps to weigh the scales in favor of inaction or painfully slow corrective programs.

Objections to environmental concern.   There is a further consideration concerning research: since so much of the pollution problem is tied to rapidly changing technology (for example, automobile emissions), there is always a temptation to believe that some new innovation will resolve our present difficulties.[31] To cite one issue, honest, technically qualified professionals are in serious disagreement concerning the construction of fission nuclear power plants. Do we construct the plants with present technology, wait for a breakthrough on cheap fusion power or low-cost solar cells, or do we insist on coal scrubbing? There is in fact much dispute concerning the wisdom of imposing environmental quality standards based on current technology. This is by no means a trivial consideration, because many environmental programs are extremely costly. It will not soon be forgotten that an end product of the catalytic converter, installed on all new automobiles at great expense, was a sulfur emittant more hazardous than the wastes it eliminated.

There are also fears that overemphasis on environmental concerns will hurt the economy and may even lead to class warfare. From the viewpoint of business and labor interests, terminating the SST (supersonic transport), stopping or slowing construction of offshore drilling and onshore oil refineries, or slowing or preventing construction of highways, polluting industries, and power plants on environmental grounds results in less business activity and fewer jobs. This is particularly so since the promised compensatory growth in pollution cleanup industries has been slow to materialize.[32]

It is all very well to argue that this is a short-sighted view, that further environmental degradation may jeopardize the future of humankind and cut years off the life of workers and their families. Certainly there is evidence that the environmental standards imposed on industry added only about half a percent per year to the double-digit inflation of 1973 and 1974.[33] When the economy is in a flourishing condition, appeals to reason, morality, and common-sense perspectives may generate broad support. But when jobs grow scarcer, as in the mid-1970s, and many business firms are facing hard times, imposing tough environmental standards promises a further slowdown in economic activity. Under these circumstances, the temptation is to rush approval of the Alaska pipeline through Congress, postpone imposition of more rigorous automobile emission standards, accelerate offshore drilling for oil, and allow western strip mining expansion without the new safeguards proposed by environmentalists.

In short there is still not a sufficient constituency for environmental protection. For a time during the late 1960s and early 1970s it looked as if environmental protection would be the new motherhood issue: everyone for, no one against. Year by year that happy vision has receded, partly because of resistance by polluters relying on a combination of weak enforcement, legal confusion and delay, and cosmetic propaganda. Even the simple, achievable programs like Vermont's billboard control or Oregon's returnable bottles have been fought to a standstill by firms and their labor allies, who would rather fight and blight than make a feasible, long-overdue change in their operations.

Toward cooption of industry.   If there is a root cause of this disappointment, it is the failure of the federal government to undertake the kind of vigorous effort that would convince the foot-draggers that resistance does not pay, and to create a countervailing corporate-labor lobby through massive antipollution/conservation contracts. As has been noted from time to time in these chapters, in America as we know it, cooption is the road to political success. In the early 1970s satirical cartoonists had pictured fat-cat corporation executives with sooty smokestacks in the background looking forward to the big money they, the major polluters, would receive for cleaning up their own pollution. Unfortunately, although there has been substantial progress on some fronts, progress has been slow in many areas. Here and there small fortunes are in the making for decontaminating auto exhausts or generating municipal heating from municipal garbage. But the very large contracts that were supposed to convert General Motors, the more prescient oil companies, and the construction workers into Friends of the Earth have simply not been forthcoming. Indeed the Nixon-Ford approach seemed to be quite the opposite—compromise, decelerate, or jettison environmental controls on the supposition that the economy will suffer unduly if oil refineries, strip mines, and pulp mills are pushed too hard, too fast toward pollution control.

This does not mean that more is not being done. Total public and private money spent on environmental capital expenditures grew from about $3 billion in 1958 to $6.9 billion in 1973. In addition to capital investment, there has been a spectacular increase in operating and maintenance costs (O & M) of environmental protection facilities; in 1973, for example, total public and private O & M expenditures were $8.2 billion, substantially greater than the $6.9 billion total annual allocation by government and private firms for investment in this field. Further major increases are anticipated in coming years; the totals projected for 1982 are almost $20 billion in capital expenditures and an astronomical $46 billion for O & M.[34]

The Council on Environmental Quality estimates total incremental pollution abatement costs at $218 billion in the period 1974 - 1983. Each billion dollars in environmental program expenditure may generate as many as 20,000 to 25,000 jobs.[35] With average expenditures of about $20 billion per year, this would mean as many as 400,000 to 500,000 additional jobs. This total makes environmental pollution control an employment factor offering twice the 195,000 jobs provided by the petroleum refining industry. Assuming that anything of this magnitude does become a reality, the result would be to create an enormous constituency for environmental protection, a kind of new version of the military-industrial complex consisting of a powerful amalgam of government agencies, unions, and corporate suppliers.

Progress in this field could be faster. At the rate of expenditure of the mid-1970s, the modest Environmental Protection Agency objectives for the nation's rivers will not be achieved until 1985, and air pollution targets will not be reached until 1980, but the trend is clearly in the right direction.[36]

Environmental costs and political appeal.   One of the principal allegations leveled against the capitalist system is that is has a pronounced, inherent tendency to place private profit above public costs. When the business firm saves money by not installing adequate safety devices, the public bears most of the burden of supporting the workers (and their families) whose lives have been crippled by asbestosis, exposure to dangerous metals, explosive materials, etc. Likewise, firms that use, at no cost, surrounding air and abutting streams as corporate sewers, pass on the cost of pollution to their unfortunate neighbors. However, this problem is by no means confined to profit-oriented societies. Soviet ecologists, for example, have complained about the pollution of Lake Baikal by the production-oriented management of timber and pulp operations.[37] All that seems to be required for this type of perverted bookkeeping is a narrow focus in which the interests of the individual firm or plant are paramount, and the more diffuse public interest is assigned to the public relations department.

There is in fact no operational decision-making mechanism in the federal government to arrive at choices based on an overall assessment of costs and benefits. And, because our system of accounts is so faulty, we delay spending $4 billion to combat air pollution when such a program might yield four times that amount in private and personal benefits from improved health and welfare. Because of weaknesses in aligning corporate profit-and-loss ledgers with a national system of accounting, we have permitted the coal industry to ravage Appalachia, concentrating pollution in that unfortunate area so that other areas may purchase slightly lower-cost coal. Environmental protection and restoration would raise the current cost per ton, since the old system tends to defer cleanup costs to later generations.

It is true enough that cost-benefit calculation is a tricky process, subject to manipulation and technical argumentation. For example, there are always disputes concerning the natural scale of second- and third-round impacts. How do you measure or separate out the effect of air pollution on the health, performance, and achievement of the affected population? How can the effect of industrial air pollution be differentiated from the effect of smoking or of automobile emissions?

By implication, the annual report of the 1975 Council on Environmental Quality (CEQ) offers a useful hint for the enterprising politician: run against cancer. The CEQ devotes (for the first time) an entire chapter to the topic of carcinogens, pointing out the following facts:

1. An estimated *$1.8 billion per year* is spent solely for the hospital care of cancer patients. Additional costs of therapy, doctors' bills, and time lost from work raise the total cost into the *tens of billions of dollars.*

2. It is estimated that *60 percent to 90 percent of all cancer is related to environmental factors.*

3. *The prudent course for cancer prevention is environmental action.*[38]

It is clear that even if one ignores the agony and death associated with this disease, environmental programs which effected a sizable reduction in the number of victims would pay for all of the cost of environmental expenditures. Other environmental issues may be as real, but the costs and benefits are more debatable. How do we set an economic valuation on aesthetics? For this reason, cost-benefit estimates, like planning-programming-budgeting, are a fertile topic for dispute among the experts.[39] But despite these qualifications, it seems clear enough that we tend to overstress the *costs* of environmental protection while neglecting the *public benefits* of such programs.

The notion that those who want to build significant developments should be required to prepare environmental impact statements is useful so far as it goes. However, this approach falls far short of a mechanism through which decisions can be reached based on a reasonable assessment of public and private costs and benefits. The word "reasonable" is used advisably. It is all too easy to get bogged down in nit-picking disputes over differing concepts of justice and equity, or in technical conflicts concerning varying approaches to time, space, interest rates, and how to separate into comparable parts complex interrelated factors to determine who is responsible and who should pay. For this reason, there must be prudence and common sense as well as some urgency in creating and using a valid decision-making process.

Is there any political mileage in such an approach? The answer is yes, properly exploited, there is. There is a broad, rough-and-ready consensus that polluters should be stopped or pay for the costs of the damage they do. Cost-benefit may sound overtechnical, but it can be translated into attractive political terms: (a) *polluters, not the public should pay,* and we will all be better off if they are made to do so; (b) *all of us benefit a lot when the air, water, and land is cleaned up,* even if it costs a great deal to get the job done; (c) *as noted, the cleanup process itself creates many contracts and jobs.*

There is a reasonable expectation that multibillion antipollution expenditures will bring into being a powerful countervailing political force to balance the polluter lobbies. And realistically, we can expect antipollution costs to be passed along to the consumer or taxpayer, as is

the case with automobile emission equipment. In a thriving economy
environmental programs tend to be viewed as just another cost of doing
business.

AN ENVIRONMENTAL PLATFORM

It seems clear that unless there is a fundamental shift in government policy, even with the help of the cancer banner, environmental
protection will tend to run a poor second to economic and urban growth,
whatever the brave talk concerning balance and reconciliation between
discordant priorities. At least this will be the case in periods of
economic recession, when environment conservation is usually regarded
as a hindrance to business expansion and job creation. The obvious
answer is to insist on sufficient federal, private sector, and consumer
outlay for environmental protection so that the cleanup does in fact
become the economic stimulus that it was hoped it would be in the late
1960s.

But is it probable? Is heavy spending for environmental protection,
unless imminent catastrophe threatens, likely to be a minority attraction and hence a political liability? The response lies in the scale of effort. If the program is big enough, the momentum of contracts and jobs
will generate the support needed to counterbalance the polluters.

The next question is, where to find the votes for this kind of fundamental shift in national policy? The answer can be found in two areas.
First, some catastrophes are indeed upon us. Interest rates may rise and
fall, but the price and supply of energy, labor, and raw materials are going to accelerate some conservationist trends: less automobile driving,
more mass transit, efforts to consume less energy for heating, less extensive land use (that is, more concentrated urban development).

To the sheer financial impossibility of continuing our profligate
ways can be added the latent but still powerful remnants of the old New
England ethic, "Make it do, use it up, wear it out," which never fully
succumbed to the vandalizing, throwaway strain in American history.
There is a widespread apprehension that the rape and wastage of
natural resources is immoral as well as dangerous, a feeling that we are
conservators for generations to come, not terminal hogs asking cynical-
ly, "What did posterity ever do for me?"

The continuing threads of schizophrenia toward the use of resources
running through American history are to a degree associated with
different traditions of different areas—conserving, thrifty Penn-
sylvania Dutch vs. wasteful, land-exhausting, southern WASP cotton

planters; jerry-built, eroded West Virginia mining towns vs. tidy New England villages. The theory that there is one profligate American tradition of polluting the rivers, razing the forests, and blighting the highways is totally false. There is an equally strong tradition of preservation, by no means confined to the affluent, the eccentric, or genteel. There is indeed absolutely no reason why a platform for environmental protection and correction could not be popular if it included such features as the following:

1. A simple, visible program (with an early target date) for removal and/or rigorous control of outdoor advertising, for undergrounding of utility and telephone transmission lines, and for collection of urban debris.

2. An acceleration and expansion of air and water antipollution programs.

3. Tax incentives and regulations to expand use of renewable resources such as solar energy.

4. Requiring manufacturing firms to build in feasible recycling (and safe disposal as well as safe use) of their products as a condition of approval for sale and distribution.

5. Requiring strip mining companies to "replace all divots," that is, to restore the area after stripping and underground mining, and to prepare a before-and-after plan with techniques like long-wall extraction to ensure against area subsidence rather than the wreckage systems of underground room-and-pillar mining.

6. Instituting and enforcing tough occupational and environmental safety regulations.[40]

7. Instituting through contractual public works major environmental restoration of urban and open areas.

8. Devising an effective tax and publicity system to penalize polluters and reward the environmental conservers and protectors, including reformed sinners.

9. Developing land use and transportation alternatives to encourage reduced reliance on motor vehicles. This could be done by giving further stimulus to existing trends toward nodal urban development, by subsidizing public transportation, etc.

The Romance and Reality of Transportation

A form of fantasizing currently afflicts the American scene, specifically in the growing conflict between automobile and truck transport and public rail transportation. To begin with, the belated recognition of the automobile as polluter and foe of the central cities has tended to obscure an appreciation of the private auto's real virtues as a liberating force, enlarging people's choice of jobs, homes, and services, and enlarging the possibilities for meeting people from farther away.

THE USEFULNESS OF AUTOMOBILES

Several facts should be kept in mind with respect to the automobile. The first is that nostalgic notions regarding the auto's principal predecessor, the horse, must be set aside. Even in the horse-and-buggy era large cities were congested with traffic, and air-blown excrement was as worrisome to public health officials then as accidents are today. Moreover, most draft animals led short, miserable lives. Grinding machinery gears may be offensive, but it is simply not in the same category as whipping, starving, and killing horses.

Second, as noted the automobile has enlarged shopping, school, social, and sexual options, and has expanded the range of job choices. Except in remote communities, a worker can afford to be more independent, less of a docile captive than when his employment market was tied to the streetcar or his walking ability. People who would tidy up urban areas by reducing cross-commuting, abbreviating the journey to work, and re-creating, in modern form, the medieval village or company town where workplace and residence are side by side, might do well to remember the heavy penalties for arguing with an autocratic boss when there is no accessible employment alternative.

There is a further reality dimension. Increasingly, transportation patterns have become diffuse. In Raymond Vernon's (a research pioneer in urbanization) phraseology, people now travel from dispersed residences to dispersed work places, shopping, services, schools, and recreation.[41] Under these circumstances, we cannot reassemble the omelet into an egg. The automobile is just about the only answer for most of our transportation needs, although there is room for such supplements as school buses, taxis, and various types of minibus and jitney (single-street, enlarged taxis) services. Even if there is some degree of intensive residential and shopping clustering in the suburbs, the diffusion of destinations embedded in past land use decisions remains. Clearly the backbone of the transportation system is and will remain the private automobile. At best, it is likely that a very few subway-elevated systems and a limited number of bus or trolley systems can be developed to meet suburban transportation needs so as to eliminate the necessity for second cars in a number of areas.

BUSES AND RAILS

Why, if this is the case, should there be any interest left in the traditional radial routes, the rail and bus spokes, focusing on the hub of downtown areas? There are several answers to this question. The first is that a very large number of trips will continue to be made within and to concentrated clusters in central cities. It is extremely difficult, costly, and perhaps politically impossible to satisfy these trip demands via exclusive use of automobiles. As noted earlier, far too much use of space, inefficiency, and neighborhood disruption is involved in ramming expressways through densely settled urban areas. Political campaigns in the United States and Canada (for example, Toronto) have centered on halting such intown roads, not on building them.

One alternative is in the direction of paralysis: no more major intown highways and no supplementary transportation improvements. This combination of zeros inevitably leads to an acceleration of urban decay in the older, larger cities. As was indicated earlier, there are those who would argue that the process of central city decline is inevitable and irreversible, and that the wisest thing to do is to do nothing. Let nature take its course, they say, and things will somehow work themselves out, thanks to market forces and American ingenuity. Politically and morally this alternative seems indefensible, since it is tantamount to writing off the sizable proportion of the electorate that lives, or exists, in large central cities. This population depends on efficient public transportation; the automobile cannot do the job in large cities.

A NEW TURN IN TRANSPORTATION POLICY?

No one has developed a perfect solution for the clogging and the friction attendant on shuffling enormous numbers of people in limited space. But clearly the old ways are better than the new. Subways, rapid transit, commuter rail lines, and properly planned and routed bus systems are more effective in moving people quickly, (usually) more safely, and at less energy than private automobiles.[42] Make-do expedients like car pools, staggered office hours, differential toll and parking fees, and tough parking ticketing policies are all helpful, but still the bullet has to be bit. Despite the risks of forcing out marginal firms, the central areas of central cities—and subsidiary business centers—will have to sharply restrict private cars.

Foreign models to imitate.   What this means is continuing heavy expenditures to modernize subway systems, bringing our older ones up to the level of Montreal, if not Moscow. We also need to retain most commuter rail lines until they can gradually be replaced by transit or express buses and to create pedestrian malls where vehicle entry is restricted to night deliveries and emergency fire, police, and ambulance vehicles. With noxious emissions reduced to the vanishing point, it may be possible to cover over a number of downtown streets for all-weather outdoor use. And lest this approach be considered visionary, suitable for an architectural magazine article but too utopian for adoption, we need only be reminded that we are using proven technologies and plagiarizing from successful examples elsewhere in the world.

One other foreign innovation is also worth copying—Japan's high-speed intercity rail line. There seems to be no reason why each of the major megapolitan corridors should not be served by a four-or-five-hundred-mile rail system providing safe, all-weather transportation at 150 miles an hour. It can be argued that the number of intercity passengers is too small for such a major outlay—a $3 billion investment is estimated to handle only 1.5 million passenger trips per year on the Boston-New York-Washington line.[43] But once again, what is the real alternative? Increasingly clogged, unsafe air corridors, crowded approaches to airports, and bitter, costly struggles to construct and to service second, third, or fourth airports at even greater distances from the nation's urban centers. Reviving and modernizing the rails may seem old-fashioned, but they can be an extremely safe and fast way to travel—as many American travelers can testify.

The elements of a sensible transportation policy might include the following:

1. Salvage and upgrade all potentially viable public transportation along with related efforts to improve the quality of life in the cities.

2. Help to group new, high-quality urban development, including housing, jobs, and services, around transportation nodes.

3.   Emphasize, as a general rule, express buses, rail transit, and light rails (streetcars); because of their greater flexibility, buses should be considered useful and indispensable unless the market justifies a heavy rail system.

The modest costs.   The cost of providing the urban United States with modern public transportation has been estimated by a source friendly to the public transportation industry at a total of $77 billion spread over a twelve- to fifteen-year period.[44] Assuming that, like most estimates, this one is greatly understated, a truer figure might be $150 billion, or $10 billion a year. This awesome total is comparable, allowing for inflation, to the $75 billion spent in the twenty years, 1956 - 76, on the Interstate Highway Program ($5 billion a year) or the $52 billion spent in fourteen years on the space program ($6 billion a year). In other words, we have spent at this pace and scale before for big, non-military projects. Converted into per capita figures, expenditures would run about forty to fifty dollars per capita annually.

The massive benefit.   By any reasonable calculation, conversion of a substantial portion of journey-to-work travel to public transportation would yield these enormous benefits:

1.   *Lives saved.* The Interstate Highway Program decreased accidents by limiting road access; transit saves lives by eliminating the need for highway travel. The national fifty-five-mile-an-hour speed limit (and higher gas prices) reduced the national toll of traffic deaths by 9,000, a decline of 17 percent between 1973 and 1974.[45] A further sizable decline in automobile ridership should result, *at a minimum*, in an equal number of lives saved. While each of these lives is precious and irreplaceable to the deceased's family and friends, it is sometimes necessary to put a price on the priceless. Insurance companies are required to reimburse the relations, and each state has a fixed schedule of survivors' lump sum benefits under the Workmen's Compensation Act. Even if we are extremely parsimonious, estimating that in view of the aged and other unemployables involved in automobile accidents, the average fatality has only fifteen years of productive work life remaining, and if the annual earnings of such persons are calculated at the nation median of $12,000 per year, the total annual saving in earnings alone is about $180 million a year. Adding at least another $180 million for reduction in accidents results in an annual total of more than $360 million, a minimum of $5.4 billion in fifteen years.

2.   At a minimum, a public transit program should result in *fuel savings* of 8 billion gallons a year, $4 billion annually at 1975 oil prices. This would be of considerable help in the balance-of-payments hemorrhage to the overseas oil producers and should therefore be supported by those with patriotic inclinations.

3.   A public transportation-land development program which substantially reduces the time spent in the journey to work would represent an enormous savings in total man-hours. Most of the working population expends less than an hour and a half each day in daily work trips, but a sizable minority travels for two hours or more. Assuming a target maximum of 45 minutes each way, total man-hours saved could run from $1 billion to $3 billion. At a modest $3 per hour, this would result in another huge saving.

4.   Other very large savings would be realized through *lessened air, water, and noise pollution* and through reduced inputs of energy and materials needed to produce automobiles.

5.   And finally, as mentioned earlier in this chapter, a higher density urban development pattern linked to public transportation is in itself a great saver in *energy, materials, and other costs.*

Factors against a transportation program coalition.   A combination of energy problems and the inflation-recession of the mid-1970s was added to the chronic traffic congestion in larger cities along with the debilitated condition of most of the larger public transit systems. The result was a heightened interest in continued massive federal subsidization of urban public transportation with a funding ratio of ninety to ten as in the Interstate Highway Program, rather than the seventy to thirty federal/local funding ratio available under the Urban Mass Transportation Act.

The efforts to build a broad constituency for such federal urban public transportation financing foundered on the following three facts. First, only about 10 percent of the United States population lives in the larger urban concentrations afflicted by serious transportation problems. Second, only about a fifth of the nation's work force spends more than half an hour getting to work. Third, urban public transportation (with the exception of commuter railroads) is widely considered an unappealing mode suitable for poor, low-status persons. In addition, the tradition of financing subways, streetcars, and buses out of the local farebox instead of federal and state gasoline taxes left such systems vulnerable to attacks and cutbacks on service and maintenance, which further accelerated the decline in volume of riders. And finally, much of the population regards automobile travel as a lifeline, the only feasible way of pursuing employment and shopping alternatives in view of the dispersion of jobs, housing, and shopping. In most areas, to be bereft of a car is to be hampered at best. At worst, it is to be virtually unable to function.

Conclusion

From a political point of view one can conjure up a myriad of opponents to each of the propositions made in this chapter. They include the airlines, downtown merchants, confirmed automobilists, oil companies, and automobile manufacturers. But the only answer to our present land use problems seems to be in a transportation-environment-livability package.

In the area of housing, there is certainly a constituency to support a state-national land use policy for attractive and livable housing, but without strong leadership such a policy would be useless. Without tough, innovative leaders, national-state land use planning will evolve into paralytic or confrontational tableaux, generating the kind of meaningless pageantry and soothing rhetoric characteristic of many planning efforts at every level of government. There is no reason to suppose that shaping land use patterns in desired directions can be achieved by more of the same type of painless, consensual, market-oriented actions undertaken by a myriad of small governments and private interests. Taking hold means just that: there must be a goal, decisions, and implementing power—and a willingness to face controversy.

As for the environment, prospects for public support of a strong environmental policy are good. Even in the absence of strong and sustained federal leadership, even without a broad consensus on the environment, even when environmental goals seem to threaten jobs and business expansion, there has been wide support for environmental action. If federal leadership is forthcoming, it can exploit a powerful current of opinion. It might be remembered that travel *is* broadening; the example of some of the European nations and some of the pleasanter areas in the United States *has* had an impact on the current of opinion. There *is* a shame factor affecting people who live in the nation's less attractive areas, who constantly apologize for their home towns.

In order to build a coalition for a transportation policy, the government could offer obvious benefits, such as heavy direct or indirect federal subsidies for the high-speed corridor rail line, combined with disincentives, like banning cars in overcrowded areas as a public health measure.[46] It should also be remembered that there are allies for a rail coalition. Though a small minority, rail commuters include a number of prominent business people with considerable political clout. Subway and transit riders, a tolerant, long-suffering constituency, and prospective riders (in unserved cities) offer another source of strength for a broad public transportation program, as do airplane passengers who have circled O'Hare or La Guardia Airport for an hour or so waiting to land.

In short, with considerable work, a coalition *can* be built for *balanced* transportation programs. These should include funds for highway improvement and maintenance and sizable sums for outlying bus and demand-responsive services as well as subway construction and operating money for big cities. Also needed are allocations for high-speed, intercity corridor rail lines on the West Coast and in the Midwest as well as along the eastern Portland-Norfolk megalopolis.

Summary

The main problem in land use today is not the lack of developable land, but the question of how the development shall be controlled. In the past, land use has been controlled, usually not very effectively, by each community. It is now apparent that land use control should be transferred to the states.

As far as the public is concerned, the central need in land use is the preservation of or creation of good neighborhoods, and a sensible land use policy will take this concern into account. Although there is some sentiment in favor of abandoning the central cities, they could be rebuilt by conserving stable neighborhoods, stressing public transportation, designing housing and neighborhoods for personal safety, improving the population balance toward more middle-class and stable working-class residents, and making better use of available space in the cities.

In the 1970s housing construction has declined as a result of the recession and the rising interest rates and costs of housing. Because of these changes more condominiums and apartments are being built instead of houses, and more wives are seeking gainful employment. The government could expand home ownership, and thus help stabilize the society, by expanding housing subsidy programs, encouraging population growth around transportation nodes, and widening housing options for working-class people.

In the past, the effect of government policy has been to subsidize land development but not to plan for or control it. Even now developers and the building industry strongly resist national land use legislation. Such legislation will need, in any case, strong leaders to implement it.

Up until now public concern about the environment has not been strong enough to be politically effective. However, it could be made more appealing by a campaign stressing the link between pollution and cancer, the public costs of private pollution, and the job-creating advantages of pollution clean-up. Furthermore, additional government subsidies for pollution clean-up are beginning to create a powerful lobby to counteract the influence of polluting industries.

A public transit program is a necessary part of land use policy. The automobile is here to stay, but dependency upon it can be lessened through improved public transportation in the central cities and between cities, and residential and shopping clustering in the suburbs.

Recommendations

- Establish strong state land use agencies with the power to guide, review, and approve plans for new towns and new subdivisions as well as for urban redevelopment. Contingencies for approval of such plans should include safety features and provisions for making the area attractive and livable, for preserving and strengthening community structure, and for making full use of the available space.

- Widen housing options for working-class people.

- Stimulate dense, high-quality suburban development around public transportation nodes.

- Encourage home ownership.

- Concentrate on a full employment program rather than on providing housing subsidies for the poor.

- Establish an environmental program, including expanding present antipollution programs, requiring industries to cooperate in reducing environmental damage, instituting environmental restoration through public works, and using tax incentives and regulations to encourage use of renewable resources.

- Establish a sensible transportation policy, including salvaging and expanding present public transportation.

Notes

1.   Martin Meyerson, William L. C. Wheaton, and Barbara Terrett, *Housing, People, and Cities* (New York: McGraw-Hill, 1962), p. 88.

2.   Melvin R. Levin et al., *Boston Regional Survey* (Boston: Commonwealth of Massachusetts Mass Transportation Commission, 1963), p. 32.

3.   See Hans Blumenfeld, "Alternative Solutions for Metropolitan Development," in *The Modern Metropolis*, ed. Paul D. Spreiregen (Cambridge, Mass.: MIT Press, 1967), pp. 38 - 49.

4.   See George Sternlieb and Robert W. Burchell, *Residential Abandonment: The Tenament Landlord Revisited* (New Brunswick, N.J.: Center for Urban Policy Research, 1973).

5.   See Mayer Spivak's discussion of the difference between adult-designed playgrounds and child-oriented playgrounds. Mayer Spivak, "The Political Collapse of a Playground," in *Cities Fit to Live In*, ed. Walter McQuade (New York: MacMillan, 1971), pp. 128 - 134.

6. Leonard Downie, Jr., *Mortgage on America* (New York: Praeger, 1974), pp. 220 - 225.

7. Henry George, *Progress and Poverty* (New York: Robert Schalkenback Foundation, 1954).

8. However, this view may be due for modification; see Gladwin Hill, "New Land Ethic: Its Spread Raises Political and Legal Questions," *New York Times*, 4 September 1973, p. 14.

9. Even before the current economic crunch, the movement away from the detached single family unit was evident. See Melvin R. Levin, "Current Housing Problems," in *Exploring Urban Problems*, ed. Melvin R. Levin (Boston: The Urban Press, 1971), p. 209.

10. Sarah K. Crim, "National Conference of Urban 'Pioneers' Show Strength of City Revival," in *Mortgage Banker* 35, no. 2 (November 1974), p. 22.

11. D. Gordon Bagby, *Housing Rehabilitation Costs* (Lexington, Mass.: Lexington Books, 1973), p. 8.

12. See Brian J. Berry, "The Decline of the Aging Metropolis: Cultural Bases and Social Process," in *Post Industrial America: Metropolitan Decline and Inter-Regional Job Shifts*, ed. G. Sternlieb and J. W. Hughes, Center for Urban Policy Research, (New Brunswick, N.J.: 1975).

13. "Housing and Community Development Act Reviewed," *Planning* 40, no. 8 (September 1974), p. 8.

14. The National Commission on Urban Problems was working with population estimates for the coming decades that were greatly in excess of current predictions. See National Commission on Urban Problems, *Building the American City* (Washington, D.C.: Government Printing Office, 1968), p. 180.

15. Downie, *Mortgage on America*, pp. 179 - 206.

16. James G. Coke and John J. Gargan, *Fragmentation in Land Use Planning and Control* (Washington, D.C.: Government Printing Office, 1969), pp. 79 - 80.

17. Melvin R. Levin, "Land Use Patterns and Problems," in *Exploring Urban Problems*, ed. Melvin R. Levin (Boston: The Urban Press, 1971).

18. Fred Bosselman and David Callies, *The Quiet Revolution in Land Use Control*, prepared for the Council on Environmental Quality (Washington, D.C.: Government Printing Office, 1971), pp. 13 - 18, 59 - 71, 85 - 87, 113 - 119.

19. For an excellent summary of issues, problems, and remedies involved in suburban exclusionary zoning, see H. M. Franklin, D. Falk, and A. J. Levin, *In-Zoning* (Washington D.C.: The Potomac Institute, 1974).

20. President's Committee on Urban Housing, "A Decent Home," in *Exploring Urban Problems*, ed. Melvin R. Levin (Boston: The Urban Press, 1971), pp. 223 - 224.

21. Bosselman and Callies, *The Quiet Revolution*.

22. Ibid., pp. 314 - 326.

23.   Anthony Downs, *Federal Housing Subsidies: How Are They Working?* (Lexington, Mass.: Lexington Books, 1973), pp. 8 - 9.

24.   Anthony Downs, *The Possible Nature of a National Urban Growth Policy* (Chicago: Real Estate Research Corporation, 1972), pp. 34 - 35.

25.   For a pessimistic appraisal of the continuing reality of racial segregation, see Karl E. and Alma F. Taeuber, "Is the Negro an Immigrant Group?" in *Integrated Education* 1 (June 1963), pp. 25 - 28. For a more recent study of the tendency for whites to flee racially changing neighborhoods, see David P. Varady, "White Moving Plans in a Racially Changing Middle-Class Community," in *Journal of American Institute of Planners* 40, no. 5 (September 1974), pp. 360 - 370.

26.   Michael Knight, "Split-Levels Giving Way to Apartments in Suburbs," *New York Times*, 20 January 1974, p. E6.

27.   President's Committee on Urban Housing, "A Decent Home," in *Exploring Urban Problems*, p. 235.

28.   Frank Lynn, "Poll Finds Economy and Taxes are Voters' Main Worries," *New York Times*, 28 October 1974, pp. 1, 26.

29.   See Paul R. Ehrlich, *The Population Bomb* (New York: Sierra Club Books, 1969); and Barry Commoner, *The Closing Circle* (New York: Alfred A. Knopf, 1971).

30.   For example, "Business Fights Pollution—and the Nation Profits," *Nation's Business* 58, no. 2 (February 1970), pp. 29 - 30.

31.   See Henry L. Diamond, "Energy and Environment as Allies," *New York Times*, 20 October 1974, p. F14; and "Detroit's Frantic Hunt for a Cleaner Engine," *Business Week*, 9 December 1972, pp. 60 - 70.

32.   An overly optimistic early view was "Science Yells for Industry's Help Against Pollution," *Business Week*, 3 January 1970, pp. 62 - 63.

33.   The Council on Environmental Quality, *Environmental Quality* (Washington, D.C.: Government Printing Office, 1974), p. 178.

34.   The estimate of what industry spent on pollution control in 1958 is probably high. It is based on the same 6 percent of total investment in plant and equipment figure of 1971. Gladwin Hill, "Estimate of Pollution Control Costs Pared," *New York Times*, 18 September 1973, p. 26. The 1973 and 1982 data are from the *Fifth Annual Report on Environmental Quality* (Washington, D.C.: Government Printing Office), December 1974, table 1, p. 221.

35.   See The Council on Environmental Quality, *Sixth Annual Report*, December 1975, pp. 533 - 536.

36.   Gladwin Hill, "Environmental Movement Registers Gains in Three Years," *New York Times*, 9 April 1973, p. 28.

37.   See "Save Lake Baikal," *Newsweek*, 21 November 1971, pp. 52 - 55.

38. The Council on Environmental Quality "Carcinogens in the Environment," in *Environmental Quality.*

39. For example, see Charles L. Schultze, *The Politics and Economics of Public Spending* (Washington, D.C.: The Brookings Institution, 1968).

40. A portent of things to come might be the state of New Jersey's claim in a recent case that it could demand compensation for harm done by polluters to the marine and animal life supported by the waterways and tideland within the state. "State Asks Right to Collect Damages from Polluters," *New York Times*, 6 July 1973, p. 27.

41. For a discussion of the complex travel pattern of one Long Island housewife, see Downie, *Mortgage on America*, pp. 85 - 86.

42. See Ed McCahill and William J. Toner, "The Long and the Short of It," *Planning*, no. 40 (January 1974), pp. 9 - 10.

43. The estimate is from a 1976 - 80 extrapolation of the 1971 $1.5 billion figure given in U.S. Department of Transportation, *Recommendations for Northeast Corridor Transportation*, Summary Report, vol. 1. (Washington, D.C.: Government Printing Office, 1971). In 1968 there were over seven times as many automobile person trips in this Northeast Corridor—Boston-N.Y.C.-Washington—as rail trips: 14.2 million vs. 2.0 million. Interestingly, despite the decay of rail transport, there were only slightly more corridor air trips than rail passenger trips, thanks mostly to remaining commuter lines. (See vol. 2 of the same report, Table 5c-1.)

44. *Energy Reporter*, Federal Energy Administration Citizens Newsletter, March 1975, p. 2.

45. "Auto Industry Resisting Costs of Pollution Controls and of Safety," *New York Times*, 6 April 1975, pp. 1, 42. Two calculations on the average value of lives saved were prepared by the adversaries on proposed legislation requiring installation of air bags in automobiles. The low estimate, prepared by a consulting firm for the automotive industry, was $189,000 per life, and the higher federal estimate was $242,000 per life. There was also a dispute over the costs of automotive injuries, the federal study estimating the cost at $7,009 and the consultants at $3,027 per injury.

46. McCahill and Toner, "The Long and the Short of It," p. 9 - 10.

4

MANPOWER:
Is Full Employment
Feasible?

We identify in this book some fundamental problems for which solution is feasible and popular, and others for which remedies are necessary but difficult and often politically risky and unrewarding. In some cases the programs are familiar—the costs and other problems can be assessed, because other nations have done the pioneering—we need only improve on proven example. In other areas (like crime) unfortunately it is we who are the pioneers, confronting problems vastly greater than those which afflict other nations. Chronically high unemployment, too, is an area in which the United States is a leader among the advanced urban nations.[1] But it is also here that a liberal coalition can combine wisdom and rectitude in an employment program and receive many, many votes.

Potential Support for the Employment Issue

At first glance, it may seem ridiculous to look for political support for full employment. Since unemployment rates have ranged between 4 percent and 9 percent in the past decade, presumably at least nine out of every ten voters are not particularly interested in the woes of the marginal worker. True, there are groups where the rate is much higher. Slum dwellers normally experience unemployment rates of 10 percent to 25 percent, and rates in chronically distressed areas like coal mining towns run 8 percent to 10 percent. Teenagers are always hard hit—white rates are 10 to 15 percent and black and Spanish-speaking 50 to 60 percent.[2] But with the partial exception of the distressed areas—a complicated story in its own right—the groups most seriously affected by spells of joblessness tend to be politically ineffective. Slum residents, a minority of the population in any case, turn out to vote in small numbers. In the slums a 30 to 50 percent participation in national elections is common, compared with the 70 to 80 percent or higher voting rate in middle- and upper-income neighborhoods.[3]

In short, the frequently or long-term unemployed have been such a minority that elections have increasingly hinged on capturing the votes of groups which normally are relatively invulnerable to threats of unemployment. An objective analyst might well have suggested that from 1950 up to the mid-1970s employment was a minor political issue. The depression may have lived on in scattered pockets of misery, but the potential for broad political support was limited to distressed-areas legislation. As far as the cities were concerned, idle, mischief-prone teenagers were not responsible for the election of candidates except through their inadvertent help for law-and-order politicians campaigning against crime in the streets.

EXPERIENCE WITH UNEMPLOYMENT
Despite these facts, it is clear enough in the mid-1970s that writing off this issue would be a serious error. What must be remembered is that *even prior to the 1973 - 1976 recession,* although only a small percentage of the labor force may be unemployed at any one time, over the course of a five-year period one out of every three or four workers is likely to have a brush with unemployment in the form of at least a temporary layoff. What the recession did was to bring home the threat of joblessness to the middle class, most notably recent college graduates.

In 1975 there were almost 9 million college students, a substantial "learning force" who with their parents represented a very large, apprehensive, and active voting bloc. True, even under recession conditions, the unemployment problem was heavily concentrated among persons with less than some college training. Also, as noted, it is most severe among the young, the single, and the poorly educated, and most especially among minorities. During the depth of the 1973 - 77 business recession, for example, jobless rates for married men with college degrees never exceeded 4 or 5 percent. In contrast, unemployment rates among black teenagers living in urban slums ranged upwards of 40 to 50 percent. Spokesmen for minority groups point out that some black youngsters had never had a job and that since the job option was effectively closed off, the remaining alternatives for such young people were continued dependence on parents or relatives—themselves exceedingly poor, existence on the welfare rolls, or escapes into drugs, liquor, crime, or vegetation.[4]

While hard times in the slums is old news, the 1973 business recession broke new ground in another area. Since the 1940s, the proportion of women in the labor force has been rising steadily to about 50 percent by the early 1970s. Often it is forgotten that the rise in the American standard of living (and frequently its survival) depends on the nation's 35 million working women. Not only are there millions of women who are the only support of aged parents or children, but many relatively affluent families can afford to live the way they do only because there is a second income in the family (almost two-thirds of working women are married). For this reason, the prescription for unemployment heard so

often in the early stages of the 1930s depression—"fire the women and
hire the men who need the money to support their families"—was barely mentioned in the mid-1970s.

By the mid-1970s it had become apparent that women were on the
front line of the employment struggle. Institutionally insulated, female-
dominated occupations like school teaching, nursing, social work, and
library work, which used to be relatively immune from layoffs, were
affected by municipal and state budget reductions and the delayed impact of the falling birth rate. Moreover, these relatively protected occupations constitute less than a quarter of the total jobs held by women.
Most employed women work in manufacturing, retail trade, and non-
government service occupations, sectors always highly vulnerable to
downturns in the economy.

What this summary suggests is that there exists a potential for a
broad coalition of interest groups likely to support a national full-
employment program. Further, even a wider backing for such an approach could be secured if businessmen could be convinced (a) that it
was an effective method of heading off dangerous unrest among a
sizable bloc of voters; (b) that tax monies would be used to hire the unemployed to perform useful public service work rather than to vegetate,
and (c) that there would be secondary economic and political benefits
from the fallout of new business activity generated by public service
employment. It is in fact possible to conceive of a Christmas tree
marketing effort which translates a job creation program into specific
benefits for all—payrolls, contracts, retail sales, and rent payments,
listed in detail state by state, county by county, and even city by city.

FEAR OF UNEMPLOYMENT
This is only part of the vote potential. As suggested above, the key
element in building support lies elsewhere, in people's emotional reactions to the threat of hard times, of the disaster that befell fathers,
friends, and neighbors in depressions and recessions. It hardly needs to
be pointed out that the prospect of very heavy layoffs, a reality in the
construction industries, 1973 - 77, has a powerful impact in resurrect-
ing these latent forces.

While it is clear that even in the periodic business recessions which
have afflicted the nation since 1945, unemployment among much of the
middle class has been minimal, limited direct experience with serious
spells of joblessness does not prevent the effect of the dark legends and
nightmares grounded in bitter family history. Underneath the topsoil of

middle-class affluence there is an enormous reservoir of generation-to-generation memories of the Great Depression. From time to time, as in 1973 - 77, this reservoir is tapped by sporadic, unexpected, and for that reason unnerving outbreaks of unemployment. These outbreaks have affected such diverse occupations as aerospace engineers, school-teachers, stockbrokers, civilians employed by the military, advertising executives, and newly graduated college students.

It is true that this unhappy experience is not an everyday occurrence; unemployment rates among married executives and professionals rarely exceed one or two percent.[5] But the rate is far less important than the widespread tremors touched off by the lightning bolt. As in perceptions of crime, a few close-to-home cases have a massive impact. Again as in the case of crime, the media, aware of the human interest value of a story about a middle-class family suddenly reduced to scraping along much like poor folk, have been quick to play up the human drama. Tales of newly minted college graduates driving taxis, waiting on tables, or queuing for the few schoolteacher openings strike terror into student and parent. A feature story on an engineer trained in some exotic specialty, reduced to working at a carwash, fleeced by shady employment agencies, dining on surplus foods, hoping that the moon shuttle, or Mars probe will come to the rescue, strikes a responsive chord among people who would be hard pressed to distinguish an analog computer from an abacus.

In short, the sentiment that there but for the grace of God go I, is widespread. Most middle-class people lack the assets to subsist more than six months to a year without a regular pay check. Given bad luck or a major slump, much of the middle class would be in the same leaky craft with the redundant ad-executive, the laid-off schoolteacher, or the failed small businessman.

Today's middle class retains tribal memories of father's depression, the *real* hard times of the 1930s. Father and uncle told grim, blood-curdling tales to children of the thirties and forties. Of the infant horror stories that linger below the surface, not the least are the real-life miseries of pinched budgets, mother's tears, and father's heavy drinking. Trips to the bank or the pawnbroker, unending marital squabbles, bleak Christmas trees, a clean brave front masking frayed poverty—all are atavistic memories, long-buried but awaiting resurrection. Even years of prosperity do not dispell an underlying pessimism, a lingering doubt that good times are here to stay. Tremors—and 1973 - 77 was more than a tremor—often have the impact of earthquakes because the fear of joblessness, if not the reality, is widespread.

Historical Background

It is worth exploring some past history, if only briefly, to illuminate the past tragedies which still shadow the present.

THE DEPRESSION

There is a remarkably rich literature reaching back to the thirties and earlier, detailing the miseries of depression and unemployment. In the thirties Jules Romains, George Orwell, and the early John Dos Passos were only three of the novelists who despaired of capitalism's ability to cope with the unemployment problem.[6] The utter bankruptcy of the establishment business leaders and economists of the day (the early 1930s) in meeting the crisis is summed up in Schlesinger's *Crisis of the Old Order.*[7]

Attitudes toward the depression.   Novelists may have despaired of the system, but for the most part, the poor blamed *themselves* for the failure to support their families, as if being out of work in company with millions of others was nevertheless a personal defeat, an action which almost wilfully harms oneself and one's family.[8] This is one reason why in the depth of the depression, in the 1932 presidential election, the Communist party picked up far less than one percent of the vote.[9] The sense of fatalism, of being subject to some mysterious plague, was portrayed in a moving passage by Henry Miller which contrasts the heroes of 1917 and 1918, brave in action against a clearly defined enemy, but struck down by unemployment during the depression. Unable to fight back, veteran soldiers were weaponless and helpless in this kind of losing battle.[10]

The motion pictures of the 1930s reflect this sense of powerlessness. While there were a few, very few grimly realistic depression dramas, for the most part there were fantasies of finding unexpected wealth, inheriting legacies from long-lost relatives, striking it rich from miraculous inventions. There were also a number of occupational dramas. These included a few bleak depictions of life on the assembly line, steel mill, or farm, but these were balanced by many more unreal pictures of sheriffs and cowboys, glamorous newspaper reporters, even an occasional department store fairytale. A strange occupational sub-genre evolved, low-budget dramas depicting highly paid working-class craftsmen in dangerous occupations, such as bush pilots, high steel construction workers, nitroglycerin truckers, deep sea divers. All featured danger on the job, camaraderie on and off the work site, a little romance, and the prospect of continuous remunerative employment—perhaps the biggest fantasy of all.

Among the propertied classes during the depression there was a pronounced tendency to think in terms of balanced budgets, eventual recovery when business confidence was restored, and the dangers of overpopulation. In 1943, the wealthy people of "Middletown" in a sociological study wished "they," the redundant out-of-work class, would go away, anywhere.[11] (Ten years later, there weren't enough people for the jobs; the unemployed were once again part of the nation's vital backbone.)

Government and the jobless.   In the latter part of the depression, there were three newspapers operating in Chicago. One, the conservative Hearst outlet, regularly referred to the out-of-work as "the needy," a phrase which conjures up genteel soup kitchens and charity baskets prepared by benevolent wealthy ladies. At this same time the liberal New Deal paper called the same group "the jobless," a term which suggests long lines of men clamoring for honest labor. But the Chicago *Tribune*, Colonel McCormick's right-wing Republican newspaper, habitually used the word "idle," calling to mind indolent loafers, enjoying lengthy vacations at the expense of the taxpayer. The difference of perceptions among the three publishers accurately reflects the different American attitudes and approaches to the unemployed.

In the beginning, America adopted much of the English poor-law system, which provided a pittance for the poor, a little work on the roads to discourage malingering, and strong hints that out of town, out west, out somewhere, able-bodied men were in demand. The out-of-work who owned a bit of land could raise a little produce. In the city as on the farm there were poorly paid jobs with employers all too ready to take full advantage of the desperate in a laissez-faire, unionless world.

To be sure, here and there was a helping hand for the poor. The big-city political machines (and the county courthouse gangs) owed their solid backing by the poor to the fact that they served, albeit crudely, as social service and unemployment agencies, with a touch of the ombudsman thrown in. George Washington Plunkitt of Tammany Hall describes his tireless labors on behalf of jobless constituents, constituents burnt out, arrested, marrying, but always poor.[12] The machine

delivered what the poor needed most, most notably jobs for the faithful
on the city payroll or with firms doing business in the city. In return for
these services, the machine received votes and a license for graft and
corruption. It was no wonder that the reformers who promised honest
government were, in Plunkitt's term, short-lived "morning glories,"
because well-off reformers attacked municipal employees as loafers but
failed to deliver vital human services. The better quality bookkeeping
and honest contract-letting beloved of the middle and upper class were
of minimal interest to the slum dweller.

The New Deal.   There is no difficulty in identifying the watershed
in government policy toward the unemployed: the New Deal, the
"hungry thirties." Harry Hopkins, Roosevelt's adviser and welfare
chief and a former social worker, upon being informed that large-scale
work relief was the wrong way to go about achieving business recovery,
replied, "People don't eat in the long run, they eat every day." Likewise
John Maynard Keynes's response, when told that his deficit spending
"pump-priming" proposals would allegedly impede sound, long-run
recovery, was, "In the long run we shall all be dead."

During the New Deal there was a problem-oriented response to
large-scale unemployment, in large measure because unemployment
had reached deep into the middle class. Large-scale federal deficits were
suffered partly to hire people to perform vital, neglected public services.
But as critics were quick to point out, some of the hastily planned work
ventures were ill-conceived, and benefits were slow in trickling down.
Public Works Administration (PWA) projects, for example, were good
news for the sewer pipe industry, but they were not a major employment generator per federal dollar. Even the Work Projects Administration (WPA), the PWA, and allied efforts all together were insufficient
to reduce the numbers of jobless below six or seven million, a jobless
rate of 10 to 15 percent in 1938 and 1939.[13]

The work programs of the 1930s offer an instructive glimpse into a
dim past and an uncertain future. For one thing, in Europe as in the
United States, penurious governments were obsessed with the need to
maintain monetary stability. Consequently, they suffered over a decade
of misery before enjoying the magical effects of rearmament and war.
Overnight, nations too broke to feed their poor found themselves short
of manpower, spending billions they did not know they had for enormous, voracious war machines. At one time the stricken capitalist
nations were so beset by insoluble economic problems that they could

offer no work for millions of their citizens. And a few years later, in the same nations, there were flourishing economies, high morale, everyone working—in fact a frantic search for fresh manpower. They were all spending, spending, spending on war on a scale they had refused to spend for peacetime needs. Even though previous, similar experience in the First World War had largely been discarded, this time it was not a lesson to be forgotten.

It has been claimed that the lessons of war prosperity were learned all too well. Trade unions in the United States were (and are) among the most vigorous, uncompromising hardliners in the Cold War, the Korean War, and the Vietnam War. While part of their anticommunism is ideological, grounded to a degree in bitter factional fights with communists for control of unions in the 1940s, to a considerable extent there was (and is) a clear recognition of the close linkage between high levels of military expenditures and general prosperity and fat payrolls. This anticommunist military WPA method of supporting the economy, which also appeals to conservatives, has regularly been given fresh impetus by some new outbreak in Berlin, Czechoslovakia, Southeast Asia, the Mideast. Best of all, military spending offers challenging, highly paid, patriotic contracts and jobs in defense of the nation's liberties. In fact so comfortable has been this relationship that a number of labor unions have been reluctant to leave an era of confrontation for an era of negotiation, detente, and cutbacks in the military budget.

Lessons of the 1930s.   In contrast to the cost-plus, if-it-moves-hire-it approach during the Second World War (a loose system of procurement that made no attempt to hold down costs but instead guaranteed a profit to the manufacturer), prewar approaches to unemployment were deficient on several counts.[14] First, they failed the test of inclusiveness. The Civil Works Administration of 1933 - 34 seemed to be headed in the direction of putting all the unemployed to work, but by 1935 the government had pulled in its horns. It was not feasible, it was said, to provide a job for everyone through civilian spending in an era of mass unemployment.[15] The WPA, at its peak, employed only two out of every five of the nation's unemployed.

The work programs of the 1930s taught other valuable lessons. For one thing, despite all the carping and sneering about makework, it was demonstrated that much good can be achieved even by quickly initiated, hastily planned programs. In the mid-1970s, the nation was still sprinkled with bridges and buildings originating in the WPA and PWA of the

1930s. It should give us pause to observe that although there have been between three and eight million jobless each year since the end of World War II, there are no similar "monuments to idleness" from these decades. Instead we have wasted in excess of a hundred million man-years.

Actually the WPA and the PWA were the third version of federal work relief. Roosevelt took office in January 1933, and by mid-May Congress authorized $500 million in relief money, the equivalent in the mid-1970s of about $5 billion. But emergency relief was not enough to get the nation through the bitter winter of 1933 - 34, and Harry Hopkins, the relief administrator, secured backing from the president and the Congress to establish the Civil Works Administration (CWA). By January 1934, at its height, CWA employed over four million persons at minimum wages. In its brief span of less than a year CWA built or improved 500,000 miles of roads, 40,000 schools, over 3,500 playgrounds and athletic fields, and 1,000 airports.

Alarmed at CWA's cost and fearful that government employment would become habit forming, Roosevelt phased CWA out and transferred the responsibility to the Federal Emergency Relief Administration (FERA), where wages were lower and the danger of permanence seemed slighter. FERA, too, made a major contribution. Among its outputs were construction of 5,000 public buildings, 7,000 bridges, and, using the skills of white-collar workers, literacy programs that taught 1.5 million adults to read and write, and nursery school programs for children from low-income families. (It may be noted that CWA workers averaged $15 per week, while FERA workers averaged only $6.50.)

The new phase of government work relief was the Works Progress Administration (WPA). Despite demands from trade unions to pay prevailing wages lest the program undercut union wage scales, WPA payments were low—$50 a month, about twice the amount available from relief. Despite its huge scale—$5 billion, equivalent to perhaps $50 billion in mid-1970s dollars—the program had to be spread out among 3.5 million workers. Moreover, since the money would go farther if it were allocated to labor-intensive activities that required few expensive materials, WPA was severely limited in terms of public works. Nevertheless the WPA was able to build more than 2,500 hospitals, 5,900 school buildings, and nearly 13,000 playgrounds. It also encouraged the arts through theater writers and art projects and provided work for jobless youth in and out of school. Considering the haste with which these programs were thrown together, the lack of substantive precedent on which to draw, and the conflicting criticism from labor and business, the depression works programs were an impressive achievement.[16]

Perhaps the reasons for the failure to make use of the unemployed since the early 1940s can be found in other lessons of the depression-era programs. It was discovered, for example, that private industry and labor unions react violently against what they regard as unfair, heavily subsidized, low-wage operations cutting into their market. One may argue that this is dog-in-the-manger reasoning and that the object of this intervention is to create new jobs. However, industry and unions reply that if there is a demonstrated need and there are government contracts to serve that need, private enterprise employing workers at normal wage rates can respond quickly and effectively. This is particularly the case when there are substantial construction contracts to let. Industries and unions fear that tax-exempt, government-operated construction organizations will undercut private business by employing hungry people at a fraction of current construction wages.

Furthermore, in the 1930s, manufacturers were fearful of low-wage labor working under special government-sponsored arrangements to produce or sell food, clothing, or furniture. They were apprehensive that a parallel economic system would evolve that would crush the private sector by pricing private business out of the market.[17] The alternative economy could conceivably do immeasurable damage by providing jobs so attractive that the labor force would flock to government work, causing a ruinous increase in private-sector wages and otherwise making life difficult for the harassed manufacturer, wholesaler, and retailer. The lack of useful employment in prisons can be traced to these roots. If penitentiaries restrict themselves to such work as manufacturing jute bags and stamping automobile license plates, it is largely due to concern that unless carefully circumscribed, ten-cents-an-hour convict labor could force private firms out of business.

It was a situation in which the government couldn't win. Its efforts were either derided as inefficient, money-wasting WPA "boondoggles" (makework) or, less frequently, feared as all-too-effective threats to taxpaying private enterprise. (To cite a well-known example of the latter, the TVA's cheap power was seen as a direct, unfair challenge to the private utilities.)

LESSONS OF WORLD WAR II

It is characteristic of great wars that they have great impact on the public consciousness. Perhaps the chief lesson of the Second World War, so far as the state of the economy is concerned, is that *no advanced ur-*

"There are plenty of jobs around. People just don't want to work."

Source: Drawing by Drucker; © 1972, *The New Yorker Magazine, Inc.*

ban nation need ever permit itself to remain helpless in the face of mass unemployment. Every westernized country now engages in constant tinkering with interest rates, taxation, tariffs, currency levels, deficit spending, price manipulation, and other measures designed to cool off, heat up, or stabilize the economy. The difference between left and right wing lies in the constant tendency of the Right to be more hopeful that stringent controls won't be necessary and, if controls are imposed, to ensure that business corporations and the wealthy are let off lightly.

The desire to work.   So far so good. But a second lesson which should have been learned from World War II was not comprehended. This was the surprising discovery (to conservatives at any rate) that when jobs are available, people really do want to work. Members of the middle and upper classes have long believed that there is a soft core of at least two, three, or ten percent of the labor force that are confirmed loafers. According to this view, well-meaning welfare and unemployment compensation policies and kindly private charities are counterproductive because they provide an attractive alternative to the threat of deprivation and starvation. These threats alone, it is assumed, force the lazy to the daily drudgery of the mill and mine and keep them usefully employed at dull, ill-paying jobs.

In particular there is a recurring worry concerning how to retain a sizable reservoir of labor to perform the most miserable, low-paid jobs—the garbage pickup, dishwashing, delivery slots that may go unfilled if something better is available. It may be recalled that part of the southern political opposition to Nixon's family income maintenance proposal in 1970 was based on the grounds that it would dry up the supply of maids and yardworkers.[18] (This fear is not entirely without foundation: every advanced nation has experienced a drastic shrinkage in the numbers of domestic servants as quickly as a reasonable alternative to domestic servitude becomes available.)

During World War II the unemployment rate shrank almost to the vanishing point—one-half of one percent of the labor force. This was far, far below the "frictional" two to three percent level thought to be the usual rock bottom minimum consisting of the sick, the tired, and the job changers. In fact, it was very much like the situation in Switzerland, Germany, and Sweden, countries where labor was so tight in the 1960s and early 1970s that they were forced to import large quantities of "guest workers" (in 1974 one-fifth of the Swiss labor force consisted of "guests"). The point is that with the exception of all but a handful of the flintiest hard core, all America was at work in 1943 and 1944. In short, domestic and foreign experience seems to offer reasonable evidence that if ever jobs could again be made available on the same scale, the nation could again mop up the deep pools of unemployment in the urban ghettos and other distressed areas as well as the peppering of unemployed in more affluent areas.

Population immobility.   This brings us to a third lesson of World War II. This was the extreme difficulty of getting many reluctant peo-

ple to move to where the jobs are. The war was a period of enormous
migrations, with armed forces shuffling back and forth on the thriving,
packed-to-the-aisles railroads, and millions relocating to California,
Michigan, Ohio, Florida, and Texas. But there were stubborn pockets of
unemployment, people who simply refused to move to places where jobs
were available. The United States Employment Service (USES), the
wartime national employment agency, provided information on
lucrative job openings, but still some refused to leave. And so the mountain went to Mohammed—ordnance plants were set up in places like
southern Illinois and Arkansas.

The Employment Act of 1946.   And then the war ended. The ordnance plants were closed, the national employment service was refrag-
mented under state control, and nine million men were demobilized. To
the surprise of many pessimists, almost all of the exservicemen went to
work or school. The expected recurrence of the depression failed to
materialize, although pockets of unemployment reappeared in urban
slums and the old distressed areas. But the expectation of much greater
disaster to come was responsible for an interesting piece of legislation,
the Employment Act of 1946.

This act grew out of the widespread conviction that the Second
World War represented only a pause in the Great Depression. Once the
troops were demobilized and accumulated wartime savings were spent,
it was back to 1930—seven or eight million unemployed and the same
old gloomy lack of prospects for workers, farmers, small businessmen,
students, and aspiring professionals. If indeed the depression were to
recur, and there were to be eight or ten million out of work, the
erstwhile heroes of Okinawa and the Ardennes would find themselves
moving from the "fifty-two - twenty club" (a maximum of one year's
unemployment compensation at twenty dollars a week for jobless
veterans) onto lines for soup kitchens. Later they would become bonus
marchers and, perhaps not long after, they would blossom into
members of radical political movements.

One of the few agencies doing any systematic thinking about
postwar problems was the National Resources Planning Board (NRPB),
an organization staffed by New Deal social scientists, but thought by
many conservatives to be the nucleus of an American version of the
Soviet Gosplan.[19] Shortly before its demise in 1943 at the hands of a
hostile Congress, the NRPB published (or more accurately republished)
a new economic bill of rights for Americans which included the right to
a decent job.

The Full Employment Program outlined by President Harry
Truman in a special message in September 1946 was less ambitious.[20] It
included an extension and enlargement of unemployment benefits, continuation of the federal USES, continued price and rent controls, a
higher minimum wage, and massive public works to take up the slack in
military spending. A strong version of the full employment bill passed
the Senate but remained bottled up in the House until a much weaker
act emerged, stripped of the basic federal commitment to provide a job
for everyone who needed work.[21]

The furor which erupted over the wording of this act concerned the
extent and nature of federal responsibility to the unemployed—or more
accurately, to the potentially unemployed. Conservatives were prepared
to go part way, but not quite so far as to explicitly guarantee a federal
underwriting of such an ambitious goal as full employment. They were
willing to make up only a small part of the difference between one-half
of 1 percent unemployed and 20 percent unemployed. In a labor force of
60 million, carrying out a promise to achieve full employment could well
mean a permanent super-WPA, employing 10 million or more. The
liberals who had pressed the case for just such a commitment com-
promised unhappily on less ambitious wording—"high level" employment. In practice this proved to mean nothing very specific, since
national unemployment rates ranged all the way to 9 percent during the
troughs of the postwar business recessions of 1948 - 49, 1953 - 54, 1957 -
58, 1960 - 61, 1970 - 71, and 1973 - 77. (The parallel to the stirring unfulfilled pledge to provide "decent, safe, and sanitary housing" for the
nation in the 1949 housing legislation is inescapable.)

The chief result of the 1946 Employment Act was the creation of the
Council of Economic Advisors. This group is directed to keep a watchful
eye on the state of the economy and to recommend growth and stabilization measures to "cool off" or "heat up" the economy through tax,
federal expenditure, and monetary policies. Over the years the council
has blended objective analysis with politically oriented pronounce-
ments.[22] From time to time particular councils have been attacked as ex-
cessively partisan and tending to confuse rather than clarify issues, but
there have also been recurring bouts of attempted emulation. However,
proposals for the establishment of a Council of Social Advisors to pursue a parallel course of action with respect to social conditions have
been repeatedly voted down. But the principal consequence of the
weakened Employment Act of 1946 was implicit: for almost thirty years
America has accepted as tolerable the fact that three million to eight
million able-bodied persons have gone without work each year. This is

an unemployment rate substantially higher than that found in any other advanced Western nation.

Recent Trends in Employment

During the years from 1946 to the present, great changes have occurred in employment patterns. But some problems are still with us.

MANPOWER PROGRAMS: 1946 - 1973

Given the reluctance of the federal government to take direct action by hiring all of the unemployed and creating work for them on the WPA model, people were pleasantly surprised at the moderate nature of the five business recessions since 1946. It is true that during this period there was in fact a good deal of makework through a kind of hot-and-cold war military WPA. Three million men were in the armed forces, and several million more were civilian employees of the military or worked for defense contractors. In addition the federal and other governments enlarged their payrolls; as late as 1950 only 6 million people worked for the federal, state, and municipal governments, but by 1973 the total had risen to 13.4 million. And other government programs helped to keep millions more out of the labor force, notably through various direct and indirect grant and loan programs to expand higher education. (The number of college students increased from 1.5 million in 1940 to 9 million in 1975.) There were also various retirement aids, including Social Security and other government or government-assisted retirement systems, which made it feasible for millions of older people to retire from the labor market.

During this period of general prosperity, it became possible to consider the benefits of area development programs, on the theory that a limited program could channel some of the economic overspill from thriving urban areas to distressed areas. The Area Development Administration (retitled the Economic Development Administration) was created in 1961 to provide loans, grants, and manpower training for distressed areas. Subsequently, the areas were enlarged, revised, and rearranged, often under political pressure, to include very large regions (such as New England) as well as hardcore slum areas. However, as has been pointed out by critics, national prosperity has made far more important impacts on the populations of economic slums than have the relatively meager benefits obtainable under special distressed-areas legislation.

The facts about manpower programs. While economic development programs created by distressed-area legislation aimed at expanding job opportunities by attracting business and industry to economically lagging areas, a more direct aid to the unemployed throughout the nation was manpower training. There have been a bewildering variety of manpower programs in the quarter century following the Second World War, including special informational activities, job-matching programs, manpower training, job development in ghetto areas, aid for vocational schools, and professional training. Several observations can be made concerning these efforts:

1. As noted above, the chief governmental contribution to employment, including jobs for the poor, has been a healthy economy. The United States, like other Western nations, has done well at the macroeconomic level. Recessions have been fairly brief and contained. Since 1946 national unemployment rates have never approached the 15 to 20 percent depression-era levels, and, as noted, jobless rates among those in professional and managerial occupations and among skilled workers have never exceeded 2 to 4 percent.

2. The most successful programs were those which were based on "creaming," drawing off ambitious, qualified young people.[23] These include the educational provisions of the G.I. Bill, assistance via fellowships, and other measures for training people to become physicians, scientists, teachers, and skilled workers, as well as efforts to identify and train motivated, talented young people, including minority youth.

The educational provisions of the veterans' legislation are particularly worthy of note, because they subsidized and extended on a massive scale the kind of easy access to public higher education formerly restricted to residents of New York City or persons located in states with good-quality, accessible land-grant colleges.[24] In particular, the student cash payments made it possible for a sizable number of young people otherwise destined for working-class jobs to move into middle- and upper-income occupations.[25] The practice has been continued, not only for the millions of veterans of the two subsequent conflicts but also

for disadvantaged youngsters through a variety of federally funded
programs which provide scholarships, fellowships, internships, or training grants. In brief, postwar programs designed to help highly
motivated, talented people have proved consistently effective.

3.   The most intractable manpower problems of the past quarter
century concern the poorly educated and, in some cases, under-
motivated, particularly those adversely affected by racial or ethnic discrimination, or those who live in distressed areas where the supply of
available manpower consistently outruns the supply of jobs. The Manpower Development and Training Act (MDTA), the Office of Economic
Opportunity (OEO) manpower programs, and the Area Redevelopment
Administration-Economic Development Administration (ARA-EDA)
distressed-area training programs have encountered serious difficulties
in attempting to bring this group into the nation's economic
mainstream. The manpower programs of the 1960s sponsored by the
OEO (Job Corps, Neighborhood Youth Corps), by the Department of
Labor (MDTA, Coordinated Area Manpower Planning [CAMPS], by the
EDA, and by many vocational school systems came under heavy fire.
Some were accused of achieving impressive results by selecting out the
most promising and ignoring the most needy applicants. Others were
charged with being far too costly in terms of their meager results. Some
were alleged to be worse than useless, training thousands of young people in obsolete, dead-end occupations. (By this time the ghetto
vocational training programs have trained armies of beauticians and
cosmeticians.) Some programs paid more in training allowances, for
minimal attendance, than was available for graduates, with the result
that trainees preferred to remain "in school" rather than take the low-
paid jobs for which they had succeeded in qualifying. For these and
other reasons, many job programs experienced great difficulties in
motivating and stimulating trainees to complete their training.

4.   Between the executives and professionals and highly skilled,
who are little affected by unemployment, and the unskilled and semiskilled, who suffer extremely high rates of joblessness, lies an inter-
mediate group, mostly skilled factory and service workers, who normally experience moderate unemployment rates.

Provisions for the middle class.   While occasional flurries of alarm
concerning oversupplies of teachers or engineers have generated modest

government efforts aimed at retreading or redirecting professional or executive manpower, by and large it is assumed that barring a major slump or a basic structural alteration in manpower needs, the middle class can take care of itself. This is, of course, an exaggeration; government programs like low-cost public higher education represent significant government aid to persons with middle-class backgrounds. But with or without modestly priced colleges and professional schools, most middle-class people can be counted on to take advantage of whatever opportunities may be available. Real poverty tends to be a threat rather than a reality for those capable of registering with good private employment agencies, of signing up for and *completing* training courses on their own initiative, and of preparing persuasive résumés. Moreover, most middle-income people are part of a helpful employment network of relatives, friends, acquaintances, and former teachers and employers. There is a loose parallel here to rural extension services and agricultural research: the well-educated farmer benefits most, while as a rule the poor farmer lacks the resources to exploit the opportunities.

A comprehensive federal manpower approach should certainly include a professional and technical component, however, because there appears to be a serious prospect that many recent college graduates are going to need a substantial transitional work period before openings develop in the field of their choice or they readjust their employment goals. Aside from this group, it would appear that short of a sizable depression which reaches deep into executive and professional occupations, there are unlikely to be many such white-collar and professional candidates for public employment programs. The exceptions in normal times are younger, entry-level persons who may prefer to sign up for a year or two of special public service employment, such as Peace Corps or Vista. In addition there are special categories of occupations where unemployment (or very low income) is endemic among holders of college degrees. Painters, musicians, actors, and handicraftsmen fall into this category, and some have found work on Comprehensive Employment and Training Act (CETA) programs. It is quite possible, in fact, to conceive of a flourishing permanent arts employment program on the order of the successful, unjustly maligned WPA arts program of the 1930s to permit such persons to pursue their calling at modest wages.

To get back to what may be one of the nation's more serious employment problems, despite its past history of success, there is a good possibility that the United States is joining the troubled nations which have long suffered from chronic and substantial surpluses of unemployed college graduates. While it seems risky to rely on U.S. Department of Labor forecasts, which have been so widely off target in previous periods, this time the arithmetic seems to be lethally clear. By the early 1980s the economy may no longer be capable of providing professional, technical, and managerial employment for the three million college graduates pouring into the labor force each year.[26] This leaves us with four alternatives: (1) persuading many college graduates that life can still be rewarding and enriching through a combination of lower-paid, lower-status jobs and stimulating avocations; (2) reducing the size of college classes to levels consistent with the supply of suitable jobs; (3) relying on market forces to take effect in the expectation that young people will adjust their sights downward without despairing or taking to extremist politics; or (4) adopting a policy to create an adequate supply of useful, suitable positions.

HARD AND SOFT CORE: THE MEANING OF WORK
In the course of past generations there has been a considerable number of predictions concerning the impact of automation (or earlier labor-saving machinery) on employment patterns. Periodically, in the midst of each business recession, Luddite talk revives, and there are dark intimations that it is the busy machines that are keeping jobless people idle. Movies on this subject include Renc Clair's *A Nous La Liberté* (1931), which ends on a happy note as workers fish and frolic while a fully automated assembly line earns their paychecks for them. Most of the depictions of the impact of automation are less happy—the machinery earnings are definitely not allocated to joyful workers. In fact, as Charles Chaplin's *Modern Times* (1935) suggested, not only are there very few beneficiaries of the system, but the remaining work is deadeningly repetititous, viciously exploitative, or both.

Automation and foreign labor.   Some have forecast a trend toward error-free, un-unionized machinery which would replace virtually all labor requiring only minimum intelligence, not only on assembly lines but in the fields, in the mines, and in building, cleaning, and maintenance.[27] In agriculture and mining this is already a reality. The work force employed in these two industries has declined by about 75 percent in the past half-century. But the prophets of doom have been repeatedly confounded by the rise of entire new industries—computers, television, air conditioning, aviation—and an enormous growth in white-collar services and research activities. As a result, the focus of anxiety has turned to another traditional bugaboo, to the threat of industrious, underpaid foreign labor in efficient plants undercutting such labor-intensive industries as textiles, apparel, leather products, electric appliances, and automobiles.

The automation threat has thus far proved imaginary. The foreign competition may or may not materialize as more of a danger in the 70s and the 80s than in earlier generations, when similar warnings were voiced. (The uncertainty does underscore one reason for the tenuous nature of employment forecasts; that is, the unpredictability of future international trade and technological developments, like the totally unexpected four-fold increase in Organization of Petroleum Exporting Countries (OPEC) oil prices in 1973 and 1974.)

Restricted opportunities for disadvantaged.   The total effect of technological and related economic changes over past generations has been to increase rather than to decrease the supply of jobs. However, some have suggested that the decimation of unskilled job openings, which has clearly occurred, has significantly restricted opportunities for the current generation of slum dwellers, blacks, Puerto Ricans, Mexicans, and Appalachian whites. In practice this particular fear seems to be exaggerated. While traditional employment areas like domestic service have shrunk, there are large numbers of low-skilled (and low-paid) jobs in services; for example, in hotels, restaurants, and hospitals. The reason that many job openings in these areas remain unfilled is that their low wage levels compare unfavorably with the alternatives—welfare, street hustling, or simply riding the unemployment compensation cycle.

The observers who see changes in the postwar occupational structure as generating new hurdles for the disadvantaged make the point that credentials barriers serve as an effective method of screening out newcomers and protecting incumbent job holders. Many of these credential requirements are only alleged to be job-related. A classic case is the fact that bank tellers in Toronto must possess a high school degree, while only an elementary school diploma is required in Montreal; differences in performance between the tellers at the bank branches in the two cities are reported to be imperceptible.[28]

One of the responses to the credentials barrier is the "new careers" concept. This combines the creation of a new class of subprofessionals, like teachers' aides, along with the creation of a continuous career ladder reaching from the lowest entry-level job to the top of the

executive-professional hierarchy.[29] This would require an extensive
system of fully accredited night courses and released-time day courses
to enable workers to advance, step by step, to the limit of their talent,
energy, and opportunities. In many ways this career ladder is analogous
to the navy system of promotion via carefully structured job ratings
from apprentice seaman through the noncommissioned ranks. The
difference lies in the expansion of the navy occupational ladder to include the civilian equivalent of commissioned officers.

To a degree, the new careers idea has been implemented through the
establishment of a new subprofessional group of teachers' aides, nurses'
aides, and security guards. So far as can be ascertained, however, little
progress has been made in integrating the professional job hierarchy
into one big bottom-to-top system. Some credentials barriers have been
rendered more porous, it is true, but a much more sizable number of
executive-level jobs have been opened up for the disadvantaged by
creating new programs, particularly the poverty agencies and model
cities. Other executive-level jobs have evolved from traditional political
pressures, which generate job rewards for leaders of politically active
minorities.

The chief difficulty with past progress is that, substantial as it has
been, it still leaves millions outside the structure. It should be remembered that the labor force is a stream, not a static pool. There is a new
group of labor force entrants every year, and the jobs opened up by attrition are not simply conferred on newcomers on a one-for-one basis.
Moreover, cutbacks in government programs have been particularly
hard on minorities which have yet to secure a firm footing in the private
sector.

Happy in your work?   The problem of absorbing newcomers is
rendered more complicated by new kinds of perceptions of the world of
work. In earlier generations the prevailing mood was gratitude for any
type of regular, remunerative labor. Upward mobility might or might
not be available to one's children or grandchildren. One's life expectations included a broad plateau of work alternating with layoffs on the
farm, in the mine, factory, or office. One counted oneself lucky not to be
among the injured, or one of those laid off in slack season, or one dismissed in favor of a younger competitor when age began to show. Part
of the widespread insecurity among middle-aged employees in westernized nations, the emphasis on youth, on dyeing one's hair and fighting
flab, is the long-term fear that the "old timer" will be labelled surplus,
fobbed off with a gold watch, and replaced with a younger man.

Dissatisfaction with employment conditions is endemic; probably only a fraction of the labor force at any time in history found work intrinsically rewarding. For most it was—is—necessary drudgery. Until recently, unpleasant work was accepted and even welcomed as the unfortunate prerequisite for eating regularly. Craftsmanship, opportunity for personal growth, or creativity and personal expression in one's job was a luxury.

HUMANIZING WORK

Even before the English Enclosure Acts which gobbled up the commons and reduced farmers to an underclass of rural or town laborers, there have been denunciations of the dehumanizing impact of capitalism. One consistent thread has been an idealization of a last golden age, in which there existed a sturdy, happy yeomanry, the independent craftsman, the small-business and cottage manufacturer.[30] Into this Eden there came the ruthless giants, men with hearts like Ebenezer Scrooge but with a powerful thrust of economics and technology on their side. Some of the responses to this inhuman system have been farm subsidizers, mini-cooperatives, or social communes. A few varieties survive: Mormons, Amish, Kibbutzim, Doukhobors (a sect which migrated from Russian to Canada in the 1890s). The majority either disappeared into capitalism like the Oneida community, side-stepped into anarchism or syndicalism, or took the USSR route and tried to out-rationalize and out-organize Western-style private enterprise.

Worker alienation.   It seems that West and East there is alienation, a loss of interest in job quality, a decline in dedication to many occupations.[31] Machinery is often shoddy, utilities erratic, appliance and home repair expensive and often faulty. Foreign products which enjoy a better reputation for quality craftsmanship and reliability have made heavy inroads into the American market.

Worker lethargy and lack of interest have been combatted in different ways in a number of Western nations. A few Swedish firms have moved on automobile assembly lines, reshaping job tasks from minute, repetitive labor to team-oriented major operations which permit workers to see the product beginning to take form.[32] Germany is attempting to bridge the decision-making gap between labor and management by requiring that labor unions be represented on company boards of directors. Attempts to revamp assembly-line operations and bring workers into management have been adopted, with varying results, by a few companies in the United States. The negative results on worker morale of a highly automated assembly line were visible in the recurrent unrest during the late 1960s and early 1970s at the Lordstown, Ohio, General Motors plant designed to produce the company's Vega.[33]

At the executive level "profit centers," "management by results," and other techniques have been adopted to recapture a sense of purpose among disaffected middle and junior managers.[34]

The extent to which things have changed in postindustrial society is evident in a wide variety of outcroppings, indicating a major heaving in the underlying bedrock. These are the following:

1.   A modest-sized counter-culture, a few of whose adherents have or are attempting to opt out of the job system through odd jobs, handicrafts, or panhandling. An even larger portion are lodged somewhere in the system but are articulate in their dissatisfaction with their jobs and prospects.[35]

2.   An even larger number of slum youths, unlike their elders, refuse to accept the menial, low-paid jobs available to them. They opt instead for street hustling, chronic unemployment, or welfare, or (less frequently) for full-time radical politics.

3.   A growing sense of "blue-collar blues" is evidenced in sloppy workmanship, reduced productivity, high rates of absenteeism, and growing addiction to drugs, liquor, and gambling. This group of workers also suffers from low morale, increasing sense of alienation, and hostility toward authority and other racial and ethnic groups.[36] (Alternatively there is a tendency to focus one's real attention on avocations, fraternal groups, or sports and to regard the workday as a necessary evil.)

4.   A parallel disenchantment among white-collar office workers is manifested by many of the same signs. Turnover is high among many lower-echelon jobs. There is a pervasive malaise, as there is among the blue-collar workers, a sense that the work lacks direction or creative product. The feeling of depression apparently extends to the junior executive and middle-management levels.

But it would not be accurate to suggest that this is purely an American phenomenon. Most of the advanced urban nations are running into similar problems. Some suggest that the answer can be found in a familiar villain—too much education, too many unrealistic expectations, a "shortage of morons" to twist the knobs, push the brooms, and pick up the garbage. Others suggest that the culprit is too much prosperity for too many years. Instead of gratitude for any honest job that sustains the family, there is spoiled finickiness, a chronic immaturity preventing serious work discipline.

5.   Ordinarily the management executive would have little sympathy for the office workers. But there is a surprising amount of fellow feeling for the sufferers perched on the lower ranks of the job pyramid, because the view from halfway up is almost as dismal. Many an executive has asked himself (much too late) if a lifetime dedicated to sales or office management is really what life is all about. He hears the siren call of the wild, envies society's dropouts—the resort area swinger-bum, the independent handicraftsman, the corporation lawyer turned full-time *pro bono.* He even empathizes with son and daughter who postpone marriage, sample yoga or encounter groups, and achieve happiness with casual work or by living in near poverty from the fruits of meaningful labor.

The upshot of the pervasive disquietude seems to be far from the traditional, transitory career menopause. Instead it appears to be part of the new generational mood—the concern about quality of life, ecology, social problems, and, perhaps most of all, consumerism. Ralph Nader and a host of like-minded colleagues have displayed to many executives the proof that they have devoted their working lives to moving shoddy, overpriced, sometimes even dangerous merchandise. While this is not precisely a new or even shocking discovery, as compared with the wilder and woolier years of the robber barons, the fact is that it seems to rankle. Brutal responses asserting that business critics are sophomoric softheads, Reds, or idealistic pansies are less in evidence. Morale has slipped. Wall Street firms have to pay more for promising young lawyers; polls show a fall in public valuation of business.

Possible solutions to alienation.   The executive alienation problem requires much the same approach as the blue- and white-collar gloom. What seems to be needed at every level below the summit is a change in the conditions of work—more decentralized decision making, more dignity, genuine consultation concerning day-to-day operations. All things considered, this is difficult but not impossible. To be sure, there is likely to be much squabbling over management prerogatives and complaints from each level of the hierarchy that decision-making power should stop there, much as cities want autonomy from the states but fight grants of authority to the neighborhoods.

A healthy federal push in this direction should meet with little resistance in many firms. Morale, workmanship, and interest in work are the difference between rejects and profits. In this connection, it will be interesting to see what role the labor unions play in this process. They have a choice between maintaining the critical-outsider, adversary posture or reaching for Yugoslav/German-style worker-management sharing of power and responsibility—and possible cooption by the establishment. In any event, the federal effort can include fact finding through hearings and research and incentives or prerequisites for contracts similar to affirmative action hiring, except in this case it would involve worker participation. But management will have to deal with its executives itself. Dispelling the middle-management blues is a problem for management, not government.

There are a number of substantive actions which can be taken to improve working conditions over and above achievement of full employment. These include the following:

1. Physical improvements in safety, lower noise levels, better lighting, and other environmental upgrading. America's occupational hazards are a national disgrace.

2. Automating dirty, unpleasant jobs. This can be achieved by introducing such innovations as fork lift trucks, continuous mining machinery, and agricultural harvesting equipment.

3. Increasing pay for unpleasant occupations. Sanitation workers in New York are now paid as much or more in their first few years as assistant professors in colleges. Nursery school teachers and domestic cleaning services are paid for doing what mothers do for no monetary wages.

4. Combining higher pay, more status, and special equipment for drudgery jobs. For example, household cleaning services which have to some extent replaced domestic servants provide tolerable wages, the uniformed camaraderie of work crews, and heavy-duty equipment.

5.   Providing psychological stroking. The socialist countries have done this systematically through awards to heroes of labor and productive mother heroines with extraordinarily large families. In the United States there is a precedent in the use of merit badges, certificates, and illusionary retitling (for example, banks have very large numbers of vice presidents who do not enjoy the powers of V.P.'s in industrial corporations).

6.   Doing without: restructuring for no growth? The best example is domestic servants. They were once a commonplace necessity for the modestly affluent, but now only the rich have the income and space necessary for maids, butlers, gardeners, and chauffeurs. If the United States, and indeed the world, is to enter an age of what E. F. Schumacher, the economic prophet of "small is beautiful," has termed "Buddhist economics,"[37] an era of conservation, smaller-scale enterprise, and diminished per capita use of resources, there will be profound implications for every aspect of the economy, including manpower needs. In practical terms one can visualize simpler "human-scale" technology, more self-help, gardening, home repairs, less emphasis on mass-scale advanced training and occupational specialization, and a new de-emphasis on traditional notions of occupational status.

Toward A Comprehensive Program

In order to achieve the goal of full employment in the United States, there is a need for a government policy that takes into consideration the objections against such a program.

A FULL-EMPLOYMENT POLICY PROPOSAL
It is proposed that the federal government adopt a full-employment policy and that the slack in jobs at all levels be taken up through federally funded contracts with private employers[38] It is recognized that substantial retraining may be involved to avoid assigning most of this work corps as casual labor to clean-up projects. The model of National Guard, second-skill training might well be explored for per-

sons in unemployment-prone occupations. This implies that there is an urgent need for government to (1) identify needed projects and services and (2) to convert these needs into numbers—skills, equipment, and funding. There are precedents for this approach in the 1930s. In periods of prosperity governments can prepare plans for labor-intensive projects and be ready for a substantial expansion in the relatively small-scale projects which are conducted even in good times to absorb the energies of the 4 or 5 percent unemployed. Hard times (that is, high unemployment) can then be viewed as periods of opportunities rather than wastage.

What seems to be needed is careful preplanning to train recession-prone labor in good times to work primarily on labor-intensive, expandable, shelf-ready projects and programs prepared by state, local, and federal governments. Moreover, there is no reason why a substantial proportion of such jobs cannot be designed for part-time workers. And there should always be ample room for needed capital-intensive construction projects. The recommended avenue for generating compensatory employment is *not* an expansion of government employment but instead *contractual, negotiable, cancellable* project contracts with private contractors. As has been suggested by Sar A. Levitan, a well-known manpower expert, a wise legislative strategy might combine outlays for quick-responding public services with appropriations for the kind of public works that formed part of the WPA's beneficial legacy.[39] It would be a disaster if the reflex response to unemployment were a simple expansion of the civil service. Chapter 8, on the ills of urban government, suggests some of the reasons why adding to the number and proportion of government employees represents a danger to effective governmental services, to the governmental fiscal resources, and to the nation's productive disciplines.

From a moral point of view the critical manpower problem is the poor and the young. For this reason, a broad effort aimed at providing direct or contracted-for employment for all of the nation's employables necessarily involves developing useful work for persons with limited skills and a spotty work record. Few will disagree with the fact that there are enormous numbers of needed public service projects and human service programs, most of which can be contracted out. Suggestions for simple, useful activities include environmental cleanup projects, particularly in slums and rural areas; twice-a-day mail delivery, redoing railbeds, service as auxiliary neighborhood police, services for aged persons, and assistance in recycling waste products.

On the whole, for valid political reasons it would seem wiser to place initial emphasis on programs which would produce physical, tangible results (such as new building, better mail delivery, environmental cleanup), leaving softer, more vulnerable programs like family counseling or big brothering of slum children for a second stage when the approach is firmly lodged in the political system.

The presence of three, four, or five million (or in 1976, eight million) jobless people is an affront to common sense as well as human dignity. Expenditures for unemployment compensation, public welfare, and other programs are required and regularly allocated to these un-employed. Therefore, aside from the public benefit to be yielded by productive effort, the costs of financing such an employment program would be incremental—not minimal by any means, but hardly horrendous. Furthermore, such a program would replace idleness with productive labor, with enormous collateral benefits for urban and environmental programs, crime prevention, social stability, and racial-ethnic peace. The proportion of non-starters, chronic drunks, the completely disabled, thieves, and persistent malingerers might approximate a hard core of anywhere from 1 to 3 percent of the labor force, basing our estimate on wartime experience.

COMPLICATIONS AND OBJECTIONS

Certainly it is true that there are no end of complications in establishing such a program. As noted, one problem is the "mollusk danger," identified in the 1930s by President Roosevelt when he phased out the CWA. That is, given an alternative between unpleasant, uncertain, low-status and often useless labor and a relatively congenial, useful public-service job, low-skilled persons might well "cross over," preferring to cling like mollusks to the project payroll. This is not necessarily bad. Private employers might well be induced to improve working conditions if such an alternative were indeed available. Nevertheless there is no denying the fact that many jobs cannot be upgraded or otherwise improved. There will be a continuing need for people to carry bedpans in nursing homes, to wash dishes, bus tables, do laundry. Certainly a good manpower program should include efforts to automate this type of work, to reduce the hours, improve working conditions, and raise the pay scales. But there is and will remain a broad gray area between the need for staffing bottom-of-the-ladder jobs and the public service alternatives which are almost certain to be more attractive.

In addition to these dangers, there are the ancient complaints from the unions and private contractors concerning unfair competition and unavoidable charges from conservatives that such an open-ended program could drain the treasury in a time of widespread unemployment. As noted, a really successful, productive program dedicated to genuinely important work at reasonable wages could permanently lure workers away from the deadening, time-wasting jobs that so many people fall into. There is the delicate task of setting wages high enough to provide a modest living, but at the same time not forcing the overall wage level up from below to price many jobs out of the market. A situation could occur such that the United States might follow the Western European model, importing desperate foreign workers to take on the menial work that domestic labor refuses to perform, taking on vital tasks at low wages and without normal job protection or promotional prospects.

There are three principal arguments against a federal full employment program: (1) cost, (2) inflation, and (3) the structure of the labor market.

Under the heading of *cost* it might be noted that the full-employment program proposed in the 1975 - 76 Humphrey-Hawkins legislation was cut back for fiscal reasons to focus on family men and to exclude teenagers. There seems to be no valid reason for this move. If it is considered that in 1975, $13 billion was expended for unemployment compensation, $128 billion for welfare transfer payments, and billions more for food stamps and various private supplementary unemployment benefit programs, it seems realistic to suggest that full employment could very largely be financed by reallocating existing expenditures rather than by pumping in many billions in new money. Certainly the $9 billion proposed in the jobs and income program suggested to the congressional Joint Economic Committee would seem to be a generous upper limit.[40] The Joint Economic Committee program calls for maximum 1975 wages of $4,600 per year for full-time, year-round work. This might provide insufficient flexibility. On the whole, a first approach linked to *unemployment compensation levels* might be one way of attacking the wage-cost problem.

Under the heading of *inflationary impact* it seems apparent that a shift of existing resources, rather than a massive input of new resources, is not calculated to fuel inflationary fires.

A more difficult problem comes under the heading of *the potential impact on wage structures*. The difficulty can be summed up in two questions: First, is it not probable that many low-paid workers might prefer low-wage but productive government jobs as compared to private menial drudgery? And second, would not the establishment of a new floor for wages above the minimum level tend to create inflationary pressure on the entire wage structure? Neither question can be answered with precision at this time. Both will remain unanswered until we begin to have some experience with full-employment programs. It is clear, however, that wage levels are not graven in stone. They can and should be adjusted for age, region, training, and emerging circumstances such as inflation.

Conclusion

There are grave enough problems to worry a generation or so of legislators and economists. But consider the alternatives: on the one hand, many millions of wasted man-years, and on the other hand, work crying out to be done. Full employment is a challenging program which bears with it great complications but also promises great results, not the least of which is greater social and mental stability. Politics, morality, and common sense, it may be submitted, are on the side of boldness, of ending the nightmare of unemployment.

What is far more troublesome is fitting a manpower program within a broader context of national economic policy and national goals. It is not hard to get a superficial response to demands for redirection—witness all the slick advertising campaigns of businesses claiming first rank in the battle for the environment, for promoting racial brotherhood, for ensuring safer products for children. But transforming this often superficial commitment to one which has some real meaning involves nothing short of a fundamental reorientation of American society. And another real problem is to reconcile business survival in the face of domestic and foreign competition, including adequate attention to generating profit levels sufficient to finance an increased emphasis on the quality of life. Fortunately much of the Western world is in the same boat; we are floundering together and there is no early prospect that Schumacher's small-is-beautiful approach is high on the political agenda, East or West.

Part of the difficulty in moving in a new direction is that the task is far broader than achieving satisfaction; being happy in one's work is in itself no guarantee of public benefit. Polls may show that doctors, college professors, and judges are leaders in job satisfaction, but fortunately there are many thoroughly satisfied persons in more lowly and less well-paid, useful jobs.[41] There are, however, a wide variety of joyful people engaged in overly antisocial activities. It is in fact not hard to conceive of a society composed of unstressful, pleasant little work units which are exploitative, decadent, or even vicious. In short, action to ensure that people are enjoying their work is not enough. As E. F. Schumacher suggests, an examination of the nation's basic activity raises fundamental questions about ends, means, directions, and goals. What kinds of machines and products are being manufactured and what are they used for? What is the end product of performing the services, filling out the forms, drawing up the contracts, finishing the training program?

A generation or two ago it might have been assumed that a kindly, invisible hand was leading the way to the greatest good for the greatest number. But decades of bloody wars, depression, and a deteriorating environment have raised serious questions regarding things to come. Clearly this examination of national goals goes well beyond work, land use, and the environment. The nature and quality of urban settlements, population, crime, education, racial and ethnic factors, and the organization and functioning of government are all part and parcel of the problem.

The foregoing discussion suggests that employment—more precisely, working conditions—is as much of a problem in mid-1970s America as unemployment. A program designed to deal with the manpower problems which cause widespread anxiety might then logically deal with job enrichment as well as joblessness, with the broader purposes of work as well as the satisfaction of basic needs for food and shelter.

Summary

The problem of chronically high unemployment in the United States is now a significant political issue, with the recession of the mid-1970s and the entrance of a large proportion of women into the labor force. A coalition supporting full employment is further made possible by the fact that fear of unemployment, if not the actual experience, is deep and widespread.

During the Great Depression, with the advent of the New Deal, government policy toward the unemployed shifted markedly, and during World War II it became obvious that full employment was possible, with government projects taking up the slack. However, since World War II the United States has tolerated an unemployment rate higher than that of any other industrialized nation. Few of the many employment programs of the 1960s were more than moderately successful, and it is clear that no action to ameliorate social problems is as important in achieving full employment as a healthy economy.

A serious government policy to achieve full employment could be instituted without great additional expenditure, inflation, or taking business or labor away from private industry. Such a policy should work through cancelable project contracts with private contractors, rather than risking permanent expansion of the civil service. Public service projects and human service programs would be well suited to such contracting.

Recommendations

- Improve physical working conditions in safety, noise levels, lighting, etc.

- Automate, eliminate, or provide greater rewards for unpleasant jobs.

- Establish a national full-employment policy, working through contracts with private employers.

- Identify needed projects and services.

- During economic prosperity, train recession-prone labor to work on prepared labor-intensive projects.

- In order to employ the poor and the young, develop useful projects for workers with limited skills.

Notes

1. Margaret S. Gordon, *Retraining and Labor Market Adjustment in Western Europe* (Washington, D.C.: Government Printing Office, 1965), pp. 9 - 10.

2. U.S. Department of Labor, *Manpower Report of the President* (Washington, D.C.: Government Printing Office, 1973), pp. 16 - 21, 157 - 158, 211 - 212.

3. Fred I. Greenstein, *The American Party System and the American People* (Englewood Cliffs, N.J.: Prentice Hall, 1970), p. 19.

4. Joe A. Miller and Louis A. Ferman, *Welfare Careers and Low Wage Employment* (Ann Arbor, Mich.: Institute of Labor and Industrial Relations, 1972).

5. U.S. Department of Labor, *Manpower Report of the President*, p. 17.

6. See Granville Hicks et al, eds., *Proletarian Literature in the United States* (New York: International Publishers, 1936). Published in the midst of the depression, the anthology only includes work produced during the previous five years. In fact, John Freeman's introduction stresses the importance of the economic collapse in driving many of the writers included into the working-class camp. However, Freeman further notes the roots of this consciousness in the output of such members of the older generation as Upton Sinclair and Jack London. Hans Fallada's German novel of 1930 expressed the disillusion with the laissez-faire West in its title: *Little Man, What Now?* Fallada's hero went Left, Germany went Right. But all over the world, those in want or those fearful of the future foresook democratic capitalism for something stronger.

7. Arthur M. Schlesinger, Jr., *The Crisis of the Old Order* (Boston: Houghton Mifflin, 1957).

8. Robert S. and Helen Merrell Lynd, *Middletown in Transition* (New York: Harcourt Brace Jovanovich 1937), p. 127.

9. Edgar Eugene Robinson, *The Presidential Vote, 1896 - 1932* (New York: Octagon Books, 1970), pp. 27 - 34. While the third-party vote in general was miniscule in 1932, the Socialists increased their vote substantially over 1928.

10. Henry Miller, *The Cosmological Eye* (Norfolk, Conn.: New Directions, 1939), pp. 8 - 46.

11. Lynd and Lynd, *Middletown in Transition*, pp. 134 - 136.

12. William L. Riordan, *Plunkitt of Tammany Hall* (New York: E. P. Dutton, 1963).

13. James MacGregor Burns, *Roosevelt: The Lion and the Fox* (New York: Harcourt Brace Jovanovich, 1956), p. 324.

14. William E. Leuchtenberg, *Franklin D. Roosevelt and the New Deal: 1932 - 1940* (New York: Harper and Row, 1963), p. 319, pp. 346 - 347.

15. Ibid., p. 122.

16. Ibid., pp. 120 - 130.

17. Lynd and Lynd, *Middletown in Transition,* pp. 120 - 122. The Lynds found that while Middletown's established citizens scorned federal aid for relief, funds for public works were more acceptable. As one newspaper editorial put it: "It is unlikely that there will ever again be an opportunity for the county to build new bridges here at a little more than half their cost to local taxpayers."

18. See Frances Fox Piven and Richard A. Cloward, *Regulating the Poor: The Functions of Public Welfare* (New York: Vintage Books, 1972). See especially pp. 132 - 135 for an explanation of the impact of AFDC payments in the South.

19. Arthur M. Schlesinger, Jr., *The Coming of the New Deal* (Boston: Houghton Mifflin, 1958), pp. 471 - 488.

20. Cabell Phillips, *The Truman Presidency* (New York: MacMillan Company, 1966), pp. 176 - 185.

21. Alonzo L. Hanby, *Beyond the New Deal: Harry S. Truman and American Liberalism* (New York: Columbia University Press, 1973), p. 60.

22. For an interesting discussion of presidential interaction with the CEA see "LBJ's Brand Goes on the Economy," *Business Week,* 25 January 1964, pp. 71 - 81.

23. Sar A. Levitan and Garth Mangum, *Federal Training and Work Programs in the Sixties* (Ann Arbor, Mich.: Institute of Labor and Industrial Relations, 1969), pp. 163 - 232.

24. For a summary of the accomplishments of veterans' legislation after twenty-five years see "A Quarter Century of the GI Bill," *School and Society* 98, no. 2325 (April 1970), pp. 226 - 228.

25. U.S. Department of Labor, *Manpower Report of the President,* p. 150.

26. "The Job Gap for College Graduates in the 70's," *Business Week,* 23 September 1972, pp. 48 - 58.

27. Glenn F. Seaborg, "The Cybernetic Age: An Optimist's View," *Saturday Review,* 15 July 1967, pp. 21 - 23.

28. For a discussion of Canada's French Canadian question, see W. L. Morton, *The Canadian Identity* (Madison, Wis.: University of Wisconsin Press, 1972), pp. 115 - 150.

29. Arthur Pearl and Frank Riessman, *New Careers for the Poor: The Non-Professional in Public Service* (New York: Free Press, 1965).

30. Even Marx and Engels flirt with this sentiment on occasion. See Karl Marx and Frederick Engels, *The German Ideology* (New York: International Publishers, 1973), p. 71.

31. "What Foreign Firms Are Doing to Fight Blue Collar Blues," *U.S. News and World Report,* 23 July 1973, p. 78.

32. "The Blue Collar Blues," *Newsweek,* 17 May 1971, p. 86.

33.   Ibid.

34.   M. Scott Myers, "Conditions for Manager Motivation," *Harvard Business Review* 44, no. 1 (January/February 1966), pp. 58 - 71.

35.   "The Job Blahs: Who Wants to Work?" *Newsweek*, 26 March 1973, pp. 79 - 84. Probably most expressive of their dissatisfaction are those individuals who sabotage the work in their own plant. In the Kankakee, Illinois Gaines Dog Food factory an entire day's output of dog food was ruined by an unknown employee's dropping green dye into its vat.

36.   For example, see William J. Roche and Neil L. Mackinnon, "Motivating People With Meaningful Work," *Harvard Business Review* 48, no. 3 (May/June 1970), pp. 97 - 110.

37.   See E. F. Schumacher, *Small Is Beautiful* (New York: Harper and Row, 1973).

38.   See Thomas Vietorisz, Robert Mier, and Bennett Harrison, "Full Employment at Living Wages" (pp. 94 - 107); James O'Toole, "Planning for Total Employment" (pp. 72 - 84); and Robert Lekachman, "Managing Inflation in a Full Employment Society" (pp. 85 - 93); in the *Annals of the American Academy of Political and Social Science* 418, *Planning for Full Employment* (March 1975); and Alan Gartner, Russell A. Nixon, and Frank Riessman, eds., *Public Service Employment* (New York: Praeger Publishers, 1973).

39.   Sar A. Levitan, "Does Public Job Creation Offer Any Hope?" *The Conference Board Record* 12, no. 8 (August 1975).

40.   See Robert I. Lerman, "Join: A Jobs and Income Program for American Families," *Studies in Public Welfare, Paper no. 19, Public Employment and Wage Subsidies*, Joint Economic Committee, Congress of the United States (Washington: Government Printing Office, 1974.). Another estimate is less precise but in the same range, $8 billion to $12 billion per year. "Goal of Democrats, More Jobs," *The New York Times*, 22 May 1976, pp. 1, 37.

41.   *Work in America*, Report of a Special Task Force to the Secretary of Health, Education and Welfare (Cambridge, Mass.: The MIT Press, 1973), p. 15. Of a cross section of white-collar workers, 43 percent would voluntarily choose the same work they were doing if they could start again, while only 24 percent of a cross section of blue-collar workers would choose the same kind of work if given another chance.

5

NAVIGATING THE
RACE AND ETHNIC
MINEFIELD

The issues that sprawl across the nation's urban panorama involve many topics, but perhaps none is so difficult nor arouses such atavistic impulses as racial and, to a lesser degree, interethnic relations. Clearly the central issue concerns the present and future status of the nation's black population.

Historical Background

It was not that the blacks were the first or only group singled out for despicable treatment. A powerful strain of racism has existed almost from the beginning of the nation's settlement.

INDIANS
Although only in a few cases did colonial Americans approach the Tasmanian record of total extermination of an aboriginal population, the nation's history contains long and bloody chapters of Indian massacres, broken treaties, starvation, concentration camps, and lynchings. Such acts were founded on two long-held beliefs: (1) the only good *wild* Indian was a dead Indian; as untamable hostiles, Indians were a species of dangerous vermin, interfering with productive, peaceable pursuits; and (2) if, and only if, he could be induced to "walk the white man's way," the Indian could assure himself a modest, safe livelihood.

After innumerable expropriations, wars and relocations, after centuries of ravages by disease and extraordinarily high rates of infant mortality, alcoholism, and suicide, the Indian population was reduced from several million—estimates go as high as 15 million—to about 800,000. It is only because Indians are relatively few in number, and because roughly half live on remote reservations, that Indian-white relations today constitute a modest-sized problem. While flare-ups like the 1973 Wounded Knee incident occasionally occur, and frictions are endemic in a few states with sizable Indian populations, like South Dakota and New Mexico, the Indians are low on the nation's list of priorities. Although the facts of Indians' condition are horrifying—unemployment, tuberculosis and infant mortality rates several times the level of the white population, and life expectancy many years shorter than both blacks and whites—Indians are too few and too far removed from urban centers to take center stage. Indian power slogans and "Custer Deserved It" bumper stickers have received considerable publicity, but Indians lack the numbers and the urban location for prime, sustained attention. That priority is reserved for blacks.

BLACKS

The importation of blacks into the Western Hemisphere was a forcible corralling and shipment of human livestock to provide a docile, hardworking labor force suitable for hot climates. When Indian tribes proved unsuitable for slavery by reason of temperament, susceptibility to disease, or unrelenting rebellion, blacks were imported by the millions, bred and sold as cattle, and held in slavery or subjection by legal and extralegal means. Despite the general acceptance of this practice, guilt over sexual exploitation and cruelties mainly perpetrated by white males, stirrings of conscience by Christian doctrine about the souls of the slaves, and agitation by abolitionists all intensified widespread feelings of guilt and fear among many whites.

These apprehensions were increased by the constant danger of slave insurrections. The culmination of these fears was the bloody and successful insurrection in Haiti led by Toussaint L'Ouverture at the turn of the nineteenth century which haunted slave owners for the next two generations. Almost from the beginning of slavery, minor incidents were distorted into major uprisings, while hangings and whippings, brandings and sales of the rebellious became a regular feature of race relations. Even after the formal abolition of slavery during the Civil War, a large proportion of the black population continued to be held in servility enforced by physical terror and economic sanctions.

OTHER MINORITIES

In comparison to the treatment meted out to blacks and Indians, America's other minorities have been more exploited than oppressed. The Puerto Ricans, Mexicans, and Orientals did not wear the color badge of slavery. However, Latin Americans were despised as feckless, Orientals were feared, and mistreatment was commonly meted out to both groups. Many were held in the grip of near peonage, but the degree of viciousness of their treatment was far less pronounced than was the case with blacks or Indians. Indeed, by 1970 the nation's half a million Orientals had drawn abreast or had surpassed white averages for per capita income and share of prestige occupations.[1]

"You're qualified. What a pity! We're trying to fill our quota for unqualified personnel."

Source: © 1976 by Mary Guarke, *National Review,* 150 East 35th Street,
New York 10016.

Discussions of minority problems in the United States understandably focus most particularly on the black-white confrontation. On the
part of some blacks there tends to be a blurring of statistical perspective, in which America is seen as a kind of Rhodesia or South Africa,
nations in which the privileged white minority owes much of its
affluence to the colonialist-type exploitation of black masses. In point of
fact, the situation is much more complex, not only because blacks and
other physically distinctive minorities are just that—minorities—but
because a very sizable proportion of the white population also perceives
itself as seriously disadvantaged. Far from considering themselves as

enjoying the fruits of exploitation, many persons of Slavic, Italian, and Irish extraction (as well as southern and Appalachian whites) view themselves as aggrieved victims of an unfair system, which reserves its best rewards for the inner circles of WASPs and other privileged folk at the top and confers unearned privileges on blacks and other minorities.

Re-examination of Minority Relations

Since the cutting edge of the minority problem concerns the status of blacks and, to a lesser extent, Latin Americans, it is useful to begin with a view of the scope of the problem.

STATUS OF BLACKS AND LATIN AMERICANS
Blacks constitute about 12 percent of the nation's population, but they are in the majority in a number of central cities and a few small rural counties. Unlike the French-Canadians, however, they do not have a sizable, contiguous geographic base for an effective secessionist movement. (The ghetto equivalent of *"Maître chez nous!"* ["Masters in our own house!"] is a hollow slogan when it means inheriting bankrupt slums or decayed central cities, as compared to the Quebec nationalism, which can aspire to vast mineral wealth and other resources.)

In 1970 Latin Americans totaled about 10 million, compared to 22 million blacks. Both groups were undercounted in the census, but because of a vast illegal immigration from Latin America, the black/Latin ratio is probably far less out of balance than it appears in census statistics. If continuing heavy illegal immigration since 1970 is taken into account, it is entirely possible that the real 1976 ratio is on the order of twenty-four to twenty. This estimate is based on a Justice Department figure, which includes 8 million "illegal" Latin American aliens added to 11 million citizens and registered aliens of Latin American origin.[2]

The traditional system.   Black/white relations in America were never idyllic, but the stereotype of the ruthless, arrogant Honky/Whitey/Man, Simon Legree whipping the field hands, was always an oversimplification. The most ruthless confrontations have always been between insecure, similarly exploited American poor whites and southern blacks. Moreover, this traditional pattern of the bitter and violence-ridden South is paralleled in northern city working-class areas. The cutting edge of racial confrontation in the northern urban areas is between the white ethnics near the bottom of the social and economic hierarchy and the blacks at the bottom or moving up. In comparison, until recently, the white middle and upper classes have almost been bystanders in the interminority struggles, largely because they did not perceive the upward mobility of black and Latin minorities as a direct threat to *their* job security and *their* neighborhoods.

The blacks' racial confrontation in urban areas differs in several major respects from the traditional black/white relationship depicted in history books published up to the early 1960s. In these historical works blacks were portrayed as unfortunate victims of history, as a burden, a litmus test of white humanitarianism, but rarely as autonomous self-conscious entities mastering history and shaping their own destinies. To the extent that it may have been mentioned at all, black nationalism was dismissed as atavistic, back-to-Africa Garveyism, hopelessly romantic and impractical.[3] Blacks were a minor problem, not a threat. There was indeed some sense of danger in the South, where racial fear and guilt were bred in the bones. The fearsome black rapist lusting after blond virgins, the vindictive black arsonist or cattle-maimer, and the politically outlawed, uppity Negro who had so far forgotten his rightful heritage as to embrace the Yankee labor unions or the communist conspiracy were rarities in fact, but nevertheless a symbolic menace. But between 1865 and 1965 blacks were usually viewed as Sambo the passive victim, happy-go-lucky, watermelon-eating, banjo-playing, slightly retarded. They were the natural clownish inheritors of poorly paid, dirty jobs and ramshackle slums, and purveyors of entertainment for themselves and an appreciative white majority.

Civil rights and urbanization.   The civil rights revolution of the mid-1960s profoundly changed this traditional race/class system. Because these changes occurred during a period of continuing demographic transformation, one major consequence was to transfer much of the friction and suffering of oppressed blacks from the rural South to urban areas, North and South. By the early 1970s, the black sharecropper had virtually disappeared, replaced by mechanical cotton pickers and other agricultural machinery, thus finally and permanently severing the ancient plantation relationship which for centuries had bound the black to southern soil.

In the cities, blacks increasingly assumed the lowly economic role, housing, and burden of prejudices born by predecessor ethnics and rural whites. At first only a few prospered, but by the mid-1970s a substantial number—in 1974 22 percent of "black and other" families (of whom 95 percent are black) had incomes in excess of $15,000—were moving into the middle class. The majority, however, remained poor. In 1974 over 40 percent of "Black and other" families had incomes of less than $7,000, as compared to only 20 percent of white families.

With respect to upwardly mobile blacks there is some disagreement concerning the continuity and rigor of color prejudice. Does a millionaire black, in one black comedian's phrase, find himself treated as a "nigger"? or is he, along with black professionals, courted and coddled as a potential lavish consumer in much the same manner as his white counterpart? The argument revolves around the permanence of racial prejudice as a *caste system* which helps to relegate all or most blacks to the bottom of the social ladder, as opposed to a *class system* which accords status and acceptability to anyone with "green power,"—money and professional or business status.

In the 1970s most blacks and Latins are at or near the lower rungs of the occupational ladder and live in bad housing in slum neighborhoods. Blacks, Mexican Americans and Puerto Ricans are heavily concentrated in jobs in the lower echelon of the Civil Service, in hotels and services and marginal manufacturing industries. Many are in low-paid, dead-end occupations, the urban equivalent of agricultural stoop labor. This kind of labor is practically reserved for low-status groups. In the South, dirty, enervating work on road gangs, sanitation services, or in the less attractive areas of manufacturing plants was termed "no job for a white man." In colonial economies, such as South Africa or Rhodesia, hard labor is reserved for the indigenous, exploited population as a matter of course. But this pattern is by no means a matter of race alone. Just as heavy, dirty work was performed in the United States by succeeding waves of white immigrant groups (and Orientals), street cleaning and similar tasks in Western Europe are the province of "guest workers" from Turkey, Portugal, Spain, or Italy.

Since the mid-1960s attempts by blacks and Latins to push up succeeding rungs to civil service jobs in the police, fire, and sanitation departments and to private-sector clerical and sales jobs have become focal points in a bitter struggle with incumbent ethnic groups which have not yet moved so far upward as to feel out of range.

TOWARD TWO SOCIETIES?

The dismal conclusion of the 1968 Kerner Commission Report was that America was moving in the direction of two societies, one larger, mostly white, relatively affluent and hopeful; one smaller, largely black, fearful, beleaguered, and explosive.[4] As far as polarization between haves and have-nots is concerned, the facts have not altered very much through history. There is always some type of hierarchy between social classes; some are well off, many confidently expect a better life for themselves and their children, while others at the bottom or on their way down are depressed and resentful. The difference in the United States, in the 1970s, is that the proportion of the population in the middle and upper classes and in the reasonably well-paid working class is much larger than ever before in the nation's history.

Depending on one's definition, 10 to 20 percent of the population now lives in poverty, compared to 35 percent in the late 1940s and perhaps 50 percent during the depression decade of the 1930s. While the proportion of poor is indeed much smaller than in previous generations, the continued existence of poverty and slums seemed an affront to justice and dignity. Given the prevalence of general affluence and enormous national productive capacity, a relatively minor reallocation of resources would suffice to provide modestly acceptable living conditions for everyone.

Antipoverty war of the 1960s.   Poverty in the midst of poverty is easier to bear than poverty in the midst of what seems to be almost universal affluence. It was in fact the relatively small proportion of the population living in poverty that gave rise to the hopes of the mid-1960s that one big push, one vigorous war on poverty, would forever slay this ancient dragon. Unfortunately, the notion that the problems of poverty and in particular the problems of hardcore ghetto areas were susceptible to easy solutions, and that one or more of a variety of income, employment, criminal justice, housing, health, education, or community governance programs would effect rapid radical transformations, died in the late 1960s. In part this was due to the belated realization that many of these problems were interrelated. Many poor blacks were victims of multiple problems—broken families, ill health, poor schooling, criminal records, lack of useful job training and job discipline—and they lived in neighborhoods suffering from physical decay and social disorganization. Also, it was not entirely clear that both the good will and the economic growth were available to welcome the newly trained ghetto people into good neighborhoods and good jobs. Certainly the minimal funding of some of the antipoverty programs raised suspicions that such action as was taken was primarily a matter of low-cost anti-riot insurance, an effort geared to cooption of potential leaders and vandals, and a placebo to pacify rebellious slum dwellers.

The 1973 - 76 recession.   Hopes of large-scale national intervention on behalf of poor blacks (or other ghetto residents) dwindled away from 1973 to 1976. Revenue sharing and block grants to be used at the discretion of local governments proved more susceptible to redirection away from the needs of the poor than the categorical grants they replaced.[5] Government revenues were down, unemployment rates were up, and in the context of a deepening business recession with spreading layoffs and sharp cutbacks in housing construction, pressures for "affirmative action" slackened.

This left in doubt the future of some aspiring minority persons still in the education/training pipeline and some of those recently hired in unionized industries governed by stringent seniority rules. Even more in question was the future of the marginal minority working class barely making ends meet within the system. Unemployment rates in ghetto areas, usually high (double the national rate) rose in 1974 - 76 to depression-era levels—20 percent or higher.[6] And most hopeless of all was the prospect for the sizable group outside the working-earnings system who face even harder times—ghetto teenagers were lucky to find any kind of work.[7] The aged and the welfare families were also badly hit by inflation.[8] Moreover, with major increases in the cost of housing, all groups found that they tended to be trapped in their neighborhoods.

In some respects, the recession of 1973 - 76 rendered more complicated the bipolar racial/quasi-class division suggested by the Kerner Commission. One group, under pressure but still relatively privileged, included the white middle and upper classes and a substantial number of minority professional and technical people who were of the right age and background to benefit from the civil rights job and housing opportunities of the 1960s. Another large group was comprised of persons too young, too unlucky, or too unwary to have purchased good housing when its cost was relatively low or to have secured a good, safe position. In this group were young, willing, and able minority people somewhere in the continuum between adolescence and the professional job market at the time when model cities were in flower, poverty programs were in bloom, and good jobs were being passed out.

Prospects for the third group, the poor, especially the minority poor, are both different and distinctly worse than for the pool of trained, temporarily disadvantaged. For the middle group a moderate upturn in the economy will suffice; when unemployment retreats to a 5 or 6 percent level their prospects are fairly good. Not so with society's underdogs, who require something approaching full employment and general prosperity before they can expect a resurgence of better job and housing alternatives.

Special Minority Group Problems

As noted elsewhere in this work, conservatives are fond of underscoring the personal and familial traits associated with the poor to explain their inability to climb out of poverty. Of course this analysis is often unfair and, more important, various forms of discriminations and societal malfunctions make it difficult for substantial numbers of stable, well-behaved and hard-working poor families—the working poor—to escape from the slums. But this fact does not completely invalidate the point that many blacks and other slum residents exhibit the same characteristics lamented in centuries past by well-meaning observers of other slum cultures. They drink too much, they desert their families, they squander their meager pay on useless frippery, most seem rather stupid, they fail to supervise their children properly, and they are prone to criminal activity.

THE EFFECTS OF PREJUDICE
All or most of these charges were leveled at successive waves of immigrants, but they took on a special twist when tailored for blacks and Latins. In addition to the backwardness and dirt, mental weaknesses and alcoholism, the two groups were assumed to have the qualities of an amusing, lovable child. Grinning, unpunctual, undisciplined, dancing and singing in their rags, speaking quaint broken English, they were not to be taken seriously as adults. The pejorative term "boy" addressed

to blacks was indicative of this attitude. One response by blacks and Latins was the Sambo ploy—confused headscratching, "no spik Inglis," a calculated saboteur's response. Treat me like a child and I'll act like a child. If you pay me a boy's wages don't expect manly effort.

There is considerable argument over whether the dependency training meted out to blacks and Latins during the years of slavery and near-peonage embedded itself into present-day behavior patterns. For example, the persistence of a good deal of desertion and female-headed black families is ascribed to the figurative emasculation practiced in slavery days, when black women were occasionally subjected to stud treatment by lecherous whites and a black family could be broken at will by sale of the husband/father or children. Recent research casts some doubt on this thesis, suggesting that on the contrary, the evidence points to stability or at most serial monogamy among black slave families rather than the learned pattern of male promiscuity within the context of a black matriarchate.[9]

Others lay more of the blame on postslavery conditions, particularly on the post-World War II mass influx to the cities. It was consistently easier for black women to find jobs. Black men, shamed by their failure as providers, were allegedly tempted to desert their spouses and offspring. One poignant short story describes the emotions of a young black boy who discovers that his housemaid-mother was really his father, forced to deny his manhood in house dresses because there were no jobs for black men but plenty of work for black cleaning ladies.[10] Another describes a black soldier, AWOL overseas during the Second World War—out of place in the entertainer's role assigned to blacks in America because "he couldn't Boogie-Woogie worth a damn."[11] For their part, deserted black women developed a pattern in which they moved in with their mothers and other female relatives and regarded black males with contempt as improvident studs, not to be relied upon as steady helpmates and serious child-rearing partners. The absence of a father model in a child's formative years led, some observers believed, to a rootless, crime-prone, exaggerated machismo among black teenagers and a repetition of the exploitative desertion pattern. Daniel Patrick Moynihan, in his pamphlet on the breakdown of the Negro family, gives as one of his reasons for recommending that fatherless young blacks join the armed forces the hope that in a rigorously disciplined environment, the strict platoon sergeant replacing the absent parent, blacks could develop a wholesome masculinity. Thus their aggressions would be released on the nation's enemies instead of on its population.

CRIME AND THE GHETTO COMMUNITY

The chapter on urban crime underscores the extent to which slum residents bear the brunt of the crime problem. The victims of crimes of violence, of police shootings, and of street crime in general are mainly poor and black. Stores owned and operated by blacks and Puerto Ricans, the elderly, children, and women have been special targets, particularly for the teenagers and young men who commit most of the crimes. In 1973 more blacks than whites were victims of murder (10,500 blacks vs. just over 10,000 whites) and the overall arrest rate for blacks for crimes of violence was ten times higher than the rate for whites.

It is of interest that the crime plague in the black population is of relatively recent origin. As one black scholar reminds us, there was a time "when black men laughed at pimps as failed men, when violent crime was the white man's thing".[12] Black (and Latin) slums as recently as the 1930s were relatively peaceful areas, places where muggers were not unknown, but still old people could walk the streets, with sensible precautions.

A change in attitude.   For a time during the 1960s, there was a certain amount of romanticizing of ghetto crime. Besides the long American tradition of transforming thugs into misunderstood heroes, there was a fairly widespread belief in the black community that these criminals were high-spirited, economically deprived youngsters, stealing from a society which offered them no legitimate opportunities. Among the ghetto population there was also a comforting myth that the criminals respected their own and did their foraging among the white middle class, thereby returning the fruits of oppression from whence they came. Moreover, appeals to law and order seemed to be code words for racism and bias, a license for bigoted, corrupt, and sadistic police to rough up or blast away at innocent teenagers entertaining each other on the streets because their homes were dingy and overcrowded.

It is not difficult to identify the approximate time when ghetto sentiments toward crime shifted decisively toward exasperation. It was after the 1972 presidential election, when a victorious Nixon had adopted the Wallace law-and-order slogans; after years of experience with police chiefs and supposed policemen who ran for office and were elected on crime-fighting platforms; after years of indecisive law-enforcement experiments. It became clear that far from transforming the police into more effective instruments of fascist/apartheid oppression, for the most part the expensive new-style law enforcement was more of the same neglect. The slums were all too often left to stew in their own juice, victims waiting up to half an hour for police cars to respond to emergency calls. Ghetto criminals and plainsclothesmen frequently coexisted comfortably in a flourishing, mutually profitable accommodation.

Part of the reason for the shift in sentiment toward law enforcement may be attributed to growing prosperity. A larger black middle class found itself a lucrative target for criminals. Another reason was the reverse trend of the 1960s—as the number of job opportunities increased, crime also increased rather than declined. The black working class, working hard for meager pay, resented being made the prey of nonworking misfits and scoundrels. There was apparently a cumulative exasperation; people whose welfare checks had been repeatedly stolen, whose children had been terrorized, raped, or robbed, grew less sympathetic to notions that local criminals were lively young "bloods," natty Superflys out to hurt the honkys in their pocketbook. Thugs were no longer viewed as pathetic political or economic victims of a malfunctioning, oppressive society. The ghetto working class and the aspiring middle class increasingly saw themselves as the victim and the neighborhood criminals as threats. Least of all did hardworking parents care to have their children follow in the footsteps of criminal role models—the pimps, pushers, and prostitutes.

Minority pressure for crime control.   The minority response to crime has been both logical and frustrated. To begin, there have been constant demands for more minority police to humanize the system, helping it to distinguish between honest ghetto residents and criminals, and to corral some high-paying civil service jobs for minority people. There have been increasing demands for police responsiveness; that is, that as taxpayers and human beings in need or danger, ghetto residents have the same right to adequate police service as residents of other neighborhoods. Certainly, it is believed, the police should be as quick to respond as the fire department. There have also been stirrings in the direction of citizen auxiliaries, neighborhood resident patrols, working cooperatively with the police for neighborhood safety.

The newer note in minority demands for anticrime action is similar to the call from much of the white community: stricter discipline in the schools, tougher sentencing by the courts, less leniency in paroles, and less plea bargaining that returns violent criminals to the streets before their victims leave the hospital. The newly appointed black Com-

missioner of Public Safety in Atlanta predicted, "Soon the greatest demand for firmer police action (to combat crime) will come from the
black community. There will be no more of this, 'I am poor, so I had to
rape that girl.'" A largely minority audience at a crowded workshop on
"Minority Groups and the Criminal Justice System" at the National
League of Cities conference "applauded vigorously."[13]

The direction in which the minority community is moving is clearly
a hopeful omen, not so much in signalling any rapid decline in the crime
rate, but in providing evidence that ghetto residents feel the same sense
of shame and outrage against neighborhood predators as did earlier
groups of immigrant ethnics. Judging from past experience, the fundamental change in attitudes will require a full generation to mature.
But in ten and twenty years there can be a reasonable hope that the
terrors experienced by children of the 1960s and 1970s will be no more
than a bitter memory.

BROKEN FAMILIES/ILLEGITIMACY

Over a third of black families are headed by a woman, as compared
to a tenth of white (defined here as nonblack and non-Latin) families.
The proportion of female-headed black families increased sharply during the 1960s. (In 1960, the black percentage was one in five.) Moreover,
in the early 1970s one in three black children was born out of wedlock,
as compared with one in nine for whites.[14]

Female-headed families.   Among white families there has been a
trend toward more divorce, toward more female-headed families, and in
a minor fashion, toward more out-of-wedlock births. This trend is
associated with (1) prosperity—as people move from the working class
they desert less and divorce more; and (2) sexual freedom and women's
liberation—the search for independence and the ability to locate and
keep better paying jobs apparently has led to more divorce and,
seemingly, to a slight increase in out-of-wedlock births.

Among minority people some of the same trends are evident, but
since a very much larger proportion are poor working-class people,
there is more desertion—"the poor man's divorce." In addition, an increasingly large number of blacks and Puerto Ricans made use of Aid
for Dependent Children (AFDC) during the 1960s. By 1973 there were
almost as many blacks as whites on the AFDC rolls, although the white
population was nine times larger. In some cases mothers applying for
AFDC were young single girls; in others AFDC was used as an illegal

form of family income maintenance. The expansion also reflected the impact of welfare rights; reformers sought successfully in the 1960s to deregulate the poor by informing them of their right to welfare, thereby forcing a change in national policy in the direction of family income maintenance by overloading the welfare system. The welfare rolls expanded partly because of considerable sloppy administration—up to a fifth of recipients were not entitled to assistance.

In female-headed families the economic consequences of a loss in male earning power are often disastrous. Small family incomes are further divided, imposing more burdens on already overstrained budgets; there are two rents, more restaurant meals, etc. The best of both worlds for slum families is fraudulent desertion, in which AFDC payments are secretly supplemented by income from the man who is not supposed to be present. It is a fact, however, that a substantial proportion of minority families would have incomes above the poverty line were it not for broken homes.[15]

Need for birth control.   The poverty problem is exacerbated when the woman head-of-household has more than two or three children. Conservatives who believe in the myth of the breeding machine, poor women who become pregnant to take advantage of public welfare, are refuted by the facts. In Puerto Rico and on the mainland, abortions and contraception may be assailed by male militants as a colonialist, establishment program designed to keep down the numbers of blacks and Latins, but their womenfolk are as aware as middle-class women of all racial and ethnic origins of the great amounts of time and money entailed in rearing children. An estimated two in five births among the poor during the 1960s were unwanted.

Fortunately relief seems to be on hand. In late 1974 the federal Department of Health, Education and Welfare was financing between 220,000 and 278,000 abortions each year, at an average cost of $180 each, for poor women, most of them on welfare.[16] This very large number of abortions represents one extremely hopeful note in anticipating reductions in poverty and delinquency in the 1980s. Moreover, in 1973 an estimated 60 percent of black families were using some form of birth control.[17]

One of the major arguments advanced by Third World developing nations during the 1974 World Population Conference in Bucharest was that historically development has preceded and should precede birth control. The theory seems to be that the high rates of population increase associated with the early, rapid stages of economic development taper off when the population becomes convinced that large families are no longer needed as a form of low-paid farm or factory labor and as a form of old-age insurance. As development progressed in countries like Greece, Taiwan, Japan, and Cyprus, children became viewed more as expense items than as assets, and birth rates fell.[18]

This argument has also been advanced for Puerto Ricans and blacks; birth rates are relatively small—equal to whites—among the middle class of these population groups, and it has been suggested that better jobs for the poor would remove the need for abortion clinics and heavy Aid for Dependent Children (AFDC) expenditures. In practice, however, there seems to be no reason why elevation into the middle class must necessarily precede a decline in childbirth, particularly since many lower-class women have reached the accurate assessment that large families are almost a guarantee of continued poverty.

The problem of the broken family.   This still leaves the problem of the minority broken family. Smaller it may be, but when the woman is on welfare or holding a menial job, prospects for the mother and children are considerably less bright than they would be if an additional steady breadwinner and role model, a father, was on hand to help with the budget, the home, and the children. Unfortunately, this pattern is susceptible to neither exhortation nor political confrontation. Despite some brave talk about the inherent strength of the matriarchal family, assisted by relatives and a growing national trend toward such families, most people regard illegitimate births and broken families, particularly in tandem, as a serious social problem. Unless this trend is somehow corrected—and on the basis of the past generation's trends, this may never happen—there is a good prospect of social division by family type rather than a racially polar society. Whole families, white and minority in the middle and working class, will be on one economic level, while broken minority families and elderly minority and white people will live at or below the poverty line. Sadly, to a degree this pattern already exists.

Minority Mobility and Preserving Community Values

Throughout most of urban history different social classes lived and often worked in close physical proximity. The obvious example is the enormous, underpaid servant class which tended to house and lawn, children, and horses. Dependent and docile, servants were live-in or work-in menials whose presence betokened status and diminished daily cares. Historically in the United States, in both North and South, racial integration was an accomplished fact, with whites mingling with black wetnurses, yardmen, house servants, and childhood playmates. Integration was also residential—a row of mansions might be adjoined by an alley or a block occupied by persons of modest means. Occasionally this kind of juxtaposed living arrangement would be capsulized in a phrase, Chicago's "Gold Coast and the Slum," but there were similar adjoining mixed class-race housing in most cities.

TREND TOWARD INCOME CLUSTERING

The physical proximity between social classes began to lessen long before the near-disappearance of the servant class with the growth of alternative opportunities during the Second World War. There were the railroad commuter suburbs, the streetcar suburbs, and later the early automobile suburbs that attracted middle- and upper-income families. These families were served, as time passed, by commuting servants from the cities. There were also substantial numbers of working-class residents employed in local factories or as municipal workers.

The housing boom of the 1920s set the pattern for the 1950s and 1960s. There was an increasing trend toward income clustering, with most of the poor remaining in central cities and satellite working-class communities, and the other groups settling in separate concentrations of upper working-class, middle-class and upper-class communities in the suburbs. Within the central citities the geographic pattern was more complex but not entirely dissimilar. Considerable side-by-side class residential mixture remained, but the basic pattern was one of increasing low-income minority concentration encroaching slowly or rapidly on resisting or fleeing white working-class and middle-class areas.

Resistance tends to be strongest in neighborhoods inhabited by fairly homogeneous white ethnic groups who lack the means or the inclination to move out to the suburbs. But the suburbs are not far behind in resisting minority influx. It may be recalled that the power of New York's Urban Development Corporation to override local zoning ordinances in small communities was stripped from the agency after its abortive attempt to construct a minimum number (1,000) of low-income housing units in ten Westchester County communities.[19]

Within the minority community there is a similar pattern of complexity. A growing minority class is trickling out to the suburbs and into middle-class city neighborhoods, often only a few years ahead of the minority working class and the pathology-prone underclass.

Between 1960 and 1970, the black population in metropolitan areas increased by 32 percent, a gain which was almost evenly divided between central cities (up by 33 percent) and suburbs (up by 29 percent). Much of the suburban growth was a move to older housing located in inner suburbs. Although some researchers predict more of the same—black purchase of older housing vacated by whites moving farther out—others suggest that black home ownership will be sharply restricted by the legacy of the past. Blacks have been mostly renters, unable to build up equity in a salable home; despite rising incomes, they lack the accumulated capital needed to purchase homes at the inflated prices of the mid-1970s.[20]

The real battleground for integration is the white suburbs where most of the nation's urban development has taken place in the past generation. The prevailing community homogeneity based on race or ethnic origin and fear of outsiders has diminished, but in its place is a kind of class discrimination. In 1975 at least half the total number of families in the nation's cities, including most blacks and Latins, were too poor in income and/or home equity to buy a house or rent a garden apartment in the suburbs.

BLACKS TO THE SUBURBS

As noted, most black suburban movement is not truly suburban in the classic sense. Instead of leapfrogging to a low-density community five to twenty miles away, new black suburbanites tend to move to high-density pseudosuburbs adjoining the ghetto.[21] East Orange, New Jersey, adjacent to Newark, is a good example. Some of the special advantages the black middle class sought to find in suburban relocation are thereby lost or diluted as they are closely followed by a portion of the black underclass. The quality of the housing, the public services (including the school system), crime rates, and open space tend to be distinctly inferior as compared to more distant suburbs occupied by Caucasian families with roughly the same income.

This raises another point. Suburban relocation for blacks is rendered particularly difficult because blacks pay more. The Kaiser Commission estimated the black families were charged a discriminatory premium for housing of about a third over the market price available for white families.[22] Other estimates of the premium are lower, depending on the area and current state of the housing market. Moreover, as is particularly the case with movement into older, close-in suburbs, much of the housing available at these relatively high prices may be obsolescent, requiring more costly expenditures to modernize and maintain than is the case with later-vintage housing.

From the viewpoint of the minority poor, the deepening pattern of postwar class segregation has been a disaster. What it has meant is either entrapment in the pathology-ridden slums or a doubling-up or tripling-up of families in housing on safer but swiftly deteriorating fringes of slum areas. Given this locking-in, it is not surprising that many minority families are eager to send their children to parochial schools, or to bus their children to schools in outside neighborhoods where they will escape the fearsome environment for their critically important schooling. And there has been consistent minority support for fair-housing legislation and administrative regulation to build new housing in safer city neighborhoods and in suburban communities. As the prime victims of the criminal minority underclass and the principal sufferers from physically and socially decaying slum neighborhoods, the law-abiding, hard-working minority family is desperate for escape. Unfortunately, in an era of colorful media crime coverage, the people fortunate enough to live some distance away from the slums and hence only infrequently victimized by roving members of this underclass are equally convinced of the necessity of preserving personal safety, school quality, and property values by keeping *all* lower-class people at a distance.

This attitude toward persons who exhibit undesired lower-class characteristics has a long history. In fact, in earlier eras, some of the grandparents of many middle- and upper-class suburban residents faced similar prejudices. Newspapers and the minutes of suburban property owners' associations one and two generations back reflect harsh comments and overt or covert action to exclude belligerent chowder-and-beer Irish, ill-mannered Jews, unwashed, crime-tainted Italians, etc. The present difference is that there has been a genuine increase in crime rates and other dangerous pathological symptoms, and that the federal government is theoretically committed to breaking down patterns of exclusion. (In practice, however, federal housing legislation from FHA, through Sections 221d - 3, often exacerbated rather than diminished segregationist patterns.)

THE LEGAL BATTLE

In the mid-1970s, with the help of various state and municipal governments, middle- and upper-income neighborhoods have been put on notice not only to cease discrimination but to take affirmative action to achieve a more representative population mix. Affirmative action is a slippery concept, however. A crafty, fearful community can easily build a plausible paper record of vigorous municipal action. It can put forth proposals which, it can be confident, are too costly for the federal and state housing subsidies that may exist or too risky for prospective developers, and hence out of reach of poor families.

Suburban residents may be castigated for the sins of hypocrisy, selfishness, callousness, and bigotry, but the suburban consensus is clearly against any significant influx of low-income families and any in-migration of multiproblem people from the slums. The local politician who advocates a new turn in land use policy to alter this pattern is in trouble. Law suits aimed at breaking down barriers erected by affluent suburbs to protect their homogeneity and stability through zoning are in the process of being struck down in New Jersey and other states, to be replaced with government action to achieve undefined "balanced" communities.[23]

But even winning law suits is easier than building low-cost housing. Great technical complexities are involved in determining "balance" in metropolitan areas on the basis of various criteria, including ethnic and racial composition, income, and the degree of dispersion throughout the community and metropolitan or county regions.[24] Given the severe cost constraints in the housing market and widespread, continued suburban opposition, it is extremely doubtful that within the next decade or two suburban dispersion of the poor in any substantial numbers can be achieved through some type of imposed housing quota. Some changes may occur if substantial federal incentives include financial carrots along with legal sticks. These extra financial subsidies would be a kind of combat pay to help compensate reluctant communities for taking on their share of a very real burden.[25]

Also, as in other problems, psychological perception is at least as important as objective fact. A "mixed," racially balanced neighborhood, from the viewpoint of whites, may be one in which the blacks constitute 5 to 10 percent of the total. Blacks often feel that a 50 - 50 split is a more comfortable balance.[26] This involves controversial questions regarding "tipping points," "blockbusting," panic flights and other phraseology describing a rapid change in racial composition. Striking a balance between differing white and black concepts of what constitutes a desirable, stable racial balance is almost as difficult as achieving any considerable suburban migration of the core-city black population.

Relocation to the suburbs would improve housing and employment opportunities for the poor but might or might not offer them attendant social benefits such as better school performance or lower delinquency rates. The most difficult problem clearly lies in bridging the widest gap, introducing *low-income blacks (or Puerto Ricans) into middle- or upper-income white neighborhoods.* Anthony Downs suggests that some of the apprehension can be allayed by adopting a policy of preserving middle-class dominance. That is, quotas could be established to ensure that the influx of low-income newcomers would be sufficiently small as not to threaten middle-class social or property values. This policy might be coupled with a difficult-to-administer but essential screening process to minimize the number of multiproblem families in any one neighborhood. For this reason it is easier to go along with Anthony Down's suggestion: concentrate, for the present, on *economic integration,* to bring low-income working-class families closer to job opportunities, even if this results—one hopes only temporarily—in creation of suburban minighettos.[27] Subsequently, as minority people advance up the economic ladder, integration policy need only surmount a single fence—race—rather than an insuperable double barrier.

BENEFITS OF BLACK DISPERSION?

As discussed in the chapter on land use, the benefits of dispersing the ghetto, parceling out poor blacks into suburban communities, are partly a matter of faith rather than undisputed proof. The expected benefits of dispersing the ghetto include access to better jobs and to improved services for the poor, and possible assistance to hard-pressed cities, which find it difficult to cope with large concentrations of poor people. A thinning out of slum populations may also offer opportunities to rebuild the ghetto at more desirable lower densities without having to displace poor people.

On the other hand proposals for major dispersion of blacks from central cities have been attacked by some blacks as leading to fragmentation and weakening of the territorial base for political power, or as an effective means of siphoning out the middle class and the steadily employed working class, leaving ghettos to welfare families and other people with serious economic and social problems. And still others suggest that the roughly forty to fifty "fair share" regional housing allocations that have been adopted since the early 1970s are largely mythical, since there is no strong legislative commitment to provide the funds for such proportionate housing dispersal.

Over and above anticipated overt and covert suburban resistance to the influx of blacks—especially low-income blacks—some suggest that not all the expected benefits of dispersal are likely to materialize. For example, the alleged mismatch between people and jobs is clearly questionable, since the shift of manufacturing industry to the suburbs has not yet adversely affected the large pool of central city, low-paid, low-skilled service jobs which have traditionally absorbed slum labor. Moreover if suburban relocation of the poor were not carefully planned, the result, as Downs suggests, would likely be the creation of mini-Harlems in the suburbs. There are already numerous examples of this phenomenon.

This discussion of the myth and reality of the dispersal issue is not intended to justify maintaining a "white noose" of exclusionary suburbs ringing black and Latin American ghettos. It does suggest that the benefits and disadvantages are more complex and debatable than some advocates of low-income, scatter-site suburban housing are prepared to concede. The furor in early 1976 over candidate Jimmy Carter's use of the terms "ethnic purity" and "black intrusion" indicates the extreme sensitivity of the issue. The consensus of the Democratic presidential candidates, once the dust had settled, probably accurately reflects majority suburban opinion: (1) Remove all racial and ethnic barriers hindering suburban relocation. (2) Attempt to reduce entrance incomes for suburban housing sufficiently to permit lower-middle-class and steadily employed persons to move in.

In practical terms this means no massive dispersal of welfare and low-income families, but wider opportunities for black families with (1976) incomes of $10,000 a year.

Race vs. Class: Definitions and Implications

Up until the 1960s, it seemed to most Americans that race relations were dominated by caste characteristics. Exploited and oppressed blacks and Latins, set off by genetically inherited physical traits, were mostly consigned to a position of permanent social inferiority, and virtually all were extremely poor. This caste relationship was so apparently unshakable that serious attention was given to the possible geographic separation of the races (partly to permit blacks to escape from a subordinate position) and minor consideration was accorded to research on bleaching one's skin and straightening one's hair to remove the badge of inferiority. Successfully passing as white was a road to wider opportunity. It ensured that an individual would be judged on his merits instead of being stereotyped—either automatically underrated or else marvelled at because one's talents were so unusual in a person of such pigment.

UPWARD MOBILITY

The civil rights revolution of the 1960s resulted in a weakening of these traditional caste barriers, the best evidence being a substantial growth in educational and occupational opportunities for blacks and Latins to the point where a modest-sized middle class had emerged. Depending on one's calculations, anywhere from a sixth to a third of blacks and Latins had achieved middle-class incomes by the early 1970s, and the qualitative indices of caste discrimination, like underrepresentation in political office, had clearly weakened. (But in 1976 blacks still constituted only .5 percent of elected office holders.)

The problem of the "underclass," a term popularized by Edward Banfield, the urban expert who authored *The Unheavenly City*, deserves special attention because it strikes at the heart of the race issue of the 1970s. If indeed the color badge is growing less significant and the status criteria of white society relating to income, education, and occupation are now being applied to blacks, the racial dichotomy is indeed being transformed into a class issue. Over time, a growing number of blacks seem to be following the ethnic pathways blazed by disadvantaged southern and eastern Europeans. This means, among other things, that while a focus on self-conscious racial pride, distinctive clothing, dance festivals, and special varieties of choral singing may persist and even expand for a few years, within a decade or two separatism and nationalism will blend into a traditional American pattern. Many black and Latin characteristics will be absorbed into the general culture (as has long been the case in the arts), and many will vanish. The residue will be sentimentalized and muted into periodic costume parties, nostalgic oratory, gastronomic loyalties, and fund-raising drives for a cause mostly won.

Since a prime feature of the 1960s and early 1970s was a significant amount of upward mobility on the part of many members of down-trodden minority groups, it became much easier to suggest that persons who remained at the bottom of the ladder had only themselves to blame if they did not grasp the opportunities eagerly seized by their neighbors. In brief, it became plausible to apply to these still-poor minorities the same comforting rationale which had previously been used for poor whites: you have only yourself (or your family or your neighbors) to blame if you fail to get the grades, get the training, and display the intelligence and discipline needed to get ahead.

A POLITICAL MINORITY

Aside from its manifest unfairness in any number of individual instances, this reshaping of views toward minority poverty as a class phenomenon, rather than as a foredoomed caste like India's "untouchable" Harijans or Japan's Etas, has certain attractive implications for political strategies aimed at improving the condition of the poor. First, this view recognizes the divergence of interests between members of the minority who have made it into the middle class and those who remain mired in poverty. The normal emotions of sympathy and contempt, felt by the successful, and the suspicion by those left behind of faithlessness and exploitation, which characterized the upwardly mobile and immobile members of other groups, are already operative. It is unlikely that any minority can remain cohesive in the face of genuine opportunities and substantive progress for minority achievers.[28] Second, focusing on the reality of class and the dimishing importance of caste would end such anomalies as the progeny of upper- and middle-income black families being accorded special privileges denied to working-class whites. As the minority middle class grows, racial or ethnic quotas lose their last vestige of political acceptability.

A third point is perhaps the most important. It is simply that a minority remains a minority. Those who claim special advantages, such as reparations, for blacks and Latins on the grounds of present suffering and past oppression run up against the fact that the majority of the nation's poor is neither black nor Latin. Moreover, it is a political absurdity to levy a bill for reparations for entire minority groups, part of which have already moved into the middle class, against a white majority, most of whom feel financially hard-pressed rather than affluent.

Logically a successful political strategy embraces the broadest possible spectrum of support and diminishes the number of opponents. A race-bound strategy seems calculated to provoke numerically and economically powerful reactions to the special claims of a minority group. In contrast, a class-oriented approach can be incorporated into a process of coalition building, and offers the attractive prospect of winning more friends than enemies. Historically, dominant elites have often resorted to the tactic of splitting the poor by exacerbating racial and ethnic jealousies. An all-black, all-Latin, or Third World conglomeration plays into the hands of the conservative power (and potential hostility) of the white poor and white middle class.

The statistics are clear: a coalition of poor people might embrace a third to over half the electorate, depending on where the poverty line is drawn. And if the appeal were broadened to include much of the middle class on the traditional Roosevelt model, three-fifths to two-thirds of the voters might be attracted to a spectrum of programs which offer something far broader than specialized aid for resentful minorities. In contrast, a black-Latin combination, if one could be fashioned, might include no more than 15 to 20 percent of the voting population. (An alternate minority strategy—political terror—has been given up by most of its former proponents as a self-destructive, one-time tactic which provokes severe reprisals by an alarmed majority.) For these reasons the discussions of potential programs and strategies in this book are framed in terms of class coalitions rather than in terms of separatist fragmentation.

Clearly, policies aimed at attracting broad coalitions in support of national reforms are likely to be more effective and far less divisive than narrow policies which are interpreted as conferring special favors on the basis of pigment or Spanish surnames. To cite three principal objectives, achieving genuine full employment, low-cost comprehensive medical care, and high-quality day care, is much more desirable for poor minority people than dissipating energy in a long, bitter struggle to force a few suburbs to permit the construction of a handful of low-income housing units or to force white neighborhoods to engage in unwanted school busing programs. Furthermore, terror tactics, including blood-curdling rhetoric, are likely to prove counterproductive. This fact of life has been recognized by former Black Panthers, Black Muslims, and other nationalist-separatist organizations, who have been converted to traditional party politics or some variety of ecumenical Islamism or Marxism.

Assuming that answers must be sought in political action, there is still a problem in securing adequate political representation for minorities. The first is the tendency of low-income people to vote in smaller numbers than their middle-class neighbors. This deficiency is aggravated by demography—poor minority people are rich only in children too young to vote, which further weakens potential minority political strength. Moreover, as noted, minorities are faced with some difficult territorial choices. The central cities in which they are approaching or have reached numerical dominance and are beginning to elect mayors are often seriously troubled, deficit-ridden hulks like Newark, Gary, and Detroit.

PROBLEMS OF BLACK MAYORS

Black mayors are caught in the middle. Elected on the basis of promised reforms—reducing crime and unemployment rates and battling alleged colonialist exploitation by landlords and merchants—they also represent a new dignity and symbolic recognition. Unfortunately, like their white mayoral counterparts, they find it easier to promise than to deliver. This failure confronts black mayors with special problems. It is part of every poor minority credo to believe that an establishment conspiracy is directly responsible for their unpleasant living conditions and that strong, honest, political leadership at city hall can effect major, rapid improvements. In practice, however, the national and local economic and employment situation is well beyond the reach of the mayor, white or black. Furthermore, he finds it painfully difficult in the face of a deepening fiscal crisis and civil service constraints to effect even modest reforms in the public schools, in police attitudes and practices, or in housing code enforcement.

As a result the black mayor, like his white counterpart, finds himself reduced to the role of "Beggar-in-Chief," pleading for special help from federal and state governments, from businesses and corporations itching to slip away to the suburbs, and from the banks wary of lending money to losing causes. He finds himself reduced to presiding over disasters, operating bad schools with unwilling pupils, and grappling with neighborhoods full of criminals and their outraged victims.

And like his political colleagues he is tempted to resort to demagogic, symbolic politics, freely denouncing Washington and the governor, excoriating criminals and venal, lazy school teachers, labor unions, and corporations, blasting corrupt, racist police and blaming parents for failing to curb delinquents and vandals.

The emerging minority middle class faces more attractive alternatives. Middle- and upper-class people can remain in the city, probably on the fringes of the slums, and play an active leadership role in the municipal and local congressional politics in which the minority represents a major component. But often the choice to remain means a continuing exposure to high crime rates and substandard schools. The alternative is black and Latin middle-class relocation to better neighborhoods in the suburbs, which in turn leads to their diminished importance in municipal and congressional politics. The middle-class option, the choice in favor of concentration or dispersion of minority power, is a critical factor in determining the future shape of American politics. Thus far the evidence points to more affluent blacks and Latins following the precedent of earlier groups, moving to the suburbs. As time passes, they will probably exhibit the complex blend of property-consciousness and sensitivity to school and safety advantages which has caused white suburbanites to fear central-city people and try to exclude them.

Alternative Solutions

The preceding discussion may have left some readers in a state of despair. The avenues upon which so much political effort and legal resources have been lavished (busing, "fair share" housing programs to open up the suburbs, "affirmative action" to reserve space for minorities) all seem costly, time-consuming, and either unproductive or outright counterproductive.[29] Does this leave us with a tired replay of Booker T. Washingtonism—"cast down your bucket where you are"—be humble, be thrifty, be grateful for vocational training, and for menial jobs, be thankful for a roof over your head?

Booker T. Washington was a counselor for turn-of-the-century survival in an age of Jim Crow and the Klu Klux Klan, and of a hostile or neutral federal government that had struck the notorious 1876 bargain with the southern white power structure to elect Hayes over Tilden. In the present era, a new generation of minority politicians, black and Latin, has learned that to get elected and reelected on the basis of issues and leadership is preferable to being a machine lackey assigned a share in the spoils of the ghetto in return for delivering the minority vote and dampening the fires of rebellion. In the mid-1970s there are 130 black mayors and hundreds of other black leaders organizing, orating, bargaining, combining on crucial votes, and bringing unrelenting pressure to bear through the party system. They can count the votes; aware that a minority, even a unified minority, is still a fraction of the whole, they have lent their support to measures aimed at helping all of the nation's poor. Although most of the people living in poverty are not black or Latin, blacks and Latins are poorer and hence benefit most from social reforms.

POLITICALLY VIABLE SOLUTIONS

The remaining alternatives—separatism, terrorism, reliance on some unlikely pressure from the militant poverty-stricken Third World, emigration, socialist revolution, life on welfare, passivity, or escape through crime or drugs—seem to be self-destructive fantasies. It seems clear this means concentrating politically on salable programs that help minorities by helping everyone. Guaranteed jobs, day care, and comprehensive health care are good examples.

It has been argued that shifting attention from busing, employment goal quotas, and affirmative action is tantamount to surrender to bigotry. If we had waited for majority consensus, slavery would be with us still. Hence, according to this view, unrelenting pressure through the courts, the executive agencies, and the legislatures is needed, for, judging from past history, such pressure can alter behavior patterns among a reluctant but law-abiding majority.

To the extent that action was taken to counter practices like lynching, barriers to voting, segregation in public places, or job discrimination, such pressures did indeed prove effective. But a majority of the majority—outside the South—was supportive of the civil rights movement. The South lost the Civil War and with it the institution of slavery largely because there were more whites in the North in favor of union and, eventually, abolition, than there were whites in the South in favor of secession and slavery.

In a phrase, reform programs which are opposed by the majority of the population are more likely to result in hard feelings, frustration, and lost elections than substantive results.

What are the political implications of this lengthy review? In terms of jobs, the following implications are clear:

1.   *Token recognition* of group power or personal merit raises no problems, partly because these appointments come in modest numbers. Ambassadorships, visible, prestigious front offices, head-table positions for minority members are all an accepted part of the political process.

2.   So too are *patronage jobs,* staff appointments by black mayors and other elected officials. There are fewer of these than there used to be, what with civil service restrictions and examinations, but they are sufficiently numerous to provide the prospect of reward for minority people among the party faithful.

3.   *Frontal assaults* on union seniority systems, merit examinations, or educational prerequisites in favor of quota systems based on race or nationality are dangerous and potentially divisive.[30]

4.   *Preferential treatment for all the disadvantaged raises no such problems.* In fact, as experience with college open admissions programs suggests, the white poor are as likely to make use of such programs as blacks or Latin Americans. For this reason scholarships and other assistance for all hard-working, deserving persons from poor families tend to be a unifying rather than a polarizing approach.

5.   *Full employment is the real key to minority progress.* For this reason absolute priority seems to be indicated for federal action to guarantee jobs for everyone who can work. Once again this is a coalition-building approach.

As for housing and neighborhood programs, they might be based on the same basic principle—help for the poor. The key issue is location. Minorities could focus their effort on one of two approaches:

1.   The first approach is *"opening up the suburbs"* through a combination of court action, legislative programs, and housing subsidies. As noted elsewhere, the possibility of a large-scale influx of the ghetto poor into middle- and upper-class suburbs raises nightmares for suburban

residents. It is likely to result in protracted legal and administrative warfare and yield minimal results. A steady trickle of middle-income minority people to the suburbs, following the pattern of earlier white ethnic groups, raises no such problems. However, the loss of this leadership might have untoward consequences in the central cities.

2.   The second approach is what is known as *"gilding the ghetto."* The prospects for refurbishing older housing, building new structures, or upgrading decayed neighborhoods seem bleak, but the prospect for preserving stable neighborhoods in central cities may be more promising. The possibilities for sound housing in central cities do appear brighter than in past years, however, because of the growing gap between the price of new suburban housing and other new construction and lagging consumer incomes. A basic decline in the nation's standard of living, embracing housing standards, would, paradoxically, open up genuine options for preservation of existing sound housing and existing city neighborhoods.

This option may entice the steadily employed, two-income minority working-class and minority middle-class family who can and will move into healthy city and close-in suburban neighborhoods. The 1980 census will undoubtedly reveal that the trends of 1950 - 1970 have continued; blacks and Latin Americans have split into two major groups. One is a steadily employed working class blending into a substantial middle class, and the other is a hardcore lower class, marginally employed, shading off into a welfare-supported, problem-ridden and problem-creating underclass.

This hardcore problem—the ghetto underclass—is unfortunately one for which absolutely no one has any solutions. At best there is some hope in the passage of time in innovative schools and in improved health care, including psychological treatment.

Realistically, the recognition of the heterogeneity of minorities suggests a continuation and expansion of traditional mortgage and construction programs. The aim of these programs would be to help moderate- and middle-income families of all races and ethnic origins to move to better housing and better neighborhoods, with an emphasis on reaching down to steadily employed families in the $8,000 to $12,000 income bracket. This stress on opening the suburbs does not imply abandoning central cities. For example, one of the more nefarious practices that requires legal and legislation action is the "redlining" by mortgage lenders of black and other ethnic neighborhoods deemed to be unworthy credit risks. In the spring of 1976 the U.S. Justice Department filed a major civil rights suit against real estate appraisers and savings and loan associations on the grounds that they had used "racially discriminatory standards" in assessing homes and making (or disapproving) loans.[31]

But it must be recognized that redlining is a contributing rather than causative factor. The availability of mortgage money on reasonable terms does nothing to alter the basic reasons for the decline of central-city neighborhoods—high crime rates, poor schools, etc. Indeed unless there are accompanying neighborhood improvements, the end of redlining may be a prelude to an increase in mortgage foreclosures, which would validate the initial reluctance of appraisers and lenders as prudence in safeguarding their clients rather than sheer willful bigotry.

The very poor, the broken welfare family, the irregularly employed, multiproblem minority persons are the most difficult group to deal with. At a minimum, *public housing projects* and other programs, such as leased housing, could provide adequate shelter for many in this category. But there is a tradeoff. Such projects cannot be livable unless there is tenant screening and rapid eviction of troublesome families. Short of such responsive social filtration, projects for low-income people will continue to be crime-ridden, vandalized jungles. This brings us to six additional recommendations, some discussed in earlier chapters:

1. *Personal and government-aided family planning,* since small, whole families are one of the greatest potential contributions to minority progress.

2. *Federal comprehensive, low-cost medical care* to cover expenditures in excess of $500 per year to protect the health of family members.

3. *Federally funded low-cost day care centers* to provide a combination of head start education (to the extent costs permit) and freedom for mothers to augment family income. And this combination of personal choice and government programming is indicated in two other areas of direct and overwhelming importance to disadvantaged minorities.

4. *Options for schooling* might well be extended by providing subsidies for ghetto families to send their children to parochial and other private schools if they wish. There has been a marked decline in

Catholic parochial school enrollments since 1965 (down from 5.5 million to 3.4 million), but substantial gains in the number of nonwhite, non-Catholic pupils has kept enrollment in central-city parochial schools at high levels. Despite the age and obsolescence of parochial school facilities and, in many parochial schools, larger classes, many poor black families are willing to pay tuition for their children for the sake of what they perceive as the greater security, discipline, and attention accorded their children at parochial schools as compared to slum-area public schools. In Trenton, New Jersey, the demand for inner-city parochial schools is reported to be so high that many parochial schools have waiting lists. That city's parochial schools, which charge up to $150 per year in tuition, have enrollments of as much as 90 percent non-Catholic, nonwhite students.[32]

Less effort might be aimed at school desegregation and more at improving city schools. Smaller classes, more remediation and tutoring, magnet schools, and effective use of audiovisual equipment all deserve support.

    5. *Measures to protect vulnerable minority people* from the depredators in schools and in neighborhoods. As noted, the chief victims of crime are disadvantaged minorities, and it is not surprising that there is growing ghetto support for tough law-and-order measures. The difficulty, as discussed in chapter seven, is knowing precisely what to do and how to ensure that whatever is done is not at the expense of disturbed children and casual one-time juvenile offenders. There is no single clear answer to the crime problem, but *guaranteed jobs,* plus *mandatory lengthy jail terms* for second-time perpetrators of violent crimes, would go a long way toward removing both the economic incentive for wrongdoing and the violent predators who menace all society but most especially their own slum neighbors. Both programs are in the coalition vein, assuming that "law and order" can be converted from a racist code slogan to a shared objective.

    6. Finally, one point bears repetition. From a serious political standpoint, nationalism and separatism for minorities are material for parades and rhetoric, not a platform to win elections. Unless reformers have some unconquerable desire for defeat, the answers to minority problems in a democratic society lie in *forming majority coalitions,* in political bargaining that yields pluralities rather than polarization, substantive results rather than emotional relief.

Conclusion

Jesse Jackson, an outstanding moderate black leader since the 1960s, has set out an agenda for blacks that is equally applicable to Latin Americans. It is based on self-responsibility, including a higher voting participation rate (only 50 percent of 14 million eligible black voters are registered), overcoming a "definite welfare mentality," curbing black criminals, restoring school discipline and stable families, and ending drug abuse. Jackson sees the model for accomplishing these goals in third-world-style political and moral mobilization which will enable blacks "to rise up from decadence." In general, Jackson is for more work, more studying, and less self-destructive behavior, including abuse of authority—for concentration on substance.[33] The goal is noble: an end to the internalization of slums.

The likely alternative, as suggested before, is a basic split within minority communities between those who can indeed set aside slum behavior patterns and those who for one reason or another are trapped and entrap their children and some of their neighbors in their futile jungle. What this means is the emergence—or more accurately, the enlarging—of substantial class division within minorities. This is a pattern very much like that which has been characteristic of predecessor ethnic groups, a pattern of individual achievement rather than a mass exodus from the slums on some sort of unified, blood-brother basis.

Summary

The problem of race relations in the United States is chiefly the present status of blacks and, to a lesser extent, Latin Americans. Throughout the history of this country blacks have suffered severe exploitation and discrimination. During the civil rights movement of the 1960s, however, discrimination in employment and education lessened significantly, and larger numbers of blacks began to move into the middle class, as other urban minorities have done in previous generations.

But most blacks are still poor, their poverty worsened by broken families. They live in decaying urban ghettos and suffer from poor schooling, criminal records, and unemployment. Crime is especially severe in urban ghettos, and there is now a strong sentiment in the black community for crime control.

While federal attempts to deal with the problems of urban blacks by improving employment and educational opportunities and ensuring civil rights have had a positive impact, other programs have been unsuccessful, and many have been discontinued. But attempts to integrate blacks and whites in urban schools and suburban housing continue, evoking strong resistance to both attempts from working-class whites in the cities and middle-class whites in the suburbs.

Especially since the recent mobility of a significant portion of blacks and Latin Americans has lessened the cohesiveness of these minorities, it is unlikely that they can wield much political influence as separate groups.

Recommendations

- Provide employment for all who can work.

- Do not give minority members preferential treatment *as minority members* in employment, education, housing, or other government programs.

- Focus preferential treatment in government programs on disadvantaged persons, regardless of race or ethnic group.

- Continue and expand traditional mortgage and construction programs to help moderate- and middle-income families move to better housing.

- Aid family planning for all low-income people.

- Provide federal comprehensive, low-cost medical care.

- Provide federally funded low-cost day care centers.

- Offer options for schooling for low-income families through subsidies.

- Make mandatory lengthy jail sentences for second-time perpetrators of violent crimes.

- Form majority coalitions, not separatist movements, to achieve solutions to minority problems.

Notes

1. Japanese-Americans are the most notable example of this phenomenon. See "Success Story: Outwiting the Whites," *Newsweek*, 21 June 1971, pp. 24 - 25.

2. "Official Urges National Assessment as Hispanic-American Population Rises Sharply," *The New York Times*, 6 April 1976, p. 13.

3. For a brief outline of Marcus Garvey's ideology and exploits, see E. Franklin Frazier, "The Garvey Movement," *Opportunity* 4 (November 1926) pp. 346 - 48.

4. *Report of the National Advisory Commission on Civil Disorders* (New York: Bantam Books, 1968, p. 22.

5. "Revenue Sharing," *New Republic*, 22 June 1974, pp. 7 - 9.

6. See "Unemployment: 8%. . .9%. . . ?" *Newsweek*, 2 January 1975, pp. 54 - 63.

7. Ibid., p. 54

8. "Who Is Hurting and Who Is Not," *Time*, 14 October 1974, pp. 26 - 27.

9. See Eugene D. Genovese, "American Slaves and Their History," in *American Negro Slavery*, ed. Allen Weinstein and Frank Otto Gatell (New York: Oxford University Press, 1958), pp. 188 - 193. Also John W. Blassingame, *The Slave Community: Plantation Life in the Antebellum South* (New York: Oxford University Press, 1972), chapter 3, "The Slave Family." Stable family unions among slaves were considered conducive to the maintenance of order and work discipline and discouraging runaways.

10. Hal Bennett, "Also Known as Cassius," *Playboy* 18, no. 8 (August 1971).

11. Nelson Algren, "He Couldn't Boogie Woogie Worth A Damn," in Algren, *The Neon Wilderness* (Gloucester, Mass.: Peter Smith, 1968).

12. Toni Morrison, "Rediscovering Black History," *The New York Times Magazine*, 11 August 1974, p. 22.

13. Ernest Holsedolph, "Blacks Analyze Roots of Crime," *New York Times*, 9 December 1974, p. 40.

14. U.S. Department of Commerce, *Statistical Abstract of the United States, 1975*, (Washington, D.C.; Government Printing Office), Table no. 77, p. 57.

15.   "More Women Head Poor Black Homes," *New York Times*, 29 December 1973, p. 22.

16.   "H.E.W. Bars Full Matching Aid for the Poor in Abortion Cases," *New York Times*, 9 December 1974, p. 18.

17.   "Study Finds Sterilization Gains Fastest of Birth Control Methods," *The New York Times*, 5 May 1976, p. 12.

18.   Barry Commoner, *The Closing Circle* (New York: Alfred A. Knopf, 1971), pp. 237 - 239.

19.   Alfonso A. Narvaez, "Legislature Approves Measure to Curb Powers of Urban Development Agency," *New York Times*, 27 May 1973, p. 38.

20.   The optimistic view (more blacks buying older suburban homes) was propounded by Bernard J. Frieden, "Blacks in Suburbia: The Myth of Better Opportunities," in *Resources for the Future, Minority Perspectives*, no. 2 in a series on The Governance of Metropolitan Regions (Washington, D.C., Resources for the Future, 1972) p. 32. Among the pessimists are George Sternlieb and Robert W. Lake, see their "Aging Suburbs and Black Homeownership," *Annals of the American Academy of Political and Social Science* 422 (November 1975).

21.   William F. Pendleton, "Blacks in Suburbs," in *The Urbanization of the Suburbs*, ed. Louis H. Masotti and Jeffrey K. Hadden (Beverly Hills: Sage Publications, 1973), p. 173.

22.   The President's Committee on Urban Housing, *A Decent Home*, (Washington, D.C.: Government Printing Office, 1968), p. 42.

23.   *Fair Housing and Exclusionary Land Use* (Washington, D.C.: Urban Land Institute and National Committee Against Discrimination in Housing, 1974), pp. 13 - 51.

24.   The United States Commission on Civil Rights, *Equal Opportunity in Suburbia*, July 1974 (Washington, D.C.: Government Printing Office, 1974), pp. 51-59.

25.   See Anthony Downs, *Opening Up the Suburbs: An Urban Strategy for America* (New Haven: Yale University Press, 1973), pp. 73, 139.

26.   For a discussion of the new black bourgeoisie, see "America's Rising Black Middle Class," *Time*, 17 June 1974, pp. 26 - 27.

27.   Ibid., p. 22. For a strong statement on behalf of relocation of the poor to suburban job opportunities, see Neil N. Gold, "The Mismatch of Jobs and Low-Income People" in *Metropolitan Areas and Its Implications for the Central City Poor*, Commission on Population Growth and the American Future, Research Reports (Washington, D.C.: Government Printing Office), 5, pp. 441 - 486.

28.   See Andrew Brimmer, "Economic Developments in the Black Community," *The Public Interest*, issue on "The Great Society: Lessons for the Future," no. 34 (Winter 1974), pp. 146 - 163.

29.   Paul Delaney, "Long-Time Desegregation Proponent Attacks Busing as Harmful," *The New York Times*, 17 June 1975, p. 5.

30.   For a vitriolic attack on preferential quotas, see Nathan Glazer, *Affirmative Discrimination* (New York: Basic Books, 1976).

31.   "U.S. Alleges Bias in Realty Deals," *New York Times*, 17 April 1976, pp. 1, 12.

32.   "Black Enrollment Soars Amid Exodus of Whites to Suburbs," *The Trenton Times*, 9 May 1976, pp. A1, A13, A15.

33.   Jesse Jackson, "Give the People a Vision," *The New York Times Magazine*, 18 April 1976, pp. 13, 71 - 73.

6

THE PUBLIC SCHOOL SYSTEM: Broken Escalator for Minorities?

The turbulent 1960s were characterized by social ferment in an extraordinary number of areas, but for several reasons education was a particularly active arena of change, contention, and frustrated hopes. There was a wave of dissatisfaction at every level: high schools and colleges were alleged to be too large and too impersonal, lacking relevance to social and vocational needs. Conservatives complained of rising costs of primary and secondary schools and their alleged preoccupation with "frills" rather than basic skills, a failure to focus on discipline, patriotism, and morality. Liberals complained of rigid educational bureaucracies unresponsive to change, to educational innovation, and to the special needs of the poor, particularly the blacks and the Spanish-speaking, disadvantaged Latin Americans.

The Continuing Problem of Urban Schools

Now, after a decade of reform, things are not much better. Although opinions are by no means unanimous, the preponderance of attitudes is still distinctly negative. One of the sixties' most prominent spokesman for school reform concluded pessimistically, after the fact and the frustrations, that "it was for the most part nonsense, foolishness based on the mistaken idea that schools really did wish to be better and freer."[1]

DISSATISFACTION WITH URBAN SCHOOLS

The dissatisfaction with school systems was compounded by a growing literature of disillusionment and alienation. It has been reflected, for example, in an increasingly widespread citizen's revolt against school bond issues. Even some of the nation's more affluent suburban communities have voted down requests for new school buildings and for sizable pay raises for teachers. But the leading edge of the education problem has remained the blacks and Latin-Americans, for many of whom the system seemed to be working badly. It was charged that hundreds of thousands of poor minority children were not being given a fair chance in life because the educational escalator which carries other youngsters smoothly upward into skilled occupations had broken down in the slums. Absenteeism, vandalism, dropouts, and truancy were the hallmarks of the system that produced functional illiterates with useless diplomas. In response, educators offered partial denials, but to the extent they admitted to a sorry state of affairs, school authorities and teachers laid much of the blame on the deficiencies of parents and the neighborhoods.

URBAN SCHOOLS IN EARLIER DECADES

An examination of almost any big-city school system uncovers major deficiencies. Typically the system is badly run, characterized by poorly trained teachers, large classes, and minimal supportive facilities.[2] But were slum schools every very much better? In the early 1970s there began to appear interesting excursions into the mythical past aimed at dispelling the nostalgia which has clouded our assessment of current problems. Through the 1920s some things were much worse—classes were larger, teachers less qualified, administrators corrupt, and facilities barely tolerable. Persons who experienced school systems in the 1930s and who have retained memories unclouded by nostalgia are not all that ecstatic, either. Memories come to mind from that particular golden age of classes of forty-five and fifty sitting rigidly at their desks, and of narrow, bigoted teachers and administrators who seem in retrospect to have been suitable as staff for reform schools. This being the case, why the furor of the 1960s?

There seem to be several answers to this question. First, there is the relatively docile nature of the slum residents during the late nineteenth and early part of the twentieth century. Many were Germans, Scandinavians, WASPs, Jews, and to a lesser extent Orientals who came with a tradition of strong family support for education and a marked deference to authority. The education-oriented Jews, it was said, had been artificially proletarianized in Easter Europe by governments which kept them outside the main career ladders. Relocating to a country in which many opportunities were open for the educated, the Jews advanced rapidly into the middle class.

For all the ethnics the weaknesses and repressiveness of the school system were accepted, since with all its faults, the system rewarded obedience, hard work, and intelligence. Quite probably the happier (or at least more placid) decades owed more to the nature of students and parents than to the quality of teachers and administrators. However, the schools were widely hailed as one of America's successful institutions. Where else in the world did a larger proportion of the population have access to virtually free education from primary grades through postgraduate degrees?

It seems likely that past success led to present dissatisfaction. The fact that preceding generations have successfully navigated their way through the system while a large part of the current slum generation was clearly not doing so helped to generate pressure for change. Just as the laurels for earlier achievements were unfairly awarded to the schools, so was the blame for failure laid exclusively at their door.

DEFICIENCIES OF SLUM SCHOOLS

Some of the dissatisfaction is not misdirected, however. Even a cursory examination of the facts reveals plenty of room for concern. For example, despite undeniable improvements in slum-area schools in the past generation, many obsolete buildings are still in use, teachers tend to be less qualified than those in middle-class areas, and overall per-pupil expenditures are relatively lower. Most important perhaps, the schools have been unable to cope with the special problems of under-nourished, underprepared, and sometimes disruptive students from overcrowded homes, students who often are victimized by economic stress and a variety of familial and social problems. Whatever the causes, the symptoms are there for everyone to see: high dropout rates, low achievement scores, and serious discipline problems.

Conditions are not much better in slum neighborhood vocational and post-high school tracks. Often vocational training programs in public schools in slum areas are poorly equipped, organized, and administered, while vocational schools are old and specialize in training programs for redundant, dead-end occupations. This was, and is, in sharp contrast to many suburban vocational schools, where new buildings, modern equipment, selective admissions, and good placement records are more common.[3]

Slum-area students who manage to work their way through high school often experience serious educational disadvantages. As a consequence of years of low standards and overly generous grading and promotion policies, unprepared students who have been denied years of needed remediation and academic rigor find themselves poorly prepared for college. Even at the college level, however, there are far too many cases of degrees being awarded out of charity, apathy, fear, or outright teaching and administrative incompetence.

The rapid increase in black academic achievement to a point where there was a gap less than one-half year between school years completed by blacks and whites in the twenty-five to twenty-nine age bracket in 1970 must be viewed in this context. Completion of a given number of

© 1976 by NEA, Inc.

"I see you have a diploma. That's good . . . er . . . Can you read and write?"

Source: Reprinted by permission of Newspaper Enterprise Association.

years of education is no guarantee of academic *achievement.* Similarly, the proportion of black persons aged twenty-five to twenty-nine with a college degree in 1972 had reached 12 percent, as compared to 6 percent in 1960. This encouraging figure also must be deflated, because far too many blacks are receiving a second-rate college education and a devalued diploma.

This is not to suggest that real gains have not in fact been achieved. The illiteracy rate in the nonwhite population was reduced by almost half between 1900 and 1930, to the point where the illiteracy rate among New York blacks was lower than that of whites in most of the South. In 1917 only 455 blacks earned bachelor's degrees, mostly from southern institutions, and a turn-of-the-century study found that most students in the thirty-four black colleges were in fact doing only secondary school work.[4] In contrast, a very large proportion of the more than 100,000 blacks who graduated from college each year in the early 1970s had completed work of acceptable collegiate quality.

Whatever the spotty improvement in the past generation, blacks and whites were confronted with serious educational problems in the mid-1970s. To cite one remarkable statistic, while total illiteracy dropped from 11 to 1 percent in 70 years (1900 to 1970), almost a quarter of adults in the United States were classed as "functional illiterates" in 1970; that is, they were incapable of reading at the sixth-grade level.

Despite the special problems encountered in the slum schools, in many ways the 1960s was a decade of great educational progress. The persistent dissatisfaction with rigid traditional approaches accounted for a wide receptivity to innovation—open classrooms, use of audio-visual equipment, close linkages to universities, greater parent and student participation, and colorful new teaching materials. In many respects schools became the most open, responsive components of government, subject to inspection, monitoring, complaint, and change in a manner unknown in the criminal justice system or indeed any other aspect of government. There was, it is true, considerable unhappiness with a persistent decline in Student Achievement Test (SAT) scores, which some critics blamed on a combination of excessive addiction to television viewing and insufficient attention in the schools to educational fundamentals. As a result school officials have been subjected to increasing pressure to stress basic reading, writing, and mathematics skills and to relate inputs to outputs, a process summarized in the word "accountability." Nevertheless, despite all of the expressed doubts concerning education, the public remains strongly convinced that a good education is the road to security and higher incomes, as indicated in table 6-1. Judging from existing evidence, they are right. (See figure 6 - 1.)

"Corrective" Action in the 1960s

As noted, the principal unresolved educational problem was a growing concern over the failure of education available to school children of slum families. This led to a variety of attempts to find effective remedies.

COURT ACTION
Legal suits were initiated to persuade the courts to end the inequities between the financing of slum area and suburban schools. One authority estimated in the early 1970s that America spent about 15 to

Table 6-1.   THE IMPORTANCE OF EDUCATION TO SUCCESS

A recent survey asked:

How important are schools to one's future success—extremely important, fairly important, not too important?

Survey respondents gave these answers:

	National Totals	No Children In School	Public School Parents	Private School Parents
	N = 1,627	928	620	124
	%	%	%	%
Extremely important	76	71	81	84
Fairly important	19	22	16	13
Not too important	4	5	2	2
No opinion	1	2	—	1
	100	100	99*	100

*Due to rounding

Source: *The Condition of Education*, National Center for Education Statistics, 1975, U.S. Department of Health, Education and Welfare (Washington, D.C.: Government Printing Office, 1975). p. 13. (Data originally from Gallup International, Phi Delta Kappa, September 1973.)

20 percent more per year per capita on the average white school child than on the average black school child.[5] Uneven but significant progress in this direction was tempered by the realization that equality in per pupil expenditures does not necessarily lead to equality in student achievement. By the late 1960s and early 1970s some deeply troubled slum schools were already expending as much for their pupils as many suburban school systems.

REMEDIATION

The realization that slum children often lag years behind children from more favored families in school achievement has led to recommen-

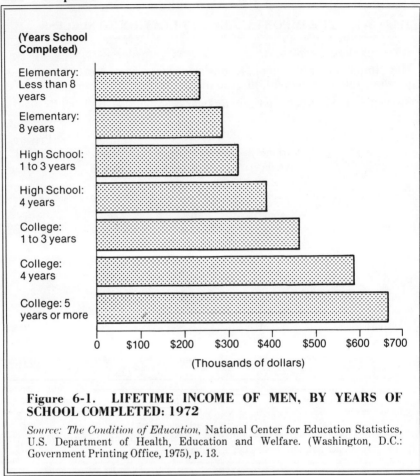

(Years School Completed)

Figure 6-1.   LIFETIME INCOME OF MEN, BY YEARS OF SCHOOL COMPLETED: 1972

Source: The Condition of Education, National Center for Education Statistics, U.S. Department of Health, Education and Welfare. (Washington, D.C.: Government Printing Office, 1975), p. 13.

dations for more strenuous efforts to close the gap. For example, Kenneth Clark has suggested that the Washington, D.C. school system devote most of its attention for an entire year to improving the reading abilities of the student body and experimenting with teaching machines, audio-visual equipment, and teaching materials especially designed for slum youngsters. Some schools have attempted to enlist the cooperation of parents through home visitations.

Beyond the guarantee of equality in school expenditures, it was argued that the cultural deprivation of slum children required extra money for remediation—for teachers' aides, tutoring, and smaller classes.

DECENTRALIZATION

Because it was assumed that slum students were doomed to failure by the unsympathetic attitudes of school administrators and teachers who treated their charges (and taught their pupils to see themselves) as uneducable animals, many of these young people were doomed to "death at an early age."[6] One effort to remedy this situation was to grant higher "combat pay" to good teachers willing to serve in slum-area schools, an endeavor which met with only modest success. A second approach was to wrest local schools from unresponsive central bureaucracies in the hope that parents would assume greater responsibility for their children's education if schools were, more or less, under their control. This resulted in a series of confrontations between small groups of activist parents and the teachers and school officials. To a considerable extent such localism proved unrewarding, often degenerating into a bitter struggle for jobs, power, and contracts with little sustained parental participation in school affairs and no improvement in educational quality.[7]

HEAD START

It became clear in the 1960s that hopes for rapid educational progress in ghetto areas were unrealistic because many slum youngsters were badly prepared for school. Middle-class children entered kindergarten or first grade with a background of parental attention, exposure to stories and printed materials, constant encouragement, and familial and peer examples. Because slum children often arrived with minimal skills it was suggested that prekindergarten training would help close this gap; hence the Head Start program. Part of the 1965 Great Society antipoverty effort, Head Start by 1972 had enrolled thousands of children between the ages of three and five, providing them with mental stimulation, structured games, stories, and other preparation for formal education.

Head Start proved popular and successful in helping slum children improve their performance in the first grades of elementary school. Unfortunately, it was found that the benefits tended to disappear by the fourth or fifth grade as the student was exposed to the deadening influence of family, friends, and the teachers available to slum children.

BUSING

Given the limitations of the slum school system, it was suggested that one quick way to improve the education available to slum children would be to transport them to better quality schools in middle- and upper-income neighborhoods. To some extent cross registration was an accomplished fact in open enrollment cities like Boston, but since it is difficult for children to travel long distances on their own, large-scale movement into schools in other neighborhoods required an organized transportation system—busing.

In practice, busing programs involving cross movement of children from different classes and races proved difficult and complicated. Parents from white neighborhoods were especially resentful of having their children bused away from nearby schools. Moreover, some of the white working-class city schools to which slum students were bused were themselves of unsatisfactory quality. A notable example is South Boston High School, scene of racial confrontation in the mid-1970s. "Southie," an athletics-oriented institution, prepares fewer than five percent of its graduates for college.[8] Further, busing accelerated "white flight," as white families relocated to the suburbs or sought other school options, adding to a growing shortage of white students in central-city public schools.

Large-city school systems in a number of northern cities are becoming predominantly black and Latin-American. While the outstanding example is Washington, D.C., where 80 percent of the public school pupils are black, other cities seem to be catching up. A preliminary 1973 census report for New York City revealed that black and Latin American children fourteen and under outnumbered white children by more than three to two—989,000 to 634,000. (This compares to a proportion of only one-third black and Latin-American only ten years earlier.) White families who could afford to do so were apparently leaving New York for the suburbs—between 1970 and 1973 the city's white population decreased by 8.3 percent.[9] To an increasing degree the remaining whites were middle-aged or older persons, or young professionals and business people without children.

Limited numbers of whites or poor quality of white students in predominantly white schools does not necessarily make integration a useless effort. Blacks who have graduated from substandard, white-dominated schools report that the experience was of great value in exposing them to white dummies—including teachers—in classes where they were the obviously outstanding performers. Their gains in morale and self-confidence compensated for their otherwise less than desirable learning experience.

The recognition that most of the white children and most of the good schools are now in the suburbs led to demands for metropolitan area-wide busing. However, in 1974 hopes of court action to mandate central-city - suburban school busing on a metropolitan area-wide basis were dampened by court decisions.[10] In any event, problems of scale, distance, and time make it unlikely that large-scale reverse commutation of central-city school children to suburban schools is a realistic possibility.

It may be noted that integration through busing was not intended as a one-way passage. A number of cities are experimenting with "magnet schools" aimed at achieving voluntary integration. These schools are designed to be so well staffed, equipped, and organized that they would attract substantial numbers of white city and suburban students to integrated central city schools. So far the results are moderately promising, but the scale is still very small.[11]

PERFORMANCE CONTRACTING

One of the attractive notions of the mid-1960s was (the past tense is used advisedly) performance contracting. The concept is simple: a private firm assumes responsibility for all or part of a school system and "contracts" to raise student reading or arithmetic test scores by a specified amount with the help of modern programmed teaching, visual aids, and other means. Failure to achieve the specified goal reduces or eliminates payment, while better than promised student scores result in bonuses.

In retrospect it appears that this approach was oversold, like so many of the social innovations of the 1960s. Some firms were not above coaching children to achieve higher scores, to the detriment of broader gauged educational purposes.[12] Moreover, the educational establishment was tempted to sabotage the approach as an unwarranted intrusion onto its turf. Most important, the problems entailed in motivating faculty and students and overcoming the serious deficiencies in the student environment proved far more complex and intractable than predicted.

MINIATURIZATION/FREE SCHOOLS

Complaints concerning overly large classes in giant schools have been leveled at the big multiuniversities and at high schools and middle-income neighborhoods. The charge that slum-area schools are inhuman partly because they are too big has been echoed in a number of books written in the 1960s and early 1970s.[13] Authors such as Kohl, Kozol,

Dennis, and Herndon all experienced exhausting, frustrating service in conventional slum school systems and achieved significant successes in teaching small groups of disadvantaged children in the face of hostile or indifferent educational bureaucracies. Drawing on this experience, one prescription for ailing slum schools is fragmentation into very small units—thirty to forty pupils—taught by dedicated, unconventional teachers unhampered by the dead weight of the administrative establishment. They have favored the nurture and growth of small "free schools" operating outside the existing system and offering custom-tailored, personalized educational experience unobtainable in large, traditional schools.

Opponents of this approach point out that all of the proponents are charismatic, highly talented personalities and their presence, or the presence of similarly gifted teachers, is essential for achieving even small-scale successes. Since such individuals are rare, it seems clear that the miniature free school is not a prescription for the salvation of millions of slum children. Most organizations are staffed by persons of modest competence, and any approach which apparently relies on the dedicated efforts of educational genuises is simply not practical for large-scale application. Despite this obvious qualification, to the extent that talent is available, these schools seem to promise every type of diversity, creativity, and choice. For this reason, while their sweeping claims to answer the ills of slum schools are clearly overstatements, free school proponents should be encouraged in their efforts.

CHITS

One suggestion for broadening the range of options open to slum-area parents is to provide them with earmarked funds to purchase their childrens' education in a school of their choice. Proponents of this approach argue that this would shake up the public school system by subsidizing various types of alternative schools and induce a healthy competition now missing from the system. Opponents counter with the argument that poorly educated parents would be fleeced by slick con artists, and that the public schools as a cohesive element in society would be fatally weakened in favor of fragmented, untested, and divisive private school businesses.

SECTARIAN SCHOOLS

One unsettled dispute concerns the future of religious schools. In many central cities, religious schools, particularly Roman Catholic schools, provide the strongly structured, well-disciplined, and traditionally oriented education favored by many working-class parents. In recent decades, sectarian schools have fallen on hard times, since they are forced to charge higher tuitions in the face of a decreasing "call" to low-paid religious vocations and less commitment to dedicated poverty on the part of lay teachers. Proposals to provide substantial public funds for religious schools have encountered strong opposition on the grounds of constitutional guarantees of the separation of church and state. However, if some acceptable legal ground can be found to laicize religious schools by separating and compartmentalizing their sectarian components, they would seem to offer an attractive alternative to many central city schools. The risks entailed by such an approach—the danger of perpetuating and exacerbating sectarianism as has occurred in French Canada and Northern Ireland—appear to be outweighed by its potential benefits in coping with a desperate situation.

DESCHOOLING/DECREDENTIALIZING

Failure to discover any simple solution to the problems afflicting slum schools and their pupils led to increasing demands that much of the educational and employment credentialing system be modified and downgraded so that the possession of a high school or college diploma need not be a prerequisite for entry-level—first job—employment or promotion. In part, the proponents of this approach echoed scholars who had long complained that intelligence tests, and indeed the school system generally, reflect middle-class experience and values, and thereby fail to accurately measure the true intelligence of slum children.[14] The courts have joined the movement by such decisions as that on the Duke Power Company case, requiring proof that a requirement for the IQ test scores or a high school diploma was job-related as the company claimed, instead of serving solely as an effective barrier to hiring disadvantaged minority persons.[15]

In its extreme frontier form, this approach goes back to pure Jacksonianism, so-called because President Andrew Jackson deliberately replaced educated experts with "plain folks" under what came to be known as the spoils system. Extreme proponents of this view assert that common sense and survival skills sharpened in poverty are far more important than such esoteric specialties as grammar, spelling, coherent writing, history, foreign languages, literature, or mathematics. Practically speaking, the Jacksonian principle has long been a feature of political life, particularly in selecting candidates for administrative posts not covered by civil service requirements. Furthermore, military service has been accepted as the equivalent of a particular credential, a high school diploma, by police departments and other agencies. There is in fact a trend in this direction. A variety of special examinations have been used by professional associations to assess the qualifications of persons with substantial practical experience and insufficient formal educational credentials.

Despite overtones of an attack on the educational system, some extreme proponents of deschooling have been asking for something different; they wish to award traditional diplomas to persons who do not possess traditional academic skills. In the view of many educators, however, granting this demand amounts to an outright devaluation of the system. In practice, there has been an uneasy, shifting compromise on this issue. Some ghetto youth have been promoted from class to class in grammar school, high school, and college without performing work of the quality required of traditional students. Others have been awarded substantial amounts of college credit for "life experience," a phrase which has been interpreted as paid employment in community agencies or even as a combination of sheer survival in slum conditions and a dollop of unpaid community service. On balance, there seemed to be less of this tendency in evidence by the mid-1970s. The pressures for easy credit diminished, partly because countervailing forces, including disadvantaged people who had worked hard to earn their diplomas, reacted against demands which seemed to threaten educational dilution.

Demands for decredentializing also appear to have slackened off because a small but steadily growing number of the ex-disadvantaged who have worked through the system are now strong defenders of traditional entrance requirements. The business recession of the mid-1970s also had an impact. As noted earlier, pleas for lower prerequisites for credentials or for total abolition are received with a certain amount of frigidity when jobs are in short supply even for experienced credential holders. Further, there is a recognition among minority leaders that minority people need genuine, substantive, marketable skills rather than suspect degrees in such fields as black or Puerto Rican studies, which offer poor job prospects for latecomers.

REMOVING DISRUPTIVE STUDENTS

From time to time in past years the media have reported on spectacular incidents of crime and disruption in the public schools, most notably riots, gang wars, murders, and rapes. The evidence indicates that the incidents which surface in the press and television are only the tip of the iceberg. Losses from day-to-day vandalism are estimated in the hundreds of millions of dollars, while a virtual reign of terror exists in many slum schools, with teachers almost as fearful as students.

Partly because of time-consuming civil rights restrictions designed to protect juveniles, school administrations have found it almost impossible to deal with the minority of disruptive students that make teaching a battle against odds, since so much energy and attention are drained off in the struggle to keep order. Secondary lines of defense—locks on school doors, pass systems, police and quasi-police guards, and various alarm-and-surveillance arrangements have proved palliatives rather than solutions. The answer, or, more accurately, one appropriate response, seems to lie in early identification and treatment of troubled children, and in the swift transfer of persistent juvenile troublemakers to alternative institutions where they can be treated and (if appropriate) confined. The argument that such institutions are presently inadequate is entirely valid. There is need for early, substantial action to create new institutions and transform existing schools and reformatories into centers for rehabilitation rather than retrogressive reinforcement of criminal tendencies. But this objection is secondary to protecting the rights of law-abiding youngsters who want to learn but cannot do so when they are exploited and terrorized by a minority of juvenile thugs and mentally disturbed adolescents.

The figures, which are horrendous, are quite probably underestimates: in 1975, 70,000 school teachers were injured seriously enough to require medical attention; $500 million was spent to repair damage by school vandals; there were 12,000 armed robberies in schools, 270,000 burglaries, 9,000 forcible rapes, and 204,000 aggravated assaults. However, extortion (bullies demanding money) is reported to be the most prevalent crime.[16]

These enormous totals do not distinguish between central city and suburban schools, but it is clear that the most serious problems are found in the slum schools. In the words of the president of the Boston Teachers Union: "Teachers who have spent years in preparation for the difficult, but rewarding task of education, quickly discover that the primary concern in many American schools today is no longer education, but preservation."[17] This suggests one reason for the relative success of parochial schools in slum areas—they have the authority to remove disruptive students swiftly.

BILINGUALISM

From time to time representatives of foreign-speaking groups have either called for the restructuring of public school education in favor of their native tongue or have sponsored private schools which stress proficiency in their native language. It was possible in some neighborhoods to preserve the illusion of residing in a European, Latin American, or Oriental land. For the most part this was a transitional phenomenon among immigrant groups—foreign-language newspapers and foreign-language schools lost clientele as foreigners completed the process of Americanization.

Hutchins Hapgood's description of New York's Jewish Lower East Side around the turn of the century offers a good capsule analysis of the transition. Hapgood depicts three groups of aspiring intellectuals: the Russian-speaking intelligentsia who dreamt of overthrowing the Czar, the Yiddish-speaking who worked for a strong Yiddish folk culture, and the Hebrew-speaking revivalists, a group combining promotion of the political aims of Zionism with attempts to resurrect Hebrew as a modern language. In contrast to these intellectuals, there were also the pushcart peddlers and other struggling businessmen, regarded as outlandish figures of fun with their mangled English and their pathetic attempts to Americanize their behavior. But, as Hapgood points out, it was they, the assimilationists, who were realists. They, not the romantic intellectuals, were the wave of the future. [18] The same pattern was replicated in other ethnic groups, with special ethnic variations. In brief, American tradition and opportunity has not lent itself to the Canadian, Swiss, or Belgian pattern of permanently established, often restless linguistic provinces.

One current example of this pattern is the tentative demand that "black English" be formally recognized and respected as a separate dialect. However, some black leaders have tended to be scornful of this notion on the grounds that proficiency in standard English is the key to advancement. In their opinion, it seems likely that students who develop black English as their "first language" will find many doors closed to them as adults.

More serious proposals have been put forward on behalf of Latin Americans. Many Puerto Ricans, Mexican-Americans, and other Latins came from disadvantaged rural backgrounds and are barely literate in Spanish. The adults have found English difficult to learn and provide little home help for their school-age children. Proposals for greater emphasis on Spanish, particularly in the early grades, with a gradual emphasis on English as the first language, have been widely accepted as a perfectly reasonable transitional entry into the cultural mainstream.

An unfortunate effect of these movements among minorities has been a growing confrontation between blacks and Latins. As native English speakers and the more urbanized of the two groups, blacks have a distinct advantage in mastering educational and political skills. Attempts to achieve substantial bilingualism, perhaps including a Latin American quota for jobs and school places, may run counter to emerging black opportunities.

The surge in the movement to have Spanish accepted as an official national language might be dismissed as a passing phase were it not for the heavy and continuing immigration of disadvantaged Latins. Since the United States population is, and will remain, overwhelmingly English-speaking, and since Spanish is not the dominant language in any sizable region of the United States, as French is in Canada, the prospects for successful, permanent official bilingualism are extremely poor. To the extent that bilingualism is fostered and perpetuated, the prospects are for a slightly altered version of the existing social and economic pattern, in which that part of the Spanish-speaking population with minimal command of English is relegated to the bottom of the ladder. Public policy aimed at transitional bilingualism through elementary school, optional in high school, would seem to be far preferable to a costly, inherently self-defeating excursion into a process outside the American tradition.

Which Way for Slum Schools?

The past decade has been marked by abortive attempts to relieve pervasive dissatisfactions about school performance—or more accurately, pupil performance—in the slum-area schools which attempt to educate the nation's disadvantaged minorities. The fact that attacks on the educational system are widespread, embracing suburban schools and the colleges, is scant comfort. But as has been noted, there *is* comfort in the fact that by many indices of change, there has indeed been genuine progress. For example, illiteracy has been reduced and the number and proportion of minority high school and college graduates have increased.

This discussion has focused on the prime cause for worry, the children in slum schools, particularly those who come from multi-problem, very poor families who can give them little or no support in their academic endeavors. The answers, if there are answers, are not the property of the schools. The Jencks study of 1973 has underscored the principal finding of the 1967 Coleman Report to the effect that family background, particularly completion of higher education on the part of one's parents, exercises a far greater influence on student achievement than school system expenditures, facilities, degree of racial integration, or even the quality of teaching. Figure 6 - 2, which compares reading scores for various categories of nine-year-old (third grade) children, points to a wide differential by race, which is linked to the differences in parental education levels.

If it can be assumed, as controversial psychologist Richard Herrnstein has suggested, that (1) there is a rough correlation between school achievement, occupation, and income levels; and (2) there is a rough correlation between parental intelligence and child intelligence, then the existence and persistence of relatively higher school achievement scores and higher rates of college attendence among higher-income families is only to be expected. Herrnstein indicates, however, that there is a great overlap in intellectual abilities by occupation and class. In particular, there is much latent talent among poor families that often goes untapped.

One of the most attractive features of American society is the extent to which poor, talented youths are afforded educational opportunities. The post-1945 veterans' benefits which provided years of tuition and subsistence were a major step in this direction. So too have been civil rights-generated programs of the 1960s like Upward Bound, which offered promising ghetto youngsters college scholarships.[19] But the problem is not so much a matter of opportunity denied for achievers but the complexity of dealing with the nonachievers. This group includes the students who require special help, ranging from remediation to physical and mental treatment, and the small, hardcore minority who require removal to intensive treatment units to permit the remaining students to learn in a tranquil environment.

In the course of past years the schools have been the subject of a number of innovations designed to improve their performance. Some, like teachers' aides and new teaching equipment, have proved promising. Others, like school decentralization and performance contracting, have been oversold disappointments. One promising approach is

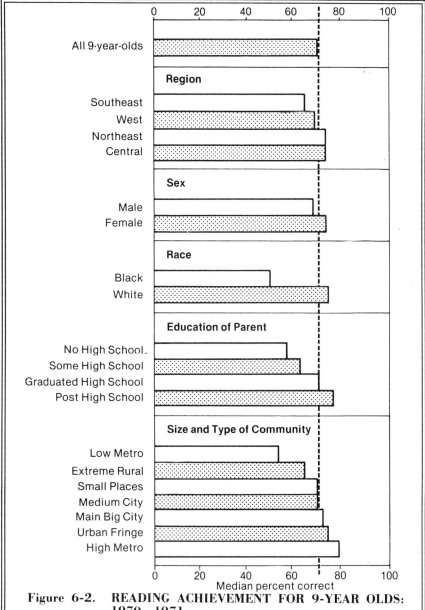

**Figure 6-2. READING ACHIEVEMENT FOR 9-YEAR OLDS:
1970 - 1971**

Source: The Condition of Education, National Center for Education Statistics,
U.S. Department of Health, Education and Welfare. (Washington, D.C.:
Government Printing Office, 1975), p. 25.

perhaps the most old-fashioned: a return to basic, highly structured education under the auspices of disciplined public schools and religious schools. In addition every encouragement should be offered to the inovators who run exciting educational alternatives, recognizing however that these are rare individuals whose successes cannot be replicated by the less talented.

One avenue which has absorbed far too much time and attention is busing. Under present demographic and social conditions there seems to be no way to assure a racial and ethnic balance in city and metropolitan area schools. "Magnet" schools designed to attract balanced school populations may be a partial answer, but with few exceptions, over the next generation there seems to be no valid, large-scale alternative to improving the quality of education in the cities.

Toward Mass and Class Education

For a generation or more Western and communist nations committed to equality in educational opportunity have been struggling with the mass-class issue. Any society has a limited proportion of executive, professional, and managerial jobs, and for the most part education is the key or the prerequisite to high status. Recognizing this linkage, egalitarian-oriented nations have been struck by the persistence of class. As was noted above, most children of high-status families do well at school, and most children of lower-class families do not do as well and hence remain in the lower class. This phenomenon has been ascribed both to genetic factors and to the opportunities, job horizons, and helping hands available to children of the middle and upper class.[20]

While the genetic factor is important, cultural and economic deprivation and lack of easy access to educational opportunity are clearly also important factors underlying the disproportionately small representation of those with lower-class origins on the higher rungs of the educational and occupational ladder. Since the latter part of the nineteenth century, the United States has been committed to open educational opportunity to a degree unknown in such socially stratified nations as England, France, or Germany. Nevertheless, a good deal of generation-to-generation transference of social and economic status occurs.

The major barrier to an open system in the United States has been
race and ethnic discrimination. Blacks in particular have been subjected
to a caste system in which their rewards for given levels of education
have traditionally been less than those accruing to whites. The dismantling of the low job ceiling for blacks during the 1960s, along with
an enormous increase in black college enrollment and substantial black
progress securing higher status jobs, suggest that the nation's most disadvantaged group (barring Indians) is at last entering the educational
and occupational mainstream. At the same time, as the above discussion indicates, a large proportion of the black population, along with
many Latin Americans, seems to be unable to work its way up the conventional educational ladder. A number of recommendations and
programs aimed at correcting this unfortunate situation have been
tried; some achieved moderate success, while others are largely in the
proposal stage. As noted, several of these seem to deserve continuation,
expansion, or experimentation.

Whatever the progress achieved in reaching the hardcore slum population, it is apparent that a schism has developed within the black and
Latin communities between those of demonstrated educational capability and the remainder. At best, success in remediation can be expected to
do no more than increase the proportion of successful educational
achievers. This leaves the basic problem of the social and psychological
implications of a meritocracy, a true merit system under which no one
with talent can deny that he (or she) was afforded repeated opportunities for educational and career advancement. Under such a system
individuals at the bottom of the ladder must face up to the fact that
there is no one and nothing to blame for their lowly status but themselves—it is not their color, not their religion, not their sex, nor their
ethnic origin, that has brought them face to face with failure. In a sense
discrimination is a great comfort to the untalented. They can delude
themselves with the notion that had it not been for an accident of pigment or ethnicity, they would be dining at the head table instead of busing the dishes. When the barriers are removed—and are perceived to be
removed—when scholarships and talent searchers produce successful
neighbors, fellow ex-disadvantaged who display every sign of advancement in a once hostile establishment, whom can the unsuccessful
blame?[21]

There is a refuge of sorts in accusation—the upward mobile can be
insulted as Uncle Toms, "vendus" (roughly, "sellouts"), traitors to their
race and class who have sold out their heritage for paltry rewards like a
good job, good schools for their children, and a good house in a safe

neighborhood. This is the standard response of those still living back in
the slums, who may also take refuge in contrasting the joys of ethnic
warmth in poverty to the relentless, ulcerating pressures of keeping up
with the Joneses, the fate of their superficially prosperous, but basically
unhappy, suburban cousins.

There is a special lesson in the merit system for women, victims of
vicious job discrimination who have begun to move into traditionally
male-dominated executive and professional occupations. Careers open
new realms of failure (as well as achievement) for a sex which has
historically found satisfaction in husband- and child-rearing. Since
most careers are, in one respect or another, ultimately disappointing,
the result of nondiscriminatory promotion through merit and discipline
will be to expose an increasing proportion of talented women to the tensions and frustrations of the workplace.

As the United States moves closer to a genuine meritocracy, particularly as very substantial numbers of the once disadvantaged move
into higher status positions, another factor should not be overlooked.
Affluent cousins and former neighbors can be counted on to extend
their face-to-face sympathies to the less fortunate, meanwhile bragging
of their new possessions, vacations, promotions, etc. Privately and
publicly, however, they tend to extol the virtues of hard work and
sacrifice responsible for their success while criticizing their poor
relations as miserable cretinous creatures, lacking in work and school
discipline and prone to all sorts of foolish behavior. More than a trace of
this attitude is already in evidence on the part of minority people who
have made it into the system.

There is a lesson to be learned from Sweden, a homogeneous welfare
state which comes far nearer to the ideal of a meritocracy than the
United States. The existence of an educational system in which students
are selected for well-financed university study strictly on the basis of
achievement, regardless of ability to pay, has caused special tensions.
As one professor stated, "We have a situation in which two-thirds of
young people feel that they have failed. And they can't blame the rich,
they can't blame the social system, they can only feel inferior. This
creates a far fiercer kind of alienation, a far harsher class system than
the old divisions by wealth."[22] Sweden may well be a preview of a mass-
versus-elite struggle in the United States in the 1980s. As the bitter
barriers linked to pigmentation and national origin continue to crumble,
a whole set of equally serious frustrations associated with class structure and a reward system based in large measure on education may
loom larger in importance.

Conclusion

The foregoing discussion may have struck some readers as an essentially negative appraisal of post-World War II educational trends and experiments. This is not the case. By and large "creaming" programs, the G.I. Bill, and scholarship programs for impoverished but talented youth have worked quite satisfactorily. Moreover, experience with the variety of programs designed to assist slum children has been mixed. The chief point to remember is that under proper circumstances, particularly when outstanding leadership and teaching skills are available and parents are supportive, most programs, including Head Start, busing, and magnet schools, have achieved substantial successes. The only program which seems designed for fraud and failure is performance contracting.

One program which has not really been tried seems worth pursuing. This is the chit system. Allied to this radical alternative is the possibility of providing large-scale direct assistance to nonpublic schools, particularly the parochial schools which provide the disciplined learning often lacking in slum area public schools. It should be frankly recognized that both these approaches pose a direct challenge to the traditional public school system. However, they represent a much-needed alternative within the broad range of educational opportunities necessary to meet the educational needs of slum children. Variety and experimentation, rather than rigid adherence to the traditional systems, should be encouraged.

Summary

In recent years there has been widespread dissatisfaction with public school systems among both liberals and conservatives, especially regarding the results of the system for disadvantaged minorities. In the last two decades there has been some improvement in minority educational achievement, but not enough. High dropout rates, low achievement scores, and serious discipline problems characterize slum schools.

During the 1970s there were many attempts to improve slum

schools, including providing increased funds, giving control of the schools to the communities, integrating the schools racially through busing, experimenting with "free" schools and performance contracting, and decredentializing. All of these attempts, with the exception of performance contracting, have been at least somewhat successful.

The problem in slum schools is not so much providing opportunity for achievers as providing remedial help for nonachievers and removing discipline problem students from the schools. Also, the fact must be faced that children's success in school depends more on their family background than on what happens in the school itself. Moreover, no amount of educational improvement can create total equality. Even in the most egalitarian socieities, class structure persists because of innate differences in individual ability.

Recommendations

- Identify and treat troubled children early in their education, and remove the minority of severely disruptive students from the schools to alternative institutions.

- Return to basic, highly structured education in disciplined public and religious schools, while encouraging educational alternatives such as "free" schools.

- Use Spanish with Spanish-speaking children in the early grades, gradually phasing over to a predominant use of English.

- Concentrate on improving the quality of education in city schools rather than on busing to achieve integration.

- Provide remediation for nonachievers.

- Give parents chits to purchase the schooling of their choice for their children.

- Give large-scale direct assistance to quality nonpublic schools in slum areas.

Notes

1.   Richard Flaste, "Embittered Reformer Advises: Avoid School," *The New York Times,* 16 April 1976, p. 35.

2.   See David Rogers, *110 Livingston Street* (New York: Random House, 1968).

3.   A 1972 survey found urban programs receiving a disproportionately small part of federal, state, and local vocational education expenditures. See Leonard A. Lecht, "Legislative Priorities for Vocational Education," *Inequality in Education,* no. 16 (March 1974), pp. 24 - 26.

4.   Clorette Henri, *Black Migration: Movement North 1900 - 1920* (Garden City, N.Y.: Anchor Press/Doubleday, 1975), pp. 182 - 185.

5.   Christopher Jencks, *Inequality,* (New York: Basic Books, 1972), p. 28.

6.   Jonathan Kozol, *Death at an Early Age* (Boston: Houghton Mifflin, 1967).

7.   See Marilyn Gittell et al., *School Boards and School Policy* (New York: Praeger, 1973).

8.   David Brudnoy, "Fear and Loathing in Boston," *National Review,* 25 October 1974, pp. 1228 - 1231.

9.   Robert Hanley, "White Exodus From the City Quickens," *New York Times,* 12 December 1974, p. 32. Interestingly enough, by the 1970s the city's annual net nonwhite migration figure had declined by 80 percent. Future increases in the nonwhite population will be due mainly to births rather than immigration. See Peter Kihss, "Migration from Metropolitan Area Called a Threat," *New York Times,* 30 January 1975, p. 39.

10.   See "Court Stops the Bus," *Newsweek,* 5 August 1974, pp. 38 - 39.

11.   See "Magnet Schools in Houston Stir Mixed Reaction," *The New York Times,* 8 October 1975, p. 37; and "Inner City School Becomes Magnet," *The New York Times,* 18 November 1975, pp. 39, 72.

12.   "Poor Performance," *Newsweek,* 14 February 1972, p. 97.

13.   Kozol, *Death at an Early Age;* Herbert Kohl, *36 Children* (New York: New American Library, 1968).

14.   Allison Davis, *Social Class Influences on Learning* (Cambridge, Mass.: Harvard University Press, 1962).

15.   Albert J. Rosenthal, "Employment Discrimination and the Law," in *The Annals of the American Academy of Political and Social Science* 402 (May 1973), pp. 94 - 95.

16.   Enid Nemy, "Violence in Schools Now Seen as Norm in Nation," *The New York Times,* 14 June 1975, p. 57.

17.   Ibid., pp. 1, 57.

18.   Hutchins Hapgood, *Spirit of the Ghetto* (New York: Schocken Press, 1966).

19.   Jencks, *Inequality,* p. 150.

20.   See "What Schools Cannot Do," *Newsweek,* 16 April 1973, pp. 78 - 85.

21.   There is an analogy here to the difference in morale between Military Police and Air Corps enlisted men during the Second World War. Noncommissioned ratings were sparse in the MPs, but overall morale tended to be high since MP units viewed themselves as misunderstood and put-upon guardians of the good name of the army in the face of a licentious, drunken soldiery. Since promotion to noncommissioned ranks was rare, an MP private could see himself as a discriminated member of a beleaguered garrison unfairly accused of sadism, arrogance, and megalomania.

Matters were very different in the Air Corps, which had at its disposal so many non-commissioned ratings that envious army divisions believed that even the barracks orderlies were staff sergeants. There were, however, honest-to-goodness privates and Pfcs in the Air Corps who could only conclude, in gloom and despair, that they had been passed over for promotion because of some personal failing. This lowly enlisted residue suffered from morale problems.

22.   Richard Eder, "Swedes, Flourishing Feel Guilt About Their Wealth and Debate Obligations to Others," *New York Times,* 26 December 1974, p. 12.

7

CRIME:
Everybody's Issue

Crises like wars and depressions are clearly identifiable; they have a beginning, a middle, and an end. Although the dates of each terminus may be disputed, certain facts are beyond argument: bombs fall, factories close, men and women are enlisted or discharged. On or about a given date a national emergency begins, and at a given time the emergency more or less ends.

The Extent of the Problem

The beginning of the crime problem cannot be so easily perceived; it seems to have sneaked up on us, spreading like a poisonous mist during the 1960s until it became one of the critical urban problems. The statistics are startling (although data on crime tend to be suspect, the errors are usually on the side of understatement): *34 million* crimes in the nation in 1960, *10.2 million* crimes in 1974. Almost 1 million violent crimes were committed in 1974, including 21,000 murders, 55,000 forcible rapes, 440,000 robberies, and 453,000 aggravated assaults. The reported victimization rate for the year was almost one in twenty—almost 5,000 crimes per 100,000 inhabitants.[1] Total public and private expenditures for crime control probably exceed $20 billion annually, an expenditure for internal security equal to over a fifth of the nation's total defense budget. Total full-time public and private security employment is probably over 1.0 million, almost as much as the 1.1 million soldiers in the U.S. Army.

A REALISTIC FEAR

The widespread fear of crime had to approach public hysteria before the liberals recognized it as a real issue rather than the bigot's euphemism for racism. Unfortunately awareness, early or belated, is not necessarily the high road to solutions, partly because of the strange, half-accepted position occupied by crime in our society. But it is important to start with the assumption that the law-and-order issue cannot be simply dismissed out of hand as disguised racism, class prejudice, or misperception. The fact is that much of the urban population is profoundly disturbed by what is perceived as a wave of lawlessness. Political victory depends, in many cases and places, on giving forceful expression to this fear and in promising to respond to it.

These feelings of apprehension are based on personal experience—
one out of every three Dayton, Ohio, and San Jose, California, households claimed to have been the victim of crime in 1970.[2] And there is a
constant barrage of colorful crime reportage in the media, which im-
mensely aids the process of terrorization. In their local coverage many
newspapers and television programs resemble a police blotter. To a
degree, crime consciousness is a matter of media highlights and
vignettes. Any sizable city furnishes a daily quota of grisly murders,
smashed windows and broken doors, broken and bleeding victims of
beatings, contagiously hysterical witnesses, and sullen apprehended
suspects shielding their faces as best they can from the cameras. The
constant repetition of this kind of news amounts to an indoctrination in
fear of crime.

While it is true that given extensive media coverage, one Boston
strangler frightened a million women with a dozen homicides, the
graphic, gory feature stories would have far less impact were it not for
the real enough substance of break-ins, snatched purses, and menacing
hoodlums. Very large proportions of city people, with or without personal experience to justify their fear, are genuinely afraid on the streets
and in their apartments. As for the parks, changes in moving picture
imagery can be instructive. For example, the last Hollywood movie
displaying a young couple strolling casually in the evening in New
York's Central Park dates back to the early 1950s. By the 1960s there
was the "Out of Towners," Neil Simon's depiction of a baffled
midwestern couple in Fun City. They are shown repairing to Central
Park for sleep after a holdup has deprived them of hotel money, only to
be haunted by a fearsome cloaked robber who mercifully departs with
no more than the husband's wristwatch.

Perhaps the people most severely victimized by crime are the
children and the aged. Adults, particularly males, have a relatively
higher crime tolerance level, partly because of the machismo swagger
required of males in American society. Young women may be fearful of
rape and assault, but many appear to accept the linkage between
central-city job and social opportunity and danger. Destructive behavior
in the classroom and playground and on the streets has given central-
city children an early exposure to vicious, dangerous crime, but it is the
old people who are most fearful of being robbed and hurt. And the consequences of their fear are far reaching: votes for law-and-order candidates, support for hard-line police behavior, flight to the suburbs, and
creation of intown and suburban fortresses complete with locks and
guards.

ROMANCE AND MISUNDERSTANDING

The romanticizing of the outlaw is an age-old historic phenomenon, partly because banditry represented one of the few avenues for the oppressed poor to strike back at the rich. Robin Hood's stealing from the affluent and allegedly splitting the take with the impoverished peasantry is widely celebrated, and there are similar folk heroes from China to the Ukraine to Latin America. There is Pancho Villa and Pugachev, Jesse James and Brazil's Lampiao, Jolly Roger pirates and Bulgarian Haiduks—populist brigands are a world staple.[3] Australia's Jolly Swagman is featured in that nation's national anthem. A number of these bandit raiders impinged into the political arena, while otherwise puritanical revolutionary groups, including the IRA, the Bolsheviks, and the Weathermen, have attempted to dip into local bank vaults or extort funds from local businesses for party activities. Occasionally, like Villa, yesterday's occasional bandit evolves into today's El Supremo.

As a nation which cherishes its real and imaginary frontier tradition, and is the product of lawless rebellion against the establishment, America has enshrined a long list of honored law breakers. Among the most prominent are the benign political outlaws: the perpetrators of the Boston Tea Party, the conductors of the underground railroad, the sit-in strikers of the 1930s, and the civil rights protesters and draft avoiders of the late 1960s. In each of these instances law breakers were eventually elevated to the status of heroes and law makers.

Even far less appealing fracturers of the legal code received a kind of posthumous benediction. Legions of industrious pulp writers and movie directors have assiduously mined the Billy the Kid and James brothers lodes. If hardly a sleazy western badman lacks his sympathetic fictional biography, numbers of eastern criminals have passed through the romanticizing fiction mill as well. Al Capone, Legs Diamond, and the Godfather are notable examples. The West and Midwest have also produced their modern candidates for the cinema in such colorful criminals as John Dillinger, Bonnie and Clyde, and Pretty Boy Floyd. Fiction is full of gentlemen jewel thieves. Clever con men and avenging gunmen are a fictional industry.

Throughout a very long history, and in most nations, it can be said that people who broke the law were frequently regarded as principled heroes. At least they were thought of as sympathetic and daring although misguided persons who were virtually forced into criminal behavior by an oppressive society. But while many nations cherish memories of bold, freedom-loving people's criminals in their distant past, crime in America is something special; compared to most nations, the United States remains violent and lawless. One index, the homicide rate, is revealing. In homicides per 100,000 population the rate in the United States is almost five times greater than that of Canada, and fourteen times higher than those of Sweden and England.

In the United States, as elsewhere, the attitude toward the criminal is often sympathetic, not only because he is a self-proclaimed people's champion or a daring entrepreneur who has escaped the deadening nine-to-five grind that oppresses the timid, law-abiding majority, but also because he is allegedly as much (or more) a victim as his victims. Often he is depicted as the product of brain damage or a cruel up-bringing, the victim of vicious penal institutions and a society which offers him contempt and near-starvation rather than gainful, respected employment. There are those, a few, who call for the replacement of prisons and traditional police-legal systems in favor of psychological and social treatment. While this is a minority position, the majority of the population no longer supports a harsh approach to the criminal. This change in attitude is exemplified by the declining popularity of ex-tralegal lynch mobs or prisons specializing in chain gang labor, starvation, and torture.[4]

Paralleling the ambivalence in attitudes toward the criminal, the attitude toward law enforcement in the United States has also been am-biguous. There was, from the very founding of the British settlements, a notion that the state, through its law enforcement arm, had the duty and obligation to regulate private morality. Punishment for drunken-ness, Sabbath-breaking, gambling, blasphemy, and adultery were visited upon the citizenry. Yet outsiders—Indians, Chinese, blacks, tramps—were often the victims of socially approved legal or quasi-legal violence which at times verged on genocide. Both the perpetrators of massacres and the outlaw were glorified; Custer and Jesse James were both folk heroes. Police behavior also reflects a certain ambivalence. Traditionally American police have been, figuratively but legally, coex-isting with law breaking in the bedroom, the barroom, and at the card table. But they have exhibited, with public approval, a harsh, often il-legal treat-'em-rough attitude toward society's chosen victims.

VICTIMLESS CRIMES

Much of the attention of the police and the legal system in general is given to enforcing a past puritanism. It focuses on alcoholism, "soft" drugs, gambling, pornography, and various aspects of sexual behavior.

Not enough seems to have been learned from the twelve-year fiasco in the attempt to control liquor through Prohibition or from the failure of antidrug, antiprostitution or antigambling legislation. Fortunately an increasingly tolerant attitude toward gambling and sex has relieved the law enforcers of some of the tedious, costly, and corrupting effort of enticing, arresting, and prosecuting prostitutes and homosexuals, Mann Act violators (interstate fornicators), and participants in card and dice games.

Despite the thunderous attacks of those who profess to see the emergence of prostitution from back streets and homosexuality from the closet as giant steps on the road to perdition, it appears that much of the nation's underside can be exposed in bottomless bars without much damage, as long as open-street infestation of whores and pimps can be dealt with under loitering ordinances. The remaining task is to finish the job of decriminalizing an overcriminalized society. This can be done by removing the penalties from victimless crimes and treating the self-destroying addict—the compulsive gambler, drug addict, or alcoholic—as a medical problem rather than as a subject for useless legal harassment. (This charge flies in the face of one recent fad, namely the effort to deal with the problem of street crime and burglary by attacking drug addiction. Exaggerated estimates of the damage done by addicts has been accompanied by portrayals of pushers as poisoners, while liquor manufacturers and distributors who furnish the material for the far more widespread and deadly disease of alcoholism are regarded as legitimate businessmen.)

One urgent task for those who believe in effective government intervention, as opposed to symbolic political expression—that is, law-and-order speeches useful only for blowing off steam and perhaps vote catching—is to develop and disseminate hard information on alcoholic and drug addiction. This should be combined with more extensive medical treatment programs for the entire range of impulse-driven victims of self-inflicted damage—alcoholics, drug addicts, and not least, the compulsive gamblers. Meanwhile, short of the most vicious forms of sexuality such as abuse of children, bestiality, and sadism-masochism, bedroom behavior can be safely ignored. And so far as pornography is concerned, one can anticipate that the market for views of naked grappling and grunting bodies will run its course, finding only a small hard core of regular customers.

The decriminalization of victimless crimes would permit resources to be concentrated on those aspects of crime which represent a genuine threat to the community. These are few enough in number: street crime, particularly mugging and other threats to personal safety, followed by robbery and burglary. This is not to suggest that crime enforcement be assigned priorities through some sort of unpopularity contest. White-collar crime—forgery, embezzlement, fraud, and stock swindles; adulterating food, drugs, and beverages; bribery and price fixing—is often invisible but can be as devastating in its effects. The spectacle of business swindlers, fixers, and political thieves strongly supporting "law and order" against slum criminals is as familiar and depressing in the 1970s as in earlier generations.

There are those who argue that this "crime in the suites" provides an excuse for the street criminal. If a vice president is known to have accepted bribes in his office and yet remained out of jail, how dare we be harsh with the mugger or burgler who lacks the law degree and access to political power to escape conviction and sentence? No one can deny that there is much justice in the argument for even-handed application of the law. But since this book is concerned with city life, it must focus on the kinds of crimes that make cities unhabitable. And they are not lucrative violations of the Sherman Anti-Trust Act, short-weighting and adulterating grain exports, or massive computer-manip-ulated stock frauds. They are not even the big-time depredations of the Mafia. They are the poor man's crimes, crimes with overtones of physical violence, violations of one's person or home.

CRIME: HARD, SOFT, AND MEDIUM
In the nineteenth century poor man's crime in the United States was pretty much a slum phenomenon, with perpetrators and victims residing in the same circumscribed territory. Successive waves of slum dwellers, often inhabiting the same decaying neighborhoods, existed un-der execrable conditions, exhibited all of the signs of deep-dyed criminal behavior, and subsequently moved up in the world and away from the tenements. Each departing group in turn deplored the inherent criminal traits of the new crop of slum dwellers. At one time or another the Irish, the Jews, the Chinese, and more recently the Italians each were labelled as a group peculiarly and genetically prone to scoundrelly activities.[5]

Stereotypically, the transition through the slums has left its mark. The Irish run the police and the prisons, Jews have become lawyers and judges, and a few Italians earn very good incomes as the big business-men of organized crime while other Italo-Americans are police, at-torneys, and judges. All three groups currently are active in demands for stern action against the disorderly street crime still characteristic of the slums but presently the hallmark of blacks and Puerto Ricans.

As always, the principal victims of crime are the slum-dwellers themselves.[6] Theft and robbery are easiest and least dangerous when performed on one's neighbors. As noted, while the children and the aged are the principal victims, teenagers and young men are the main population reservoir of the criminals.[7] Moreover, the young hoodlum risks very little—a study revealed that only 4 percent of juveniles (fourteen- and fifteen-year-olds) arrested for violent crimes in New York City were sent to institutions.[8]

Urgency for crime control.   If history is our guide, if we are confronted with no more than another phase of a transitional historic phenomenon, why the fuss? Give the blacks and Latins another generation of education and mobility, it is argued, and they too will move out of the street-crime class and join the establishment in attacks on the filthy hoodlums that infest the slums and spill over into other neighborhoods to threaten decent, hard-working folk.

The reasons for urgency can be found in two areas. The first, as was mentioned earlier, is the presence of the media. Far more immediate and penetrating than the garish *Police Gazettes* of the 1890s, television strikes home in a way that even the sensational tabloids of the 1920s and 1930s could not manage. The public is sensitized to crime in a manner and to an extent that was simply not possible before television. And there is plentiful grist for the TV mill in films of middle-class and working-class victims, struck down in everyday surroundings by thugs.

The second reason for the alarm is that crime is no longer perceived as something that happens to "them" in Harlem, Brownsville, Little Italy, or the Five Points, an activity of strange slum animals, prone to drunkenness and violence, destroying each other. Crime has come out of the slums to the middle class. City stores, parks, offices, homes, and persons are viewed as unsafe from crime, vulnerable to attack by criminal elements foraging out from the tenements. In short, the time has passed when violent crime was a subject for middle-class wonderment or amusement. Its worst manifestations are no longer confined to the decaying sections of the core city, or to the rare crime of passion among the rich, or to the juicy political scandal.

In New York during the 1880s the police cordoned off the Wall Street area, shooing away all shabbily dressed outsiders, thus reserving the street for the stock frauds so characteristic of the period. Western communities frequently enacted a "dead line," a boundary street which legally separated the respectables from the cowboys, gamblers, and prostitutes. Now these geographic deadlines are gone, but there has been a new growth of residential fortresses in outlying neighborhoods, tiny enclaves that have continued and expanded the time-honored practice of screening out suspicious-looking strangers.

Faced with a perceived threat to life and property, a large part of the urban citizenry and its leaders have reacted in a fashion which might have been predicted from earlier law-and-order campaigns to rid western towns of infestations of bad men. In the West no-holds-barred sheriffs, occasionally helped by deputized posses, cleaned out the law breakers by swift and brutal terror, thumping heads freely and having frequent recourse to gun and noose, unencumbered by excessive concern for civil rights or for overwhelming proof of guilt. And, following the traditions of the violent South from which some of the westerners had emigrated, there was often a sliding scale for justice. The more heinous the crime (such as murder or rape of a respected citizen, or rustling) and suspect the defendant (that is, if he were a member of the local discriminated group), the less weighty the evidence needed to convict and hang.

Crime as entertainment.   It is true that crime remains a source of entertainment as well as terror. The legendary West is still celebrated in national folklore—the elements of bad man, sheriff, posse, vigilante, wild bunch, and range war all remain staple fare for movies and paperbacks. Similarly, the eastern tales of organized and disorganized crime and crime fighting represent a sizable branch of the publishing, movie, and television industries. Criminals, detectives, gangs, and private investigators provide a steady source of entertainment and amusement. A step or two removed from the reality of the *French Connection* and the *Godfather*, many of the semirealistic crime genre convert grim and vicious people and nasty behavior into light entertainment, manufacturing melodrama, sentiment, and comedy from genuine agony.

One possible consequence of this type of fictional treatment seems to be a desensitization of much of the public to the reality of crime. In fiction it is usually portrayed as a game of wits, and even in the news media crime is always a step removed from reality. The TV news camera turns perfectly ordinary people into actors and extras in a near-realistic drama. Onlookers and participants bask in publicity; smiling teenagers point to the cameras, ignoring the mangled corpse being carried away on a stretcher just a few feet away. Paradoxically, the extensive media coverage which helps to scare the daylights out of the viewer also makes the real event seem less real. The criminal is a nonperson, an incomprehensible manacled figure, head bent, trying to hide his impassive face. He might as well be a visitor from Mars. This situation has given considerable force to the argument for the hard-boiled solution—or, more accurately, reaction. Who can object to having these alien vermin shot, incarcerated, beaten, exterminated?

The conservative approach.   Insofar as a distinction can be drawn between liberals and conservatives in their attitude toward crime, it lies in this area. The conservative does not pretend to understand the criminal, who he tends to think is either a brain-damaged animal or a greedy, callous ethical weakling. The answer he sees to such subhuman behavior is harsh, certain punishment, with jails providing bleak places for lengthy suffering and penitence to instill fear in the potential repeater criminal. Approaches to crime based on childhood diagnosis and treatment, teenage therapy, or environmental changes have little appeal. The idea seems to be to frighten the wavering adolescent or, failing that, to wait until he commits a crime and then catch him and punish him severely. The criminal must reform, be executed, or spend most of his life in prison, removed from the society he has harmed. The conservative's basic approach rests on the morality of punishment as a consequence of crime, and on instilling terror of the police, the courts, and the prisons as the only language the criminal animal can comprehend.

The principal drawback to this tough approach is that for a number of reasons, it does not appear to work very well. And interestingly, when conservatives are faced with failure, their answer is usually more of the same: hire more police and even elect police chiefs as mayors.[9] But the resounding electoral triumphs of hard liners like Mayor Rizzo of Philadelphia have had little effect on basic crime rates. To identify the main reason for this failure, it may be instructive to return to the scene of a similar disastrous effort in pacification—Vietnam.

REASONS FOR URBAN CRIME

In Vietnam moderate pressure on a guerrilla rebellion met with little success. Subsequently, urged on by tough-minded militarists and Cambridge scholars, the United States poured more money and personnel into Vietnam until the American constabulary forces passed half a million and native allies fielded a million soldiers and policemen. Yet the enemy, poorly armed, decimated in years of battle, appeared, in the then Secretary of State's words, to have "the recuperative powers of the Phoenix." Even a civilian destruction program (cleverly titled Operation Phoenix) aimed at wiping out the opposition infrastructure failed in its mission.[10] In the face of a population mistrustful of a brutal and often corrupt pacification force, which increased rather than reduced social and economic imbalances and suffering among the native people, rebellion flourished and pacification barely held its own.

Fortunately, we are not presently confronted with a well-organized, politicized revolution in our slum areas. And even if there were such a development, America's criminal poor (unlike the rebels in South Vietnam) are a tiny minority of the population. Nevertheless, the analogy is painfully close in the following ways.

1. The law breaker is often sheltered and shielded by a population mistrustful of the police and frequently more fearful of the criminal than of the law.

2. The police often are brutal and corrupt, harsh on some law breakers but protective of others through secret, mutually beneficial arrangements with favored criminals.

3. The population has legitimate grievances which may be expressed in some types of banditry with at least a touch of genuine or professed Robin Hoodlumism.

4. Places of incarceration for apprehended criminals often serve as crime schools; there is little or no opportunity for education or learning legitimate occupations. So the law breaker perfects his criminal skills, often coming to jail as an opportunistic amateur but leaving a hardened professional who hates the establishment and is psychologically ready for revenge on it.

In earlier years, it is probable that most of the nation's liberals would have been unsympathetic to a billyclub approach, partly because of a guilty conscience, a belief that the criminal is a starving man condemned by an unjust society for sleeping under bridges and stealing bread. However, in the late 1960s and early 1970s there have been certain changes. One of these was certainly the combination of a real increase in both the number of crimes which the middle class has actually experienced and in the similar (or worse) crimes they experience through the media.

There are, of course, explanations relating to the social problems of the present occupants of the slums.[11] There are also suggestions that the increased crime rate is a demographic phenomenon; that is, some theorize that we are still suffering from the effects of the post-World War II baby boom, and the teenage bulge will begin to contract in the late 1970s. Since teenagers form the bulk of the street criminal population, we can hope for better days in the 1980s.

It is also suggested that crime is a last-ditch substitute for legitimate labor. Who can blame the desperate, unemployed man who steals to clothe his children, or the jobless girl who turns to prostitution to feed her family?[12] But this tolerant attitude is partly past tense. Despite continuing elements of romanticism and compassion, the 1972 election returns and the 1976 presidential campaign suggest that a sizable share of the population, including blacks and liberals, regard societal explanations for crime as deceptive rationalizations. They are apparently ready to accept the notion that most criminals must be combatted as outright enemies of the people, not viewed as a misguided fellow citizen (there but for the grace of God!) susceptible to reason and reform. The fact is that despite the failure of old-fashioned repression, many liberals are prepared to vote for law-and-order candidates. From their point of view sympathetic rehabilitation does not seem to have worked (however much reformers and the slum population may claim that it was never really tried). In the absence of alternatives, they are ready to support traditional police practices.

Clearly, the bipartisan consensus on the crime problem has significant racial overtones. Much of the white public is uneasy at the sight of a group of black teenagers on a poorly lit street. Mugging, violent robberies, and indeed most of the crimes which are perceived as physical threats, as distinct from the high-powered stock frauds and other big money thefts, are seen as emanating from the black—and secondarily the Puerto Rican—population. It is interesting to speculate on the extent to which the rash of black Superfly crime movies of the early 1970s, applauding the exploits of dudish studs as pimps and cocaine dealers, tended to reinforce unfavorable stereotypes.

HARD FACTS ABOUT CRIME
So far as most of the public is concerned, learned arguments over causation and cure are of no great interest. The question is, what do we do now? Moreover, liberal failure to recognize the legitimacy of the concern over crime or the need for response leaves a major urban con-

stituency ripe for the demagogue, racist, or political patent-medicine salesman peddling placebos and counterproductive slogans.

The first task obviously is to establish the facts. In 1973 there were almost five million arrests in the United States, almost one million for serious crimes (murder, rape, robbery, assault, burglary, larceny, and auto theft). Over one-third of these arrests for serious crimes were of persons under the age of eighteen. Full-time employment in various crime-fighting activities was over 900,000, almost 600,000 of them police, and total public expenditures for these activities approached $13 billion. Crime rates varied widely—businesses located in ghetto areas were twice as likely to be victims of vandals, shoplifters, or burglars as suburban businesses, although both suffered almost equally from bad checks and employee theft. The clearance rate for crimes (crimes solved and perpetrator caught) ranges from a high of 81 percent for murder to lows of 29 percent for robbery and 16 percent for auto theft.

In 1973 the two large cities with the highest rate of violent crimes were Baltimore and Detroit. New York and Washington, D.C. were close—all four had rates for violent crime approximately seven or eight times higher than the United States average for very small cities of under 10,000. Larger cities also differed. San Francisco's rate for violent crime was three times higher than San Diego's, Chicago's three times higher than Milwaukee's, New York's twice as high as Philadelphia's. In 1973 there was a total of 205,000 adult prisoners and 75,000 juveniles in detention homes and other institutions.[13]

Another important fact about crime is that the real victims are the blacks. A black teenager in a large urban ghetto faces fairly heavy odds: one chance in three of picking up a police record, one chance in eight of dying violently.[14] In 1973 more blacks than whites were victims of homicide, despite the fact that the white population was nine times larger. The data on robbery and rape further support the theme of black victimization—blacks are twice as likely to be victims as whites.

It is clear that by all rights, blacks should be the principal supporters of effective law-and-order campaigns, and indeed by the mid-1970s black politicians were fully cognizant of that fact. If there were some way to separate crime control from the personnel and operating practices of existing police forces, a sizable portion of the black population might well be enthusiastic backers of a crackdown on criminals.

The battle against crime in slum areas is complicated by one significant but often overlooked statistic: crime means jobs and money. It is estimated that one in five young men in some slum areas are employed full-time in criminal activity, while another of the five receives part of his income from part-time criminal activity.[15] Furthermore as slum residents have taken over organized criminal enterprises, particularly in gambling and drugs, a variety of slum capitalism has flourished, mostly by keeping local money in the neighborhood, but also by catering to middle-class vices.[16] At least some of this accumulated capital seems to be going into such legitimate businesses as bars, restaurants, and real estate. To a degree, the future of black capitalism may depend on criminal entrepreneurs in the slums. If they emulate previous generations of prudent criminal bosses, they will convert surplus funds into respectable enterprises which provide opportunities for families, friends, and neighbors.

Two other points are worth mentioning. Heroin is not the bogey nor the crime generator that some suppose it to be. While it is certainly associated with thieving, most of the addicts are too passive and too withdrawn for organized gang activity, armed robbery, or mugging. Addicts get the money for drugs from honest employment, minor theft, their families, and prostitution, but mostly from hustling drugs.[17] Moreover, most were criminals before they took to the needle.

It is true that the heroin trade and use has generated some increase in violent crime, including gang activity, but for the most part the "war" on heroin is a publicity-rich fringe attack on the crime problem which is likely to have minimal impact on the amount of street crime.

A second point: the amount of recorded crime is extremely low compared to the real figures. It is estimated, for example, that the number of burglaries is at least three or four times as high as the number reported to the police. Most people simply do not report minor crimes because it involves too much trouble and there is virtually no chance of recovering the stolen property.[18]

Before leaving the subject of criminality and taking up the problem of the police—not a great leap in some respects—two further statistics might be noted. The majority of homicides (nearly 7 in 10) are committed with firearms, a circumstance which should give powerful support to tough gun-control legislation.[19] (There were 18,520 victims of firearms in 1972).[20] Second, most homicides are private crimes involving family, "friends," and neighbors. In a surge of passion or in a drunken argument someone reaches for an uncontrolled firearm, and, depending on his aim, another corpse or two is added to the roster. The fact that the perpetrators and victims are often related by blood or other close ties is also important. If one does not want to be shot or wounded he is in little danger from strangers; it is usually his family and friends he has to worry about.

The Criminal Justice System

In many ways the system constructed to deal with crime—the police, the courts, the prisons—is as much of a problem as crime itself.

THE POLICE: WYATT EARP AND HENRY PLUMMER

The nation has been continually vacillating between diametrically opposed views of the police (and other upholders of the legal system). On the one hand the police have been seen as thuggish, corrupt pigs, tools of a vicious and grasping establishment. They have crushed trade unions, beat young people, oppressed the poor, the blacks, and Puerto Ricans, while ignoring the misdeeds of the rich and fellow policemen, who were permitted to buy or influence their way out of justly deserved punishment. On the other hand, police have received more than equal time in the media portrayed as warm-hearted, brave, and underpaid guardians of the law-abiding majority, a thin blue line holding off the subhuman criminals.

The daily evidence of a dual role of the police as law enforcer and lawbreaker which surfaces with every investigative commission has deep historic roots. On the one hand there is the Wyatt Earp tradition—honest and fearless lawman guns down lawless gunmen. But there is also a Sheriff Henry Plummer tradition, in which a law enforcement official runs a criminal gang. This police gang uses its inside information and legal weaponry to prey on the very people—in Plummer's case, Idaho miners—that official has sworn to protect. America has its share of both police heroes and police burglars—police who protect and police who steal and riot.[21]

In the media "Dragnet" was a notable example of a show which portrayed the Los Angeles police as stern but humane, even-handed guardians of law and order, sadly misunderstood by the only occasionally grateful public they served. "Barney Miller" maintains this tradition for law enforcement in New York City, although the new breed is witty as well as brave and compassionate. Other media examples, such as the film "Serpico," have attacked the police as racist and crooked—pretty much the opposite of what their supporters claim.

As usual, the truth is complicated. Police forces vary greatly from city to city. It has been argued that police behavior varies in a number of ways and that lax or tough, communities pretty much get the kind of law enforcement they really want (as opposed to what they say they want).[22] Some police departments, particularly in small working-class cities, are composed of barely educated, underpaid, sometimes corruptible incompetents. Others, particularly in large cities, contain a sizable but still fairly small proportion of college graduates and highly proficient professionals.

Alienation from slum population.   But in every variety of police department there is a pronounced tendency to view the underclass as a loathesome breed whose evil is fully comprehended only by the police who meet them in their natural habitat and by their victims. As seen by the police, the betrayers of justice are the bleeding hearts, the judges, lawyers, and social workers who handle the subdued criminal after his apprehension when he is harmless, well scrubbed, and full of false promises to sin no more. There is, in addition, an element of fatalism in police attitudes toward criminals. Like their nineteenth century predecessors, modern police are convinced that crime is endemic in certain population groups. Arguments that time and history alter the nature and composition of the underclass are met with outright denials or rationalizations. ("Things were different in the 1930s; these days there are plenty of jobs.")

The alienation of the police from the slum population is compounded by the fact that increasingly, in many cities, the police department has become an Irish preserve with a significant Italo-American component. To the poor Irish in the 1930s, the police were not "them" but "us"; they were not the imcomprehensible, brutal occupying power that the police represent to the blacks or Puerto Ricans, today's slum dwellers. (This harsh portrait is obviously overdrawn; attitudes toward the police are as mixed as the roles they play. In one real-life episode they are heroes rescuing old people from young hoodlums; in another they indulge in a needless display of arrogant contempt and brutal force.)

"And when Murphy leaves, I'll have outlasted eight commissioners, three mayors, and two investigative commissions."

Source: Drawing by Modell; © 1973, *The New Yorker Magazine, Inc.*

It is not surprising that policemen often feel the people they protect are ingrates; they forget or never really comprehend the history underlying ghetto neighborhood suspicion and hostility. Just as they find it difficult to differentiate between harmless high spirits and dangerous thuggery, so the ghetto citizenry tends to lump them all, grafter, sadist, and decent patrolman, into a faceless, alien force.

Minority recruitment.   In the past decade there have been a number of attempts to make police departments more representative of the populations they serve. To a degree, this has been achieved in terms of education. The age of grammar-school cops lingers in the rural South, but in most big-city police forces a high school diploma is a minimal entrance requirement. Moreover, attracted by high salaries, federal incentives such as Law Enforcement Assistance Administration (LEAA) support, and the improved chances of promotion for the educated policeman, college graduates have begun filtering in. But this trend is far from reaching a critical mass; widespread antiintellectualism among police has not yet been converted into casual acceptance of a college degree as the norm.

In contrast to rising educational levels, minority recruitment has lagged. While there has been some progress—the proportion of minority police in big cities rose markedly in the late 1960s—the minority proportion has stabilized in the 1970s.[23] Black police are no longer rare—in Philadelphia and Newark the black proportion of the force is 17 percent, in Atlanta 22 percent, in New York 7.6 percent, in Washington, D.C. 40 percent. Blacks are still lagging—the 25,000 black policemen out of 500,-000 in the nation are still less than half of the black 12 percent of the national population. But the 25 percent gain in the five-year period from 1969 to 1974 suggests that the tradition of white-cop-beating-black-suspect may be slowly fading into the past. The slowness in assimilating blacks into the police has been a case partly of institutional foot-dragging, based on the understandable assumption that a job that pays as well as a policeman's should be reserved for one's friends and relatives.

The question of physical attributes is also raised when found useful. A police lieutenant who believed that height in a patrolman helps him keep the peace (this officer was six feet, four inches) suggested that undersized Latins who were demanding a reduction in the height minimum to five feet, four inches could be usefully employed only to inspect the undersides of automobiles, to rescue tots from wading pools, or to sneak into bar rooms without disturbing the upper halves of Dutch doors.

Running counter to the trend toward a better-educated policeman is the demand from minority groups that police forces drop the requirement that applicants have high school diplomas and no police record (and be able to swim). In practice, these criteria combine to wipe out a goodly share of potential lower-class black applicants. As for highly qualified blacks and Puerto Ricans, less hostile environments and more lucrative employment opportunities than the police force are available to them. In addition, business recessions increased the number of applicants for secure, high-paying careers; minority applicants are facing stiffer competition from whites with college training. The pressure is increased by the simple statistical fact that police departments are not expanding and their attrition rates are low. One study in Boston discovered that even if half the anticipated number of annual vacancies could somehow be filled with minority applicants, it would take more than ten years to make the racial composition of the police proportional to the city's 1970 racial makeup.[24]

Why not join the police department?   A spate of news stories in the early 1970s concerning police shootouts with roving killer squads of black nationalists brought police departments a good deal of favorable publicity. Fortunately for police forces, casualties from this kind of sniping, and indeed in regular police work, are by no means as high as one might infer from media impressions. In 1970, for example, the police death rate was roughly equal to construction workers and farmers, but well below the rate for miners.[25] In 1973, 127 policemen (out of almost 600,000) were killed by felons; 42 more died in accidents. In the same year 132 coal miners (out of a total of 144,000 miners) died of injuries on the job. Since police assignments call for exposure to bad weather, a high sickness rate is common, but overall the casualty rate through illness, accident, or confrontation does not seem to discourage the increasing number of applicants who show up each year for the examination.

The examination itself is not particularly taxing. Average IQ's for New York City patrolmen, for example, range around the 100 level, although in a bad year (1969) the average dipped to 93.[26] Moreover, once the applicant was past the examination, job security used to be almost absolute. Few recruits were flunked out of police academies, and except for those caught in the most flagrant dereliction of duty, police were almost never fired. This happy situation altered drastically in the mid-1970s, when police were laid off by the thousands in New York and other cities. Unfortunately the layoffs are made by seniority, not by attempts to sort out the good, poor, and indifferent.

Police pay scales are very, very good. Few people realize just how much an ordinary patrolman earns in many big cities. Total annual earnings, salary plus special bonuses for night work and special assignments, often range between $15,000 and $20,000 a year.[27] When we consider that this is the return for a high school graduate of average intelligence who is still in his early twenties, this salary level is remarkable. A beginning patrolman earns as much as a junior executive, more than a social worker or a school teacher with a master's degree, and certainly more than most criminals. It is no wonder that many have been able to move out to the suburbs.[28] But the fact that police are well paid and of a different nationality than the ghetto residents is not the heart of the police-crime problem. The key to it is a combination of remoteness, incompetence, brutality, and corruption. Often the police in high-crime areas are perceived as motorized bwanas cruising, hunting, and foraging among the natives in the urban jungle.

Deficiencies of the police.   One difficulty is that as a group the police are of average intelligence and therefore tend to bungle many cases. Partly in compensation for sloppy police work, there are attempts to force confessions out of suspects or simply to vent general frustrations on the public, or even on fellow officers, including oneself. (The suicide rate for policemen is considerably greater than for the general population.[29]) The fact is that the police are not carefully screened for potential psychiatric disorders, and all sorts of potentially dangerous individuals are issued guns and other lethal equipment in an operating environment which they regard as vicious and threatening. It is not surprising that the police are charged with killing or maiming persons simply because they perceive these persons as dangerous, suspicious, or merely disrespectful. This last deserves a special note.

For obvious reasons, police tend to be extremely sensitive concerning the low esteem in which they are held by much of the public. A verbal insult from a slum dweller or college student can trigger off a violent reaction out of all proportion to the stimulus.[30] People in high-crime areas are also hostile to the men in blue because of the pervading atmosphere of corruption which surrounds law enforcement agencies. This is not a new phenomenon—the Knapp Commission in New York City, which concluded that a substantial proportion of New York City policemen were "meat-eaters" (actively seeking out extralegal opportunities to augment their salaries), was only the latest in a series of investigations reaching back at the very least to the turn of the century. All reached essentially the same conclusion: crime among the police was common and was consistently covered up by superiors and fellow officers.[31]

This dismal excursion into New York history is significant on two counts. First, the New York story, with local variations, has been duplicated elsewhere.[32] Police collection of protection money from gambling, prostitution, and narcotics, payoffs for changing testimony or losing evidence, and bribes for minor infractions like speeding and illegal parking are so common as to arouse no surprise at the charge or the conviction of policemen and detectives. Police burglary rings have surfaced in Chicago and Denver, among other cities. The theft by narcotics detectives of the heroin rounded up by an honest policeman, in the New York "French Connection" case for example, has been a matter of considerable embarrassment to that department.

The point of this recitation is that the legal system has many deficiencies, but one major problem is that the cutting edge of the war against crime is soft. It is no wonder that expenditures for private police have risen sharply in the early 1970s. It is a matter of fact that in 1972 more private policemen were reported to be employed in San Francisco and Detroit by business firms and institutions than were employed by the city police department.[33] This voluntary double taxation to provide the security the public law enforcement agency was incapable of offering is both an indication of the seriousness of the crime problem and a judgment that the police department cannot deliver security despite all of its manpower, its high pay, and its new equipment. Unfortunately the chief victims of crime, the slum population, cannot afford their own private police, although presumably they would hire them if they could. Quite clearly they do not consider most of the police who operate in the slums as their own people in background, sympathies, temperament, or trustworthiness.

The modernization of police departments was one of the primary aims of the various federal agencies, commissions, and research studies which flourished during the 1960s and early 1970s. At first it was assumed that as experienced crime fighters the police knew what they were doing. The result was a substantial increase in police manpower, police salaries, and police equipment, and a modest improvement in management, planning, and community relations capability. Serious problems remain, as for example in the lack of commitment to serious research by policy makers and weakness in study and design methods.[34] But perhaps the most surprising tentative conclusion of the 1960s was the apparent marginal impact of the police on crime rates—which leaped upward in the midst of this crime-conscious era of bigger police budgets.

OTHER WEAK LINKS IN THE CRIMINAL JUSTICE SYSTEM

While the police are the most obvious representatives of the law enforcement system, the rest of the system is also seriously flawed.

Penal institutions.   The penal institutions are overcrowded, fail to discriminate effectively between novice and hardened criminals, and offer insufficient education and training, and hence no meaningful reform. Understandably, the recidivism rate is high, partly because the preparation for any legal, reasonable postpenal occupation is absent, as are effective drug and alcohol treatment programs.[35] The probation system is poorly run and subject to corruption. Sentences for identical crimes are often extremely uneven and unfair, and the corrections system is badly flawed. As one commentator noted, although each innovation in prison reform has been hailed as "extremely successful" in rehabilitating offenders, to date there is no hard experimental evidence proving that any of these innovations really worked. This assessment includes earlier methods—religion, solitude, hard labor—as well as modern counseling, probation, and therapeutic techniques.[36] Furthermore, employers are usually reluctant to hire exconvicts, particularly when they have few skills to offer and there is a plentiful supply of alternative labor.

In passing, the observation that crime pays fairly well as a relatively low-risk small business enterprise is quite true, but largely irrelevant to the problem at hand. While highly skilled professional burglars, safecrackers, and, even more, conmen and forgers may operate for years with little chance of apprehension, the semiskilled criminals who engage in the type of high-risk crime that terrorizes urban neighborhoods—opportunistic crimes like small stickups, mugging, rape, and apartment robbery—are usually panicky bumblers who do get caught and convicted. They rank lower in status, IQ, education, and earnings than the real professionals and hence are much more vulnerable to arrest, just as they are far more prone to the kind of unnecessary violence which leads to a trail of evidence, shootouts, and long prison terms.

It can be noted that of 142,000 jail inmates surveyed in 1972, only 10 percent had completed high school, and almost 90 percent had a prearrest annual income of less than $7,500.[37] The workings of the prison system may have little impact on big business and organized crime, but it can have an important impact on society's losers, the hoodlum element which commits the type of crime which renders urban neighborhoods unsafe.

A 1974 report on the New York State prison system revealed a five-point rise in the recidivism rate between 1971 and 1972—from 11.9 percent to 17.1 percent. Moreover, 75 percent of inmates did not have jobs lined up before their release. Sixty-one percent of the inmates of maximum security facilities, where two-thirds of the state's inmates are housed, receive no vocational training at all before release. Moreover, 91 percent of inmates known to have drug or alcohol problems did not participate in any rehabilitative program.[38]

Perhaps the most devastating indictment against the penal system concerns the treatment meted out to juveniles. Many of these young people are helpless victims of neglectful families, a classic source of juvenile and subsequently adult crime. Many who suffer from moderate to severe mental deficiencies, or outright mental disorders, are thrown into institutions with neither the trained staff nor the facilities needed to ameliorate their problems. Reform schools and other large institutions are in fact so bad that, like adult prisons, they make bad things worse.[39] As a result judges often refuse to sentence juvenile offenders to such places in the belief that the institutions are worse alternatives than being out on the street. What seems to be lacking, unfortunately, is an adequate supply of good foster homes or community-based facilities. Along with early screening and treatment, such alternatives could offer some hope of preventing serious delinquent behavior before the potential offender gets much beyond the stage of school truancy.

The courts.   The courts, the other principal component of the law enforcement system, are almost as inefficient but probably have less impact on urban crime than the police and the prisons. With overcrowded calendars, and sometimes lax, punitive, or corrupt judges who sell justice to wealthy offenders and give short shrift to the poor, the courts represent another element in the urban crime problem.[40] The principal attacks on the system concern its glacial slowness, while complaints concerning judges usually involve their alleged leniency toward criminals, based on the critics' supposition that lengthy sentences deter prospective law breakers. Moreoever, many judges actually are unfair in sentencing—criminals guilty of identical offences may receive erratically different sentences. Improved organization of the court system and more and better judges would be helpful, but these improvements must be accompanied by upgraded police work to produce the convicing evidence that will secure higher conviction rates.

What To Do until Civilization Returns

As students of urban life have noted, over time each group of high-crime slum dwellers moves up in status, leaving the old neighborhood and loudly deploring the behavior of the succeeding crop of rapscallions who now occupy the tenements they vacated. There is every reason to believe that the same pattern will take place again, and that in a generation or so the blacks, Puerto Ricans, and other groups who now furnish most of the street criminals will advance to middle-class virtues, non-violent, middle-class vices and white-collar criminality. There are of course some who see the present slum occupants, particularly blacks, as the eternal underclass, permanently excluded from the kind of changes in mobility and status improvements which have so profoundly changed predecessor populations. However, as chapter five suggests, such pessimism seems peculiarly unjustifiable after two decades of substantial progress. And, so, for those who can afford to wait, the year 2000 may see more peaceable cities—always provided that whatever group rests at the bottom of the pyramid at that time is relatively law abiding.

There is additional hope that this may indeed be the case because a major cause of juvenile delinquency, which often leads to adult criminality, is on its way to substantial improvement. This is simply the large number of unsupervised children from broken homes who roam the slums, and later the other parts of town, looking for excitement, trouble, and other people's property. With the decline in birth rates at last reaching down to the poor, the supply of delinquents will diminish. The parent who has no chance of supervising five or six children may do a perfectly adequate job with one or two. For this reason alone—the prospect of near zero population growth among the poor—there is hope for the year 2000 or possibly even for the late 1980s. But to a pensioner at 65 with a life expectancy of perhaps another 15 years, there is scant solace in the faint hope that he or she may be able to hobble outside on the street in some safety for a few weeks before he expires. Nor is this much comfort to the parents of school-age children who get held up on the street or in the school for their lunch money. In short, what do we do while we wait?

Goals for the 1980s

A 1973 national commission on crime proposed simple goals:

1. A reduction in homicides by 25 percent by 1983.

2. A reduction in forcible rape by 25 percent by 1983.

3. A reduction in aggravated assault by 25 percent by 1983.

4. A reduction in robbery by 50 percent by 1983.

5. A reduction in burglary by 50 percent by 1983.

To achieve this goal the commission called for a number of steps, including better criminal justice planning, manpower programs, improved community-police relations, swift trials, higher quality staffing and facilities for penal institutions, and tough controls on handguns.[41]

We take it as given that many cities are in a race with time to see if their slum populations become civilized before they wreck their homes, their families, their neighborhoods, and the rest of the community. Black, white, or Spanish-speaking, all the law-abiding who possess ambition for their children and hope for safety for themselves will abandon or attempt to abandon the core cities to a residual, problem-prone underclass.

Certain principles for dealing with crime in the cities can be established at the outset:

1.   Elements of an anticrime program should start with a redefinition of crime—marijuana, prostitution, alcoholism, and gambling do not wreck a city. Neither does crime in the suites, however reprehensible. Embezzlement, adulterating grain cargoes, and violations of antitrust laws are criminal acts that require prosecution, but they too are not immediate personal threats to life and property.

2.   A first task is to focus on the crimes that do violence to the city: crime in the streets, stores, schools, homes, and public places. It is axiomatic that the thrust of a crime enforcement system aimed at saving cities should focus on this type of city-destroying law breaking. *Stiff, mandatory, equalized sentences* for violent criminals would be a useful beginning.

At first glance this would appear to be as repugnant as it is unworkable. Shipping the perpetrators of a million violent crimes each year off for lengthy prison sentences seems a violation of conscience and a sure way of creating a prison system so vast as to rival the Gulag Archipelago. In practice, the prospect is far less appalling. The repeater, the hardcore mugger, arsonist, robbery-with-violence criminal is a minority of offenders, perhaps no more than 5 or 6 percent of the total. At least half the violent crimes are committed by a group that probably numbers no more than 100,000, at the outside. To the extent that these violent recidivists are off the streets, crime rates will decline. And their lengthy removal will serve as a deterrent, channeling remaining criminal inclinations into safer aberrations like shoplifting. As for the morality of harsh punishment, one can only suggest that it is totally immoral to expose old people, children, and the general public to repeated depredations by thugs.

3. *Early prevention and treatment, including adequate prenatal care,* is essential. Brain-damaged, mentally disturbed, or delinquent children should be identified early and psychiatric counseling should be provided for these children and their families. It is assumed that the number of seriously disturbed children and families is sufficiently small to permit this kind of intensive treatment.

There does not seem to be much merit in belabored argumentation over causation. Obviously some crime is committed by the genetically defective. Some can be traced to unstable or disordered family relationships, notably the violent, compensatory machismo of the fatherless adolescent. Much is learned behavior in groups and areas in which crime is widespread and "normal." Some is undoubtedly due to the malfunctioning of economic and social systems. The point is that no single cause or cure exists, and some means must be found to protect a peace-loving, productive majority from a minority of menaces. There is no reason to believe that Americans will buy a police state—in any case, a pass system, lengthy preventive detentions, and harsh punishments have not worked all that well in the USSR or South Africa.[42] The more effective Cuban and Chinese approach, which involves quasi-religious, total surveillance and constant exhortation, holds few charms for most Americans. This leaves us with some difficult problems.

4. One of the most troublesome problems, the juvenile gang must be dispersed or coopted. Youth cultures can foster attitudes in which

delinquent behavior is the norm and the conscientious boy who does his schoolwork is the mutant. No one in this country has mastered the art of breaking them up, coopting them, or diverting their energies into such harmless channels as the Police Athletic League. One obvious approach is to enforce strict curfew regulations and to form corps of juvenile police adjuncts, pre-cadets to work with the police out of idealism (and pay) to restrict the criminal behavior of the more vicious gangs.

5.   Another obvious contribution to reducing the level of violence for adults as well as juveniles would be strict gun control, not simply through legislation affecting sale and possession but through a rapidly escalating scale of punishment. Just as the burglar who is caught with his tools is given a much heavier sentence, a criminal who uses a gun—or knife or other weapon—would be given additional time.

6.   A fruitful approach is the provision of two certainties— *guaranteed gainful employment, available on a part-time basis for all persons as young as age twelve* and *a guarantee of tough punishment for violent lawbreakers.* In short, as in other social components of crime, the best answer lies in a combination of a productive alternative and improved policing—the carrot and the stick.

Technological innovations of different types can play a major role in assisting the police in this endeavor. Continuous street surveillance through television monitoring, rapid communication systems to ensure quicker police response, and changes in design of buildings and open spaces can be helpful. At a minimum, streets in the relatively small downtown areas can be lit, supervised, and rendered safe.

7.   There are persuasive arguments for *redesigning building construction and site planning* to provide fewer temptations for opportunistic crime, the kind that teenagers, short of cash, find inviting.[43] To those who rightfully object that all this may lead to a fortress mentality like Johannesburg's, mingled with an unhealthy dose of Orwell's 1984, one can only reply that the alternative is waiting and hoping for at least a generation, abandoning much of the normal use of the core city in the interim. The point is to discourage the violence-prone criminal who makes life intolerable for the law abiding. Surveillance and controlled ingress and egress to buildings and open spaces is a far cry from preventive detention, vigilantism, and other police state measures which may

otherwise be incorporated into a law-and-order platform. It is also clear that failure to adopt deliberate, restrained measures of this type leaves the field to law-and-order demagogues whose self-righteous racism and wild promises and accusations are matched by their failure to achieve substantive results.

BETTER POLICE?

Various suggestions have been advanced to improve the image, status, and behavior of the police. Police spend most of their time in paper work and a range of social service activities, intervening in family disputes, for example, rather than in crime fighting. One natural result of this reality has been a substantial increase in the number and proportion of civilians employed by the police department as auxiliaries in the neighborhoods, to man some of the desks, and to operate new communications equipment.

The police have had some hard knocks in recent years. There have been the frequent scandals involving everything from ticket-fixing to thievery, from drug-peddling to unjustified violence, up to and including murder. And there is a growing suspicion, not least among some of the police, that many crimes like juvenile gang violence, burglary, and the use and sale of illegal drugs occur according to their own mysterious rates and timetables, unrelated to the extent or quality of the local police force.

The response to the second reality of police operations has been slower in coming but appears to be well on the way. This is a fundamental change in the image and function of the police from a semimilitary, threatening law enforcement system to a peace-oriented public service network. Special training in coping with troublesome, often dangerous family problems, and training in minority relations, in handling juveniles, alcoholics, and drug users are becoming increasingly common, spurred on by financial inducements for college training and special ratings.[44] It is hard to judge just how much of the reformation to date has been real and how much purely cosmetic. But the tide seems to be strongly in this direction, to turn the police force into a modern version of the friendly, honest neighborhood men-on-the-beat.[45]

It may be noted that one reason for the acceptance of unorthodox approaches has been the crime statistics which reveal that plain-clothesmen and detectives have much higher arrest records than their uniformed colleagues. It may well be that much of the traditional crime-fighting role in the future will be assumed by detectives, backed up by special uniformed units like the tactical police. Certainly police cruising seems to have little or no effect on crime rates. Meanwhile the policeman in the slum neighborhood would act and be regarded by his assigned precinct as a helping hand, a source of protection and assistance rather than an alien menace. This would require a step backward in time—most police might well be required to work out of small neighborhood offices in their assigned districts rather than out of precinct armories. But this approach would, it is hoped, enable the police to know the slum neighborhood, to gain the trust of law-abiding poor people. Among other benefits, this would open up possibilities of crime prevention through work with juveniles.

It would also tap new sources of information. While it is true enough that most people in middle-class neighborhoods do not possess much in the way of useful tips on lawbreakers, this is emphatically not true of people in slum areas permeated by overt criminal activity. Newspaper reporters have been escorted on guided tours of high-crime spots by slum-area school children. A police force with strong local roots should be able to make serious inroads on the slum crime problem. On the other hand, realistically, police cannot be forced to live in the slums, but will continue to commute in from middle-income suburbs and city neighborhoods. They nevertheless can develop close neighborhood ties, particularly if they act as ombudsmen, counselors, and quasi-social workers to make themselves generally useful to the community.[46]

Two other allied trends need accelerating. The first is a rapid increase in college graduates—black and white—in police departments, coupled with stringent measures to weed out police corruption. Perhaps it is too much to ask that police departments, like Caesar's wife, be above suspicion, but surely no one expects them to behave like Caesar's bookie. The argument that despite what it says, the public in many cities really wants a loose, corrupt system of selectively enforced policing reflective of the real character of urban society is growing thinner. There is no tolerating police burglaries or shakedown artists who add $5,000 to $10,000 a year in graft to their $15,000 and higher salaries, and there is no tolerating the combination of harshness toward the poor and acquiescence or complicity in the crimes of the affluent.

The police could be expected to put up powerful resistance to most of these reforms. Indeed, they have already done so. But the alternative is almost as unpleasant for the police as internal change: a ceiling on hiring, dehydration through attrition, and an increase in private, more responsive police units, possibly stimulated through tax credits or

citizen chits. In short, the answer to static, costly, unyielding bureaucracy is a bypass mechanism operating around and behind a structure
which cannot be dismantled but which can be ignored.

We have seen this resort to the private alternative with the growth
of private school enrollment in central cities as a replacement for the
public school system; now the same trend is taking place with the police.
The total number of private policemen in the nation is variously estimated to be between 500,000 and one million. But whatever the true
figure (and making allowance for part-timers), their total number is
larger than the 440,000 public police officers. The two largest firms,
Pinkerton and Burns, employ almost 70,000 guards, a force larger than
that of many national armies. Although poorly trained and poorly paid
for the most part, private security guards provide tailor-made service
for apprehensive clients.

Once private policemen were largely confined to warding off union
organizers and light-fingered customers and company personnel, but
now one of the fastest growing segments of the private security business is protection against street criminals.[47] And despite their limited
powers and meager police equipment, they appear to be effective in
curbing opportunist muggers and thieves. This fact suggests that a low-
cost, high-employment, and fairly effective way of using law enforcement funds would be to issue chits to neighborhood and block
associations to employ their own security guards to supplement the
public police force.

WHY NOT THE MOB?

Some readers may raise objections to the attention given to the petty retailers of crime, the adolescent thieves and muggers, as compared
to the neglect of the grandees of organized crime and their business and
political allies. The reason, as explained earlier, is simple: it is the activities of the two-bit youngsters that are most threatening to most city
residents. Therefore, this type of criminal deserves a degree of attention
all out of proportion to the size of his take.[48]

In its traditional role of purveyor of illegal goods and services to the
straight world, organized crime does contribute substantially to urban
problems. There is the discouragement of business through extortion,
the continuing pressure on the law enforcement system through bribes
and threats, and the presentation of a vicious, lucrative life style, an illegal success model, to admiring, ambitious youngsters.

The attack on large-scale criminal organizations has been very much of a hit-or-miss affair in the past. Fortunately, now that there is ample proof that subscribers to the code of *omerta* (silence) can be converted into blabbermouths, the organized crime problem seems reasonably vulnerable to attack.[49] In fact, success is far more probable with organized crime than with the vast, shapeless army of unorganized petty criminals. There is a military analogy that applies: the war against the North Koreans was a clear-cut affair in which enemies were separated from allies, and hence this war was manageable. In contrast, the war in South Vietnam was fluid—the enemy was unidentifiable in an ocean of incomprehensible, hostile, or terrorized natives. And in the war against crime, just as in Vietnam, victory depends on winning the hearts and minds of the population. (It can be hoped that we will be better at this process at home than we were in Southeast Asia.)

Conclusion

While we hope and work for better days there are a number of temptations, easy solutions which are no solutions at all, which should be avoided. These include:

1. Loud, get-tough talk from elected officials and police promising that more police of the same kind and rougher treatment of apprehended criminals will cut the crime rate.

2. Side-show gimmickry, like expending great amounts of energy chasing drug pushers, pornographers, or ideological extremists as the critical threats to urban society.

3. Confusing the battle for public safety with a one-shot spectacular. Solving the crime problem is not simply a matter of rounding up the Godfather and his relatives, severing the French Connection, or cornering John Dillinger and resting on one's laurels. It is much more of a daily guerilla war against a relative handful of civilization-wreckers—a war which cannot be won without the active cooperation of the slum population which furnishes most of the criminals and most of the victims. Hence the urban need for a new breed of police.

4. The degeneration of law-and-order platforms into the equivalent of addresses at a Klan convention—racist, ethnocentric attacks against supposed subhumans. Fortunately, with the
growth of a middle class among blacks and Latin Americans,
genuinely even-handed law enforcement will no longer seem
biased—provided that the law enforcement machinery is
perceived as fair, and that it contains a really substantial
representation of minority people.

As is the case with most urban problems, there are no short cuts, no
miracles. And politicans who promise quick results in this or other
areas are contemptible charlatans.

We need not conclude on the grim note of a generation of turmoil
ahead—we can find a few rays of sunshine amid the gloom. First is the
obvious indication that there is sufficient optimism among both
affluent city residents and people of modest means to stay on and invest. This is not true of all cities, but there are widespread indications
that white ethnics are remaining—at least the ones who inherit the
property. There are safe, substantial working-class and lower-middle-
class neighborhoods in which street crime and house-breaking are
rarities and which seem utterly stable. Moreover there are rebirth
areas—Park Slope in Brooklyn, the Capitol Hill area in Washington, the
South End and Prudential Center area in Boston—in which young
middle-income people are locating, accepting what they perceive as a
legitimate tradeoff. That is, they can live in substantial well-located
neighborhoods in return for a moderate risk of criminal assault, which
can be rendered less likely by reasonable precautions. In short, the
prediction that the cities will be turned into terrorized wastelands by
vicious criminals seems to be overdrawn. But no one can deny that the
reality is bad enough and effective action is long overdue.

Summary

Crime—both actual crimes committed and public fear of crime—
became a critical urban problem in the 1960s. One reason for the inten-
sity of public fear is that street crime is no longer confined to the slums
(although slum dwellers are still the principal victims), but is affecting

the middle class. Also, news media coverage of crime, as well as the use of crime as entertainment in movies, television programs, etc., intensifies public concern.

Attitudes toward criminals in United States society are conflicting. On the one hand, criminals are romanticized; on the other, they are viewed as an animal subspecies responding only to harsh punishment. Also, the vestiges of a puritan concern with regulating private morality wastes time and money by using the police to control victimless crimes. Police resources should be concentrated on street crime, since these are the crimes that destroy the cities.

In the nineteenth and twentieth centuries successive waves of slum dwellers of various ethnic origins have exhibited criminal behavior, then moved up the economic ladder to the middle class. This process is now occurring among black and Latin American slum dwellers.

Public sentiment, even among liberals and blacks, is in favor of tough law enforcement to combat crime. However, this approach so far has not been effective, since the police do not have the cooperation of the slum communities, and the police are often corrupt and poorly selected for their jobs. The lack of public faith in the police is shown by the growing number of private security businesses. Penal institutions are also ineffective, as is seen by the high recidivism rate.

Recommendations

- Decriminalize victimless crimes such as marijuana possession, prostitution, and gambling, while providing information and treatment programs for alcoholics, drug addicts, etc.

- Institute a full-employment policy to lessen the appeal of crime as a way of making money.

- Promote tough gun-control legislation, with punishment for gun possession.

- Recruit minorities for police forces in order to make police more representative of slum communities.

- Reform police departments to eliminate corruption, and retrain police to function as ombudsmen, counselors, and quasi-social workers operating out of neighborhood precinct offices.

- Establish a system of early screening and treatment of potential juvenile criminals, along with foster homes and community-based facilities.

- Establish stiff, mandatory, equalized sentences for violent crimes.

- Disperse or coopt juvenile gangs.

- Redesign building construction and site planning to minimize opportunities for crime.

- Issue chits to neighborhoods and block associations to employ their own security guards.

Notes

1. U.S. Department of Commerce, *Statistical Abstract of the United States, 1975,* (Washington, D.C.: Government Printing Office, 1975,) table 248, P. 150.

2. U.S. Department of Justice, *Crimes and Victims* (Washington, D.C.: Government Printing Office, 1974), p. 23.

3. For an excellent summary of this phenomenon see Eric Hobsbaum, *Bandits* (New York: Dell, 1969).

4. Richard Maxwell Brown, "The American Vigilante Tradition," in *The History of Violence in America,* ed. Hugh Davis Graham and Ted Robert Gurr (New York: Bantam Books, 1970), pp. 154 - 217.

5. For a discussion of the nineteenth century American stereotypes of Irish and Italian immigrants as revolutionary papists and knife-wielding rowdies, respectively, see John Higham, *Strangers in the Land* (New York: Atheneum Press, 1969), pp. 26, 90.

6. President's Commission on Law Enforcement and Administration of Justice, *The Challenge of Crime in a Free Society* (Washington, D.C.: Government Printing Office, 1967), pp. 35 - 39.

7. Ibid., pp. 5, 56 - 57.

8. "Juvenile Justice Found Deficient in New York City," *The New York Times,* 3 May 1976, pp. 1, 26.

9. Especially notable indices of this trend were the election of an obscure detective, Charles Stenvig, as mayor of normally liberal Minneapolis in 1969, and Frank Rizzo's ("the toughest cop in America") victory in the 1971 Philadelphia mayoral contest. See "God is My Co-Pilot," *Newsweek,* 23 June 1969, p. 32; and "What the Voters Wrought," *Newsweek,* 11 November 1971, p. 28.

10. Allan E. Goodman, *Politics in War* (Cambridge, Mass.: Harvard University Press, 1967), pp. 224 - 231.

11. President's Commission on Law Enforcement and Administration of Justice, *The Challenge of Crime in a Free Society,* pp. 60 - 64.

12. Ibid., pp. 75 - 76. In general, the President's Commission exercises a degree of toleration seldom found these days.

13. Data from U.S. Department of Commerce, *Statistical Abstract of the United States, 1975,* tables 251, 264, 266, 269, 271, 287, and 290.

14. Orde Coombs, "Three Faces of Harlem," *New York Times Magazine,* 3 November 1974, p. 44.

15. U.S. Department of Labor, *Manpower Report of the President* (Washington, D.C.: Government Printing Office, 1971), p. 98.

16. See Francis A. J. Ianni, *Black Mafia* (New York: Simon and Schuster, 1974).

17. James M. Markham, "Heroin Hunger May Not a Junkie Make," *New York Times Magazine,* 18 March 1973, p. 40.

18. President's Commission on Law Enforcement and Administration of Justice, *The Challenge of Crime in a Free Society,* p. 22.

19. U. S. Department of Justice, *Crime in the United States, Uniform Crime Reports for the United States, 1972* (Washington, D.C.: Government Printing Office, 1973), p. 6.

20. Ibid., p. 9.

21. "Making Police Crime Unfashionable," *Time Magazine,* 6 May 1974, pp. 88 - 90.

22. For example, see John A. Gardiner, "Wincanton: The Politics of Corruption," in *Criminal Justice: Law and Politics,* ed. George F. Cole (North Scituate, Mass.: Duxbury Press, 1972), pp. 101 - 131.

23. William K. Stevens, "Black Policemen Bring Reforms," *New York Times,* 11 August 1974, pp. 1, 35. Only in cities such as Detroit and Atlanta, with black populations approaching 50 percent have the proportion of minority policemen increased to near parity with their group's general population portion.

24. Melvin R. Levin and Joseph Slavet, *Police Recruitment and Personnel Policies: New Goals for the Seventies* (Boston: Learning and Planning Associates, Inc., 1971), p. 23. This was a report prepared for the Boston Police Department.

25. Ibid., p. 18.

26. Ibid., p. 13.

27. "Salary and Employment Trends of Firemen and Policemen," *Monthly Labor Review* 95, no. 10 (October 1972), pp. 59 - 60.

28. David P. Riley, "Should Communities Control Their Police?" in *Police and Law Enforcement, 1972,* ed. James T. Curran et al. (New York: AMS Press, 1972), p. 187.

29. Sanford Labovitz, "Variations in Suicide Rates," in *Suicide,* ed. Jack P. Gibbs (New York: Harper and Row, 1968), p. 69.

30. James Q. Wilson notes that the average patrolman is unable to distinguish disrespect directed at him as he fulfills the role of policeman from that aimed at him divorced from this social role. James Q. Wilson, "The Police in the Ghetto," in *The Police and the Community,* ed. Robert F. Steadman (Baltimore: The Johns Hopkins Press, 1972), pp. 70 - 71.

31. *The Knapp Commission Report on Police Corruption* (New York: George Braziller, 1973), pp. 3 - 11, 61 - 64.

32. Paul Carpenter, "Police Corruption: Endemic to the System? . . . Or Holdover from the Feudal Past?" *Sunday Times Advertiser,* Trenton, New Jersey, 21 July 1974, II, pp. 6 - 7.

33. "Living with Crime, USA," *Newsweek,* 18 December 1972, p. 34.

34. Mathematica Inc., *Reviews and Critical Discussions of Policy-Related Research in the Field of Police Protection* (Maryland, October 1974).

35. *New York Times,* 14 July 1974, p. 24.

36. Leslie T. Wilkins, "Introductory Note, Five Pieces in Penology," *Public Administration Review* 31, no. 6. (November/December 1971): pp. 596.

37. U.S. Department of Commerce, *Statistical Abstract of the United States, 1975,* table 289.

38. *The New York Times,* 14 July 1974, p. 24.

39. Leslie Oelsner, "Juvenile Justice: Failures in the System of Detention," *New York Times,* 4 April 1973, pp. 1, 86.

40. For a further discussion of the courts as well as the general problem of crime in the United States today, see James Q. Wilson, *Thinking About Crime* (New York: Basic Books, 1975).

41. National Advisory Commission on Criminal Justice Standards and Goals, *A National Strategy to Reduce Crime,* (Washington, D.C.: Government Printing Office, 1973).

42. Walter D. Connor, *Deviance in Soviet Society: Crime, Delinquency, and Alcoholism* (New York: Columbia University Press, 1972) presents an in-depth analysis of a political deviance in the context of extremely high levels of social control.

43. See Oscar Newman, *Defensible Space: Crime Prevention Through Urban Design* (New York: Macmillan, 1972).

44. Charles B. Sanders, Jr., *Upgrading the American Police* (Washington, D.C.: The Brookings Institution, 1970), pp. 79 - 151.

45. Of course, first steps in this direction have been shaky. For example, see Terry Eisenberg et al., *Police-Community Action: A Program for Change in Police Community Relations* (New York: Praeger, 1973) and Donald F. Morris, *Police-Community Relations: A Program That Failed* (Lexington, Mass.: Lexington Books, 1973).

46. President's Commission on Law Enforcement and Administration of Justice, *The Challenge of Crime in a Free Society*, pp. 97 - 101.

47. See Clark Whelton, "In Guards We Trust," *The New York Times Magazine*, 19 September 1976; and Milton Lipson, *On Guard: The Business of Private Security* (New York: Quadrangle, 1975).

48. President's Commission on Law Enforcement and Administration of Justice, *The Challenge of Crime in a Free Society*, p. 18.

49. "Ganging up on the Mob," *Time Magazine*, 2 May 1969, p. 76.

8

GOVERNING URBAN AREAS: Managing the Unmanageable?

From time to time political scientists have pointed out the failure of the nation's big-city mayors to advance to higher office during the past decade. The mayor's office is less a stepping stone than a political grave. Mayors are the bearers of bad news—higher taxes, rising crime rates, increases in transit fares, deteriorating public schools, abandoned housing—and they are accorded the unenviable fate reserved for those who transmit ill tidings. Astute analysts suggest that these political pariahs should instead have tried for Congress or the Senate, where the incumbent can lay low in hard times, emerging at discretion to seize the glory when there is a contract to announce, a bill to sponsor, or an occasion for ceremony, including the laying on of hands at a construction opening or completion. The mayor cannot hide, and the result is that many a promising politician has found the post a dead end, if not a ticket to oblivion.

This is not meant to suggest that political leadership in the state and federal governments is, in comparison with the cities, some sort of paragon of efficiency, honesty, and responsiveness. And there is a lengthy history of corporate disaster proving that chiefs in the private sector can be just as callous, incompetent, and crooked. The point of this chapter is not to pick on everybody's favorite fall guy, big-city government. It does zero in on the day-to-day concerns of the people who live in troubled cities, large and small. While many of these anxieties can be relieved only (if at all) by state or federal action, the cutting edge of the most vexing city problems—crime, streets, schools, land use—are municipal responsibilities.

Overview of Urban Government Problems

If the troubles besetting the big-city mayor could be summarized in a single sentence, it would be this: There is a growing lack of public confidence in municipal government, based on perceptions that higher taxes seem to purchase lesser amounts and poorer quality of urban services. Despite promises to the contrary and attempts at reform, municipal government does not seem able to cope successfully with the most pressing urban problems—high crime rates, deteriorating schools, decaying neighborhoods. Many city residents feel that not only are they paying more and getting less, but that there is no end in sight to this nasty trend.

Moreover, up to the 1973 - 77 recession, wages and salaries of municipal employees rose faster than the private sector year by year. Equally important, so did municipal pension and fringe benefits. With city employees being paid more handsomely for minimal effort than most city residents for working hard at *their* jobs, municipal government is perceived as a kind of giant racket, a cozy conspiracy between politicians, city employees, big real estate operators, welfare cheats, and other unscrupulous insiders, submerging their differences to squeezing more and more out of the ordinary taxpayer and working man. It is not surprising that given their druthers, most Americans would prefer to live away from cities in rural areas or small towns.

STAFF PROBLEMS

There are serious difficulties in doing much to alter this discouraging perception of city life. One major problem is staff. Mayors have tried with only limited success to improve municipal employee productivity through the use of modern management tools. Alas, experience has shown that business-style productivity measures are often hard to develop and even harder to use. There are few fully defensible, objective measures to gauge performance of school teachers or policemen, to cite only two difficult examples. And even if indices are available, as in the case of sanitation workers, the power of civil service tenure and municipal unions is so great in many of the larger cities as to make it almost impossible to increase output. This is especially so if the proposed changes involve layoffs of the less competent.

A 1975 report on municipal productivity published by Georgetown University's Public Services Laboratory summarizes the problem: Even in the dozen or so cities which have tried to develop links between measures of output and individual employee performance ratings, there is no proven track record and no accepted evaluative process. Unions and civil service practices are reported to be barriers to changes, but even here the evidence is more subjective than analytical.[1]

CONTROL OF WELFARE

Another aspect of municipal efficiency, control of welfare rolls to ensure eligibility, has proved almost as frustrating. For at least two decades there have been recurrent welfare scandals, with estimates of ineligibles ranging from 5 to 20 percent, but they all seem to fizzle out in exchanges of recriminations between state and municipal officials and a few well-publicized prosecutions. While the bulk of welfare costs are carried by the federal and state governments, there remain substantial local burdens, some financial but others relating to the impact of broken welfare families on the quality of neighborhoods. The monthly checks may originate with federal and state agencies, but the localities pick up the tab for crime and school problems.

None of this is meant to suggest that fiscal stress or misgovernment is characteristic of all cities. But for every well-run Minneapolis there are dozens of cities in trouble, ranging from multimillion giants like New York, Chicago, and Philadelphia downward to small, grimy, industrial cities like Camden, New Jersey or East St. Louis. Cities in the 40,000 to 200,000 class can be disaster areas, petite but authentically dismal. However, there are a few cities that no amount of maladministration seems to faze. Private investors appear to be pouring money into some cities which have been badly misgoverned, just as they have done in other uniquely attractive cities like Boston and San Francisco and Minneapolis. But the concern here is not with the successful exceptions but with the many cities that possesses few advantages that cannot easily be duplicated in surrounding suburbs. In such cities, governmental quality can make all the difference.

FINANCIAL PROBLEMS?

From a tactical point of view, mayors have found it more expedient to argue that the real problem of urban government is the sheer lack of financial resources. Unable to set their house in order partly because of their prudent refusal—in past years—to risk head-on clashes with municipal unions, the mayors have made constant, fervent pleas for more state and federal money. There is a persuasive case for more help. The tide has been running against the cities. Much industry and commerce and much of the tax surplus-yielding middle- and upper-income citizenry have left for the suburbs. A good deal of the municipal plant is obsolescent and in need of replacement, and support from federal and state governments is helpful but inadequate. The political scientists' maxim, "The Feds have the money, the states have the power and the cities have the problems," is an exaggeration, but not by very much.

If money alone were the problem, the solution would be simple—a domestic fiscal imbalance of this sort can be corrected by reordering of resources. Redistribution—larger scale revenue sharing could be one answer. Or, as has been frequently suggested, the federal government could assume all welfare costs while the states assumed all responsibility for school finances.

If money is not the real problem, what is? It can be suggested that it is the basic weakness is of the city in dealing with the intractable bureaucracies. Intergovernmental fiscal arrangements toward redistribution might indeed eliminate, for a time, the chronic tax problems confronting the cities, but there is no certainty that increasing expenditures on schools or crime prevention would result in commensurate improvements in outputs and service quality. Furthermore, there is a reasonable guarantee that having more money available would be likely to accelerate the tendency for municipal unions to take command of their agencies. It would also probably strengthen their grip on municipal expenditures and services. Up until the 1974 - 75 recession the municipal agencies had, in many larger cities, seemed virtually impervious to outside control.

The recession resulted in a trend which would have been unthinkable a year or two earlier. It caused sizable staff layoffs, pay freezes, and renewed interest in productivity. The layoffs and pay freezes proved possible, albeit extremely painful. The third item, increases in productivity, proved a much more difficult proposition, partly because productivity measures are hard to come by in evaluating school or police operations, and partly because civil service layoffs are made on the basis of seniority, a practice that tends to retain tired drones while firing promising younger workers.

THE FOUR MAIN PROBLEMS

This chapter examines four problems directly linked to the growing loss of confidence in municipal government:

1. Equity. There are constant complaints that some groups seem to be hogging the jobs, the contracts, and the cream of the services, while other groups receive short shrift.

2. Efficiency/productivity. Municipal governments cannot seem to get enough good-quality work done, despite higher salaries, expanded staffs, and rising taxes. Without commensurate efficiency and productivity, adding personnel and funds achieves very little.

3. Fiscal pressure. Municipal government appears to be a bottomless pit. Taxpayer "watchdog" committees railing against

"confiscatory" levies or property taxation failed—up until 1974 - 75—to have much impact in halting year-by-year increases in the local tax burden. Even then, holding the line was achieved only at the cost of painful service, construction and maintenance cuts. In short, increasing local expenditures seems to have little positive effect, while reductions cut to the bone.

4. Political/social impacts. The demographic and political changes taking place in larger cities seem to be creating—or, more accurately, are linked to—profound alterations in the economy and the society at large. In particular, these trends raise disturbing questions concerning the extent to which an increasingly urban nation has fallen victim to an irreversible trend toward uncontrollable governmental bureaucratization.

The concentration of poverty and the city employee political clout in the core cities have led directly to costly attempts to use municipal government as a mechanism to redistribute income. This practice induced cities to live beyond their means. Through a variety of measures, including higher taxes, rent control, and deteriorating services, cities accelerated the flight of their middle-income people and much of their remaining business and industry.

Equity

From time to time residents of low-income areas remind those of more affluent communities that one of the principal causes of filth on streets, sidewalks, and alleys is the fact that they receive substandard garbage collection. Similarly, slum schools tend to receive less qualified teachers, school buildings are less well maintained, and city police and health departments are slower to respond to calls for help in slum areas. And there are never-ending complaints from poor areas concerning discriminatory practices by landlords, by local stores, and by the municipal government in filling and placing jobs and contracts. Colonial analogies, such as those made by Frantz Fanon, the African revolutionary, are sometimes used to explain the differential treatment in services. For example, middle-class areas are clean because they are cleaned; slums are dirty because they are not; teachers in middle-class schools teach, while in slum schools teachers try to keep order, etc.

JUSTIFICATIONS FOR INEQUITY

There are two standard responses to these assertions. The first is to blame the victim. As noted elsewhere in this book, blacks, Latins and other slum dwellers are alleged to create their own problems because they are prone to crime, airmailing garbage from windows, vandalism, and playing with matches. They are also allegedly hard to educate and are unqualified for either steady work or business contracts. When the disciplined, saving, gratification-postponing poor do succeed in achieving requisite skill levels, this argument goes, they are swiftly rewarded in public school and subsequently placed in the civil service jobs for which they have qualified themselves. Hence the residue slum population remains poor because it—they—have rejected the opportunities for free schooling, vocational training, and advancement through the merit system proffered by a generous society. They have chosen instead the primrose path of drunkenness, drugs, welfare, and crime. They wreck their lives, their children's lives, and their neighborhoods, and they break the cities as they do so.

The second response is slightly more technical. In the 1940s and 1950s there was a passing fad for cost/revenue studies aimed at measuring and comparing tax returns and municipal expenditures in various urban neighborhoods. Again and again it was demonstrated with numbers and graphs that commercial and industrial areas yield substantial revenue surpluses, that affluent residential neighborhoods more than pay their own way, and that the slums absorb far more in municipal expenditures than they generate in taxes. Such futile comparison studies are rare these days, but the attitudes linger on. The slum can conveniently be viewed as a sinkhole, absorbing government expenditures like some giant sponge. It follows then that charges that the poor are inequitably treated meet with incredulity. In April 1976 most of the respondents in a national poll agreed with the statement that the "government has paid too much attention to the problems of blacks and other minorities."[2] In the mind of the middle class, a welfare and crime culture wallowing in public housing, poverty programs, and welfare payments and requiring a costly criminal justice system is already receiving a disproportionately large share of government attention. How dare they cry foul!

EXPLOITATION OF THE POOR

However, the inequity argument is sustained by two sets of statistics concerning the exploitation of the poor. The first concerns charges of "creaming." It is alleged that organized crime, larger retail stores, and residential buildings in slum areas are controlled by outside carpetbaggers who skim off much of the residents' earnings and welfare payments. What the establishment reluctantly gives with one hand, it quickly and brutally takes away with the other.

To a degree, time has altered this simple colonial model. Many businesses owned by suburban sahibs have departed, or have been burnt out or robbed out. The fabled slumlord is becoming extinct, since the profit margin on slum tenements vanishes when landlords are forced to keep obsolescent structures in a reasonable state of repair, when some tenants organize, some vandalize, and others refuse to pay their rent. The result is a growing trend toward abandonment of core-area housing as ex-landlords convert their capital into investment in commercial buildings or into middle- and upper-income residential units.

Increasingly, however, exploitation of the slum population has taken on less of a special "colonialist" character and more of the kind of generalized fleecing which has traditionally been accorded to poor people. Some industries benefit from paying low wages to slum residents; the liquor, gambling, cosmetic patent medicine, automotive, and movie industries, to name a few, reap sizable profits from catering to specialized, gullible markets. And as noted, municipal government tends to give grudging, substandard service to the slums. The fact that executives in government agencies and nonprofit industries serving the poor are themselves in the middle- and upper-income brackets means that the slum population, to an even greater extent than the rest of the nation, is manipulated as helpless consumers.

In the middle class the response to this persistent hoodwinking and overcharging has been sophisticated. There has been a growth of neighborhood associations, buyers' cooperatives, consumer magazines, discount organizations, and Nader-type consumerism. In this context, the continued exploitation of the poor represents an inability on the part of low-income groups to organize and mount effective countervailing pressure against public- and private-sector exploiters.

ATTEMPTED SOLUTIONS

One response to the problems of the poor has been subsidized advocacy—legal aid programs to give guidance to the poor in fighting off city plans and city agencies, private enterprise, landlords, and legal systems. Through a variety of programs, the urban poor are given special technical help in securing vocational training, finding adequate jobs, and getting better medical care and higher welfare payments. The poverty and model city programs in particular have been vehicles for the federal government to pressure the cities to give the slum dweller a stronger voice in municipal government.

Aside from the fact that these two programs have been virtually phased out, neither program succeeded in altering the deep-rooted institutional resistances to change in traditional city agencies such as the police department and the public schools. It can be argued, in fact, that not only is providing standard quality housing and safe neighborhoods beyond the financial resources of the cities, but they find it almost impossible to reorient their municipal agencies even enough to provide a tolerable quality of services. This is not, as some have alleged, solely a problem in staff laziness and incompetence. On the contrary, a principal reason for the failure of welfare and education bureaucracies is their orientation toward business-like efficiency, in which conformity to elaborate administrative rules and procedures seems more important than the needs and feelings of the client. Spontaneity, creativity, and even humanity tend to be suspect, and innovation is stifled. The bureaucratic machine is encrusted with civil service barnacles who are hostile and unresponsive to outside (or inside) criticism. The client's "failure" is attributed to personal deficiencies rather than societal failure or agency weaknesses.[3]

One alternative method of achieving minimal agency responsiveness has been the institutionalization of "Little City Halls," which, among their many functions, help aggrieved slum dwellers through the maze of municipal procedures and delays. This approach seems to have had some success in Boston.[4] In addition, a modified form of leverage is the pressure brought to bear on agencies by local politicians. Service-oriented political officials maintain storefront offices to act on the complaints of local residents. Occasionally a local newspaper or television station will operate a complaint service on such matters as potholes or abandoned tenements.

In Denmark the system includes a public official charged with snipping red tape, termed the Ombudsman. Versions of this Danish system to promote government responsiveness have also been adopted in the United States in some areas. American ombudsmen, usually working out of the mayor's office, provide an alternative channel for hearing and resolving grievances when no city agency seems to want to take responsibility for such commonly neglected needs as removing abandoned automobiles or cleaning mountains of trash out of vacant lots. Certainly political or ombudsmen assistance can be extremely helpful. Nevertheless, there are basic areas of friction, like the criminal justice system and the public schools, where it is difficult if not impossible to evoke adequate responses without first achieving basic changes in staff and agency philosophy.

LEGAL ACTION

Partly because of disillusionment with results achieved through such agencies as poverty and model cities programs, some members of disadvantaged minorities have taken legal action to force an increase in the pace of change in municipal agencies. Police departments, fire departments, and the public schools have been selected as special targets, specifically with regard to altering discriminatory personnel policies. Although this type of legal action is not a post-1965 phenomenon—the National Association for the Advancement of Colored People (NAACP) and other groups have brought legal suits at the federal level for many years—the massive frontal legal attack on municipal government dates from the 1960s.

In addition to lawsuits, some of the militant poor have resorted to two major types of political pressure to effect changes in municipal government. The first is the use of traditional political muscle. Voting power is the simplest and most direct method by which blacks and Latins have obtained political offices, city jobs, and improved services. A more recent trend, which began in the 1960s, is the pressure to decentralize central-city government to give poor areas more control over agency activities affecting their neighborhoods.[5] The second approach is an end run; that is, using political leverage at the national and state level to pressure the cities. Here one of the main objectives has been to link federal aid to municipalities with an improvement in municipal government services and affirmative action in employment and housing.

REASONS FOR PROGRAM FAILURE

It cannot be denied that the combination of these approaches has had some effect. There are more blacks in the police and other city agencies than there were in the early 1960s. Blacks and Latins have received recognition in political appointments, in school curricula, as students in institutions of higher learning, and in private hiring. But whatever the gains, expectations have consistently outrun delivery, particularly in slum areas, with the widest gap in the crucial area of neighborhood quality.

Some of the difficulty in satisfying city constituencies is attributable to the fact that employment, housing and, to an even greater extent, crime rates and public school quality are not really under the control of municipal authorities. To cite one crucial example, meeting the job needs of slum areas is beyond the power of the city. A few municipal discretionary (non-civil service) positions barely make a ripple in an ocean of unemployment, and the steady expansion of the city civil service was halted and reversed by the 1973 - 77 recession.

It is not that the federally funded programs of the 1960s have borne no fruit. They proved a training ground for a new breed of leaders, some of whom were subsequently elected to public office. A modest number of slum dwellers have been elevated into the middle class through executive jobs in poverty agencies, model cities, and public or private agency affirmative action programs. But since these successes have whetted the appetite of those who have not been similarly blessed, it is not surprising that this effort has been dismissed as a form of moderately expanded tokenism. Moreover, the upward movement in the world of part of the slum population has had a dismaying impact on the old neighborhoods from whence they fled. Increasing the geographic and occupational mobility of the more disciplined and better educated slum families has tended to leave behind in core-city slum areas higher concentrations of hardcore, multiproblem families and individuals.

The question arises, why did the Great Society not have more impact on the urban poor? Extensive critiques of the poverty programs of the 1960s suggest that the original expectations have been largely unfulfilled, partly because of inadequate funding, but also because neither the city agencies nor the parallel poverty and model city agencies were capable of coping with the monumental tasks to which they were assigned. The attempt to establish an autonomous, community-oriented activist organization to sensitize education and welfare agencies floundered on the opposition of career executives and rank-and-file personnel in old-line agencies. It was also hampered by continuing shortages of funds, inadequate employment opportunities for graduates of job-training programs, indifferent leadership, and the sheer magnitude of the problem of altering the ill health, passivity, self-destructiveness and other troublesome characteristics of the slum population. While the aims of the model cities agencies were more modest, focused mainly on physical improvements in slum areas, their conflicts with old-line housing and renewal agencies and other components of the municipal administrative establishment were frequent and bitter. Of all the poverty projects initiated during the period, only the legal aid services seem to be moderately successful.[6]

When all is said in criticism, perhaps the principal reasons for failure lie outside the poverty war and its warriors and the model cities program. Since 1945 the national economy has not provided the level of full employment—less than 1 percent jobless—needed to provide work for the marginally trained slum population. High level employment might have had an impact on urban ills which have some linkage with unemployment—crime, high welfare rates, broken families, decaying housing. But city administrations are guilty of not providing equality even within their own areas of control. And it is this failure to do the simple, homely chores—to sweep slum streets, clean the playgrounds, tear down vacant firetraps, and offer honest law enforcement—that exacerbates the ever-present paranoia of slum dwellers. Employment may be too much to ask of the city, but they know they are being shafted when the tangible, visible evidence of municipal neglect is all around them.

Improving Efficiency and Productivity

Alexis de Tocqueville suggested in the 1830s that democracies, as compared to aristocratically governed countries, place a lower monetary value on top leadership positions. Also, to the degree that democracies are controlled by common folk, they tend to pay comparatively higher salaries for positions at the bottom rungs of the public service job ladder.[7] He noted as well that neither the aristocrat nor the commoner is particularly oriented toward efficiency. Aristocratic disdain for dull technical details is matched by a lower-class willingness to accept sloppiness in agency administration and execution as a tradeoff for job opportunities. It follows then that the main proponents of measures to improve governmental efficiency are drawn from the middle classes. It was the businessmen and professionals who generated most of the support for the turn-of-the-century reform movement in the cities, for the battles against big-city machines and the current variations on time and motion studies—Planning, Programming, and Budget Systems, (PPB), Zero Base Budgeting (ZBB), and accountability and output measures.

While the nation's middle class and its educated professionals were a small minority, reform movements could come and go. Like the "morning glories" in George Washington Plunkitt's phraseology, they soon withered, while the public business remained in the hands of full-time, shrewd professional politicians and dullard bureaucrats.[8] But with the great increase in affluence and education since the Second World War, public expectations have risen. An agency full of fumblers and bumblers is no longer an acceptable and inevitable cause for merriment, or fatalistic resignation. In the United States in the mid-1970s, there is a seething exasperation and suspicion that the cities are going broke because bureaucratic parasites are rewarded for their chronic mismanagement while human needs go unmet.

A LACK OF COMPETITION

In theory, techniques which have proved their worth in private business can be successfully applied to the public sector. If what works at DuPont is good for General Motors, why can't the same methods work for the police and schools? The prospect of such transferability has been the fond hope of businessmen newly arrived to government. But the difficulty in simply applying private corporative techniques to the public sector is that government is a different animal. As its critics have charged, and as its friends have explained, there is no comparable test of the market place. That is, unlike small businesses, inefficient agencies do not go bankrupt. In fact, not only do badly run agencies survive, but they often flourish despite a dismal record of mistakes and incompetence.

Moreover, cleaning out the bumblers is often impossible because, as reformers quickly discover, many key executives are civil serviced into place and cannot be fired without enormous, frustrating effort. Below the executive level, many government employees are members of strong trade unions, and therefore attempts to engage in mass firings or even to improve productivity are often effectively resisted. And, as if all this were not enough, the agency's constituents, its political patrons and the groups it serves or to whom it awards contracts, are most reluctant to support sweeping change. The result of this immobility is a stifling inertia.[9]

Often the progressive reformer, the hard-driving businessman, the tough military officer trying to take charge in municipal government finds his new broom shredded or, more accurately, rotted by the permanent bureaucracy and its powerful supporters. Changes tend to consist of a combination of bold rhetoric, mingled with resounding catch phrases like "vigorous leadership," "modern business practices," or "management by results," and a few surface innovations. Normally a new agency head will only be able to choose a handful of top administrators to work with him. Unless circumstances are unusually propitious, the top echelon finds itself captured and worn down by the long-service agency bureaucrats, the "permanent government" which they are supposed to lead.[10]

"Why," an executive in a mayor's office was asked at a university seminar, "why doesn't the city remove tree branches that have grown over street lights?" He replied, "I think we have a truck and a five-man crew assigned to cleaning branches away from street lights, but they were last seen going into a bar in 1937 and they haven't been heard from since." That was funny, but no one laughed as the city official began to cite one case after another of untouchable municipal barnacles, which in return for absorbing municipal funds impeded work which might far better have been contracted out. For example, the parks and recreation department, he said, contained two college graduates in addition to a vast array of superannuated, semiprofessional athletes. Unlike his learned colleague, who had a bachelor's degree, one of the two college men in the parks department was often sober, but unfortunately he hated kids. It seems he had some sort of phobia about boys urinating on soft surfaces, so he had insisted on retaining hard-surfaced asphalt or concrete under the playground equipment rather than softer but absorbent (and tempting) tanbark. And then there were the assessors and the housing inspectors who took bribes and did favors, to say nothing about the cops. They, he said, were a story all by themselves.

PROBLEMS OF MEASUREMENT

The shoddy quality of government and its outputs at the municipal and state levels have been profoundly affected by the persistent tendency to use public agencies as a refuge from the competitive world. While single comparisons are unfair and inaccurate, there can be no doubt that the overall quality and speed of output tends to be higher in the private sector than in public agencies. Where comparisons are possible, examples are legion: municipal repair services are slower and more ex-

"Either shape up or ship out!"

Source: © 1974 by Paul Szep. Reprinted by permission from the *Boston Globe.*

pensive, sanitary pickup is more costly, construction work is slower, etc.[11] Whatever the defects of the market place, competition does exert some influence in relating pay scales and promotions to some sort of measurable output. In a truly decadent bureaucracy (of which there are numerous examples in the private sector), promotion and tenure and the rest of the reward system is often removed from merit and instead linked to sheer length of service, political connections, or skill at intra-agency maneuvering. The test of battle or simulated combat in field problems identifies capable military officers; the test of the market serves the same purpose for private-sector executives. Both tests are absent in the public sector. Instead the system is often run by and for employees, with only the most tenuous linkages between inputs of money and staff resources and product outputs, including client satisfaction.

The miracle is that the system works at all. It is a fact that somehow buses run, pay is issued regularly, schools operate, fires are put out, garbage is picked up. Because of the low caliber of personnel there is much lurching, many false starts, enormous wasted effort and inefficiency, but in spite of it all the machinery somehow functions. Surely in view of municipal bureaucracy's systematic, long-term avoidance of intelligence and progress, there must be some Higher Power at work, a kindly deity who has decreed that a collection of mediocrities led by a moderately competent executive corps can operate governments—at great, great cost.

Over the years there have been periodic attempts to devise accurate measurements of agency and bureaucrat performance. Cost-benefit and PPB are only two of many techniques which were developed to inject new perspectives into overly routinized agencies which had lost sight of their objectives and lost control of their staff. For a number of reasons, some of which have been discussed elsewhere, not much has come of these efforts to improve governmental systems.[12]

Just as prisons are run by the inmates, agencies are often run by and for their employees rather than their clients—most libraries are still closed on Sunday because it suits the library staff. The much touted "new" emphasis on preventive health and social programs never seems to alter existing patterns with which the staff is comfortable, and accountability measures to gauge teacher or police effectiveness remain mired in disputes with teachers and police (who don't want outside evaluation) over the relationship of alternative types of public investment to pupil achievement and crime rates.[13] In short, there is much frustration in store for those who attempt to improve the quality of public service.

BYPASS MECHANISMS

Faced with a record of fruitless, exhausting efforts at reform, critics have proposed three types of bypass mechanisms (reflecting in large measure their lack of faith in either piecemeal or sweeping government reform). The first is service contracting: hire private firms to run the fire department, to pick up the trash, and to operate the payroll system; and fire the contractor if he is more expensive or less effective than his competitors. At a minimum, reverse the traditional yardstick principle in which a public enterprise like TVA serves as a check on the private sector—develop a system in which private firms serve as yardsticks and pacesetters for public agencies. For example, contract out trash removal in sample neighborhoods of municipalities and gear public sanitation workers' raises to their matching private work standards.

The second proposal carries this process one step further, to the point of substitution: municipal government should avoid or withdraw from providing specific service functions, dismantle the bureaucracy as it is presently developed in urban areas—or do not permit it to build up—and cut taxes. In many suburban communities trash removal is a matter of private arrangements between householders and contractors, and many cities and towns use volunteers to man fire departments and emergency ambulances.

The final, end-of-the-road bypass mechanism has been the subject of considerable discussion in recent years. Acting on the principle of the G.I. Bill and the Social Security Program, it aims at eliminating intervening layers of bureaucracy by providing funds directly to individuals, leaving them free to spend the money pretty much as they see fit. Family income maintenance programs and housing rental allowances are other examples of this approach, and there have been suggestions that this free choice concept be incorporated in our educational system.

The education issue has been complicated so far by constitutional prohibitions concerning the use of public funds for parochial schools or for support of the lily-white private academies which have emerged in response to desegregation of the public schools. But since no similar limitations are placed on college students—the G.I. Bill provides support for veterans at Ohio Wesleyan, Holy Cross, and Yeshiva University—it seems likely that legal obstacles to a choice system of lower-grade education are not insurmountable. But whatever the approach adopted, alternatives to public agencies may very well provide the needed galvanic shock to produce significant improvements in efficiency and productivity in the public agencies. At present these agencies behave like insulated monopolies, defending their turf with silent or overt job action—enforcing work rules to the point of paralysis—using freely and effectively political muscle.

Fiscal Pressure: Bankrupt Cities?

A great deal has been written in recent years concerning the fiscal plight of the cities. As already mentioned, the mayor's attention must be devoted to wringing financial sustenance out of a reluctant state government and a balky, unpredictable federal establishment. It may come as a surprise to some that this problem which occasioned so many nightmares for mayors is really one of the simplest and easiest to solve—at least in the short run. As noted earlier in this chapter, the avenue to solvency is enlarged revenue sharing, combined with federal/state assumption of public school and welfare costs.

NO METROPOLITAN ALTERNATIVE

Is there a *metropolitan* fiscal alternative to state and federal intervention? It has been suggested that the answer was a pooling of resources, with the financially enfeebled cities buoyed by suburbs enriched by expensive residences and a growing commercial and industrial base. The difficulty with this approach is that most suburbs do not feel particularly affluent. Their citizens, struggling to meet mortgage payments and other expenses, have taken to voting down local school bond issues in recent years. And if there are special needs they prefer to have them met by special districts, not by one big government.[14] People who skimp on community schools—the pride of the suburbs—are not likely to perceive their municipal budget as rich in fiscal fats which can be trimmed off for the use of the financially undernourished cities.

Using its superior powers of tax generation and collection, the federal government turned over $5 billion in 1975 to the cities. Estimates are that the figure will be in the $6-billion-yearly range through 1980.[15] Past experience suggests that revenue sharing will be most helpful in municipalities which retain a sizable tax base; it may barely serve to keep afloat blighted, improvident communities.

As New York City's travail in 1975 and 1976 suggests, some cities are beyond the reach of revenue sharing in its present form. Philadelphia, Chicago, and a number of smaller cities are apparently in much the same condition of pernicious financial anemia. But regardless of the specific details (or the scale), the revenue-sharing concept provided proof that the municipal fiscal crisis is partly a matter of bookkeeping rather than a national shortage of financial resources. Given a reasonably healthy national economy, the intolerable fiscal strains on the municipalities and the heavy property tax burdens on the city home-owner and city business can be lifted by a figurative stroke of the pen. *As long as any layer of government has, or can raise, large amounts of money, financial starvation in another part of government is an artificial condition.* The remedy for undernourishment is to change the rules of the fiscal game, either by allocation of funds collected elsewhere in the system or by a shift in financial responsibility for particular functions.

BASIC ELEMENTS OF FISCAL REORGANIZATION

The Advisory Commission on Intergovernmental Relations, pointing out the obvious—that cities have the expenditure problem in today's federal system—outlined the basic elements for fiscal reorganization, including:

1. Sharing of a percentage of the federal personal income tax with states and major localities.

2. Assumption by the federal government of all costs of public welfare and medicaid.

3. Assumption by state government of substantially all local costs of elementary and secondary education.[16]

The assumption of most welfare costs by the federal government, and to a lesser extent by state government, has been helpful to municipalities. A complete takeover of the burden of school costs, as has been frequently suggested, would relieve most of the pressure on the local tax base. A combination of enlarged revenue sharing and a transfer of welfare and school financing costs could, in fact, effectively dispell the gloom which clings to city halls like a poisonous mist—always provided municipal expenditures can be kept within reasonable limits. Naturally this happy solution depends on a healthy national economy and even more, perhaps, on a willingness to cut through the encrusted prejudices and traditions which have made city finances such a painful problem. But among the ills which beset the city this one is most susceptible to swift and effective remedy—at least in the short run.

The Long-Term Problem

While changing the tax distribution system would make the fiscal prognosis for the short and medium term favorable, there is no light at the end of this particular tunnel. Some years ago, when revenue sharing was still on the horizon, a municipal budget director pleaded for quick passage of the proposed legislation as a life saver for his beleaguered city. But was this really much of an answer? he was asked. Considering his city's recent history—major strikes and job slowdowns by school teachers, police, and sanitation workers, leap-frogging pay raises by firemen and policemen, with lavish pension settlements and fringe benefits for all city employees—wouldn't a mere employee raise (or two) wipe out the anticipated gains from revenue sharing?[17] If city employees were perfectly willing to bring the community to its knees when it was broke, what would they do when some honest-to-goodness federal money was available? His answer was simple: We need the money *now*. Anyway, he claimed, who said state or federal government is any better? And after all we live one year at a time, getting from one budget year to the next. In a more cynical mood he delivered his clincher: Let tomorrow's troubles rest with their natural heirs—let the next administration worry. (Author's note: it did.)

Political and Social Impact

From the start of Roosevelt's 1936 campaign, most Republican candidates blasted away, almost by reflex, at big government and big-government spending and pointed the finger of derision at government "payrollers."[18] By definition, persons employed by government agencies were the object of scorn, irritation, and, less frequently, fear. They were insulted as "parasites," interfering busybodies, unrealistic, socialistic, a drain on the public purse, and a blot on the free enterprise record of this nation. Some hardcore conservatives professed to believe that New Dealers were wittingly or unwittingly paving the way for socialism or communism through such measures as the Social Security Program. There were going to be dogtags around every neck, and TVA would be the beginning of the end for the private utility industry.[19]

CHANGES IN POLITICAL ATTITUDES

Little by little the scoffing and panic slowly died away during the 1950s and 1960s. By 1968 only the quasi-populist George Wallace was in the field to mount a frontal attack on "pointy-headed" federal bureaucrats who had been forcing resentful local communities to adopt all sorts of unpopular practices, like desegregating the public schools. If elected president, Wallace pledged, he would throw all their briefcases in the Potomac, thus protecting the people from threats of school busing for the purpose of "race mixing." A different approach was taken by the other right-wing candidate, Richard Nixon. Although Nixon was never known for his timidity in assaulting vulnerable targets, he rarely mentioned government employees except to refer in a few laudatory phrases to these "dedicated public servants." Why this unusual forbearance in a conservative? The reason may be that there were now too many government employees; a broadside attack on a major portion of the electorate would be suicidal.[20] Even at the height of the 1976 campaign, with Carter, Brown, Reagan, and Ford all inveighing against the tyranny and inefficiency of Big Government, there were no clear pledges to fire specific numbers of employees. Moreover, the focus on Washington and its federal iniquities in favor of government "closer to the people" at the state and municipal level left most government employees with the impression that while heads might roll into the Potomac, the state capitols and city halls were protected territory, civil-service sanctuaries.

RISING POWER OF GOVERNMENT EMPLOYEES

In the political arena, campaign funds are spent where they seem to yield the most results, and every effort is made to maximize the amount of contributions and the numbers of voters. The enemies list should be small, identifiable, and isolated. Therefore, President Nixon had no intention of insulting the nation's millions of civilian government employees and their families and friends. In short, while this kind of broadside was an acceptable political tactic in the 1946 through 1956 congressional and presidential elections, when the numbers and proportions were smaller, it was a prescription for political suicide by 1976, when one out of every six employed persons in the United States worked for federal, state, or local government.[21] Add to this total spouses, older children, and sympathetic relatives, and the number of voters who can be driven into the enemy camp by blood-chilling vows to cut wages, trim fat off the payroll, and clean out the dead wood may approach 20 or 25 million, at least a quarter of the electorate. Considering the tendency of people to vote their fears—that is, to turn out in large numbers in response to what they perceive as a direct threat—the civil service can easily tip the balance of power in national elections. Municipal employees already do so in some cities. Certainly securing or at least not antagonizing the combined government employee vote has become absolutely essential in many municipal and state electoral contests, and they could be decisive in a close presidential race. Hence the focus of political attacks on faceless Washington bureaucrats.

In many respects the cessation of overt, humiliating insults to government can be regarded as a sign of maturity. The Republican mainstream of the 1930s, 1940s and 1950s, like the Wallacites, clearly reflected more than a touch of unthinking antigovernment sentiment. It is all to the good that government is accepted as useful and indeed indispensable, rather than as a species of parasites dreamed up by scheming or unrealistic New Dealers. During their long political drought, 1932 - 1952, many Republicans professed to view government, particularly federal agencies, as an excrescence which could be swiftly removed through determined surgery and rollback of the civil service, just as the Russian occupiers of Eastern Europe supposedly could be rolled back to their 1939 borders by Dullesian brinkmanship. In the event, both 1952 campaign promises proved to be sheer bombast. Not only was Dulles a dismal failure as secretary of state, but so were the early Eisenhower efforts to dismantle the federal agencies.[22]

IMPLICATIONS OF GOVERNMENT EMPLOYEE POWER

The new realism in the Republican ranks is welcomed as a portent of a new maturity, more skeptical of sweeping promises to make fundamental changes in basic institutions swiftly and painlessly. But, as in other areas, there is a tradeoff of bad with the good. The end of the era of cheap insults was also a danger signal that the number of governmental employees had expanded to the point where they consituted a pivotal factor in national, state, and local elections. One consequence has been a growing imbalance between government salaries, vacations, pensions, and fringe benefits as compared to those in the private sector. The figures are impressive. In 1974 Detroit paid its public school teachers an average yearly salary of almost $23,000, and Los Angeles policemen earned almost $16,000. A typical sanitation worker earned almost $16,000 per year in New York City, and firemen averaged almost $18,000 in San Francisco.[23]

The fact that the controls over output of government units are increasingly feeble means that the labor cost of government has risen much faster than in private firms and far more rapidly than can be justified by tangible gains in output or by any reasonable yardstick of performance. Where political muscle has proved to be insufficient, municipal employees have used the strike weapon. Cities have discovered, to their cost, that the National Guard can prevent looting following natural disasters, but it cannot collect garbage, teach schools, or put out fires.[24]

The implications of the growing power of municipal employees are twofold. First, there is the impact on tax revenues. The wage and pension bill for city employees constitutes a bottomless pit capable of absorbing virtually any conceivable amount of property taxes, payroll taxes, and revenue-sharing allocations. America may be a wealthy country, but it will find it difficult indeed to foot the bill if the levels of wages, fringe benefits, and pensions available to highly paid municipal employees become the national pattern in the coming decade.[25] Because government is an unpressured, more secure, and better-paying place to work than most private corporations, there is likely to be a continued scramble for government jobs, especially during business recessions, and further pressure to safeguard existing jobs and add new ones. It is true that employment growth in the federal sector has stabilized and employment levels in municipal government tapered off with the 1974 - 1977 recession cutbacks and the trend toward a decline in public school children. In many cities, however, there is nevertheless an inherent, widening gap between population size and composition, revenues, and services which simply cannot be tolerated. The population grows smaller and poorer, but municipal spending continues to rise or at best levels off. This situation is particularly dangerous in cases where the agency bureaucracy has grown so large that the stranglehold is almost unbreakable.

Some Modest Suggestions

One solution, or more accurately one effective approach in dealing with municipal unions, is fiscal brinkmanship. The severe business recession of 1973 - 76 led many cities to do the unthinkable—they fired city employees, froze salaries, reduced services, and postponed capital expenditures, all very much in the tradition of the hungry 1930s. New York City's brush with financial disaster caused considerable comment during much of 1975, particularly because other cities were also close to the edge. But there is every reason to suspect that reforms and cutbacks adopted under the threat of bankruptcy are not likely to be permanent. Once the economy begins to recover, the municipal bureaucracy may revert to its previous size and power.

There are two primary obstacles blocking effective action. The first is the inherent resistance of the "permanent government," or "pyramidal mass" of the hard core of career officials.[26] Large bureaucracies often degenerate into an ecology of "nay sayers," in which there are dozens of negative checkpoints where minor officials are rewarded for "prudent review" or "further examination," or for their penchant to brake forward movement at any point in the burearcratic labyrinth. It has been suggested that there are psychological explanations for this phenomenon—pathetically, the only way for a lowly official to force a big bureaucracy to notice that he exists is to say no. Yea sayers are ignored as routine rubber stamps.[27] This predilection for negativism places an enormous premium on doers like Edward Logue, the former director of the Boston Redevelopment Authority, and Robert Moses, New York's former public works and parks commissioner, who can actually get big jobs done, and alternately on various bypass mechanisms, which to some extent avoid the strangling red tape and multiple layers of the bureaucracy.

The prospects for reform of the federal bureaucracy, a prerequisite for overhauling the municipal and state agencies linked to federal funds and federal monitoring, appear to be rather dim. It is suggested that although a coalition of antibureaucracy votes can be assembled to win an election, the agencies have powerful legislative strength, media constituencies, and the *sitzfleisch* (politely translated, "staying power") to outlast the prospective reformers—and to make life miserable for the political office holders. As one observer suggests, reform would require subordination of "virtually all other political considerations" to assembling a coalition to battle the federal unions and the social welfare establishment. "Even, then, it will be one hell of a fight."[28]

In some respects, the task of reform is easier in financially hard-pressed local and state governments. As the events of 1974 - 75 prove, civil service staffs can indeed be cut back in dire emergencies. But firing provisionals and relying on attrition and retirement to thin the ranks is dehydration, not reform. The end product may be slightly less costly but still incompetent baronial gerontocracies, not effective government.

It is clear that thoroughgoing reform of any institution implies hard work, most likely reductions in the labor force, and violent disruptions of comfortable patterns of thought and behavior. Past history repeatedly demonstrates that all too often after the spirited rhetoric ends, and after an initial flurry of activity, optimistic assaults are swallowed up by the impenetrable bureaucratic jungle. The action leadership and their protégés are eventually worn down and depart for the private sector, for academia, to the foundations, or to the political arena—anywhere to escape more difficult, hazardous, and frustrating confrontations with the agencies' staff. This leads to the conclusion that the focus of reform must be on locating and developing appropriate bypass mechanisms to circumvent, shock, or replace inert bureaucracies. These mechanisms include:

1. *Temporary Task Force.* "Authorities," "projects," "councils," and the like have been created to get a job done in such fields as housing, redevelopment, transportation, and poverty. They offer the prospect (if not the reality) of rapid disassembly when the job is completed, an alternative to civil service constraints in staffing, and a greater responsiveness to public pressures and complaints, since they lack civil service protection. The danger is that "temporary" agencies will not voluntarily self-destruct, partly because they operate in areas where, by definition, the "job" is never done. Moreover, freedom from civil service restrictions opens the door wide to appointment of political hacks. In time the new agency may sink to a level as debased as the agencies it was meant to replace or to galvanize into action.

2. *Miniaturization.* In theory, very small agencies in very small communities should be more responsive than big agencies in big cities because there are fewer places to pass (or hide) the buck. Like the old Model T Ford their operations are highly visible, simplified to the point where they can be mastered, or at least understood, by even a moderately adept layman.

While there has been a good deal of wishful thinking with respect to governmental decentralization into small units, fragmentation of a number of urban functions seems to be well worth trying, particularly if the governing population can be reduced to absolute minimum levels, perhaps 5,000 to 10,000. Clearly, functions such as running a public transportation system or combatting water pollution cannot effectively be subdivided, but functions such as operating recreational areas, libraries, and (more important) police systems can be allocated to small governmental units.

Naturally there are two fundamental risks involved in this process. It may be a blank check for petty tyranny, for rigid authoritarian bigots who seek to run things their way. And there is some risk of a decline in productivity and efficiency as new governing bodies grapple with unfamiliar responsibilities and assign key jobs to friends or relations with even less than the present regard for qualifications or performance. Moreover the proliferation of midget kleptocracies, government agencies operated by bands of thieves, is also possible. We have seen examples of this, notably in police units and smallish machine-run cities and counties.

Nevertheless, the gamble seems worthwhile. If there is ever to be a closer link between the governed and their government, a reduction in size appears to be a necessity. Few people have the talent, knowledge, or ego to interact as an equal with a mammoth bureaucracy—public or private—but ordinary people can cope with very small, human-scale endeavors. Indeed, there seems to be every reason for continuing the process into the private sector, to miniaturize the operations of as many corporations as possible. It seems clear that one reason for the pervasive sense of alienation in America and the host of evils associated with this attitude is that everything has grown too big to be grasped or controlled. The surge into suburbia reflects, among other aspirations, a desire to move into communities where the citizen has some prospect of influencing his government and his environment. Contrary to the trend of much of the last century, as E. F. Schumacher suggests, smaller may be better, not only in economic enterprise but in government and automobiles.

It is clear that the promise of miniaturization can be oversold. Decentralizing jurisdictions can produce less rather than more citizen participation if, as in thecase of some school districts, a tiny, vocal minority seizes control. And it may be true that most people do not really want to become intimately involved in policy formulation or government operations, and few possess the competence to make much of a substantive contribution to most issues.[29] But conceding that smallness is not a recipe for a flowering of active, expert citizen participation is not a reason for dismissing the approach. Some already existing models can be examined—government in smallish cities and suburbs is *perceived* as more responsive, more honest, and more human in scale than big municipal, state, or federal government. Surely enhancing citizen confidence in the government process is a worthy goal.

3. *Quais-Public/Quasi-Private.* From time to time a private corporation will be converted to a public or quasi-public agency. In theory this approach should be attractive. Unfortunately this conversion usually occurs as a form of socialism by bankruptcy, as in the case of transit lines which start to lose large amounts of money.[30] Governments have traditionally been generous to the stockholders of bankrupt transit companies, railroad, public utilities, and mismanaged defense contracts. But governmental kindness and consideration is not restricted to aggrieved stockholders. Government is usually more than fair to the employees of the decaying corporation. (For example, bus drivers' wages usually rise steeply after a public takeover.)

The upshot is that a vital service is retained but only at great and rising cost, partly because the changeover to a civil service bureaucracy tends to worsen the management failures which were at least partly responsible for accelerating the demise of the enterprise. Over and above the need to make lavish payments to bondholders, the now public enterprises are plagued with featherbedding and resistance to improvements in productivity and management. Public transit authorities, for example, are notoriously weak in market research, slow in complaint response, and lacking in aggressive sales development. In short, a private corporate disaster which becomes a public takeover frequently produces a secretive, unresponsive, expensive hybrid combining the worst features of both systems.

The trend toward private-to-public conversion has been decelerated by an increasing tendency toward outright heavy subsidization, as in the case of Lockheed Corporation and other defense contractors, or in the creation of a quasi-public amalgam such as the National Railroad Passenger Corporation (AMTRAK), which is responsible for operating much of the nation's remaining intercity rail passenger service, but leases the equipment and uses the personnel of the private railroads. After a few years of operation, AMTRAK seemed to share many of the problems identified above in connection with municipal transit systems. If anything these problems are even more serious because so much of the roadbed, equipment, and operating rules AMTRAK inherited should long since have been modernized. But perhaps the greatest obstacle to success is the tendency to operate through most of the management structure responsible for the "wreck of the Penn Central" and for other

lesser known corporate castastrophes.[31] In short, public takeovers, in
many instances, seem to be a classic case of the folly of providing fresh
cash for the very mismanagers heavily implicated in the decades of
decay which end in the plea for public help soon after the last drop of
private profit has been squeezed from the carcass. All things considered, socialism by way of corporate bankruptcy is not a preferred
answer to approaching urban problems. George Washington Plunkitt
was prescient. Unlike other politicians who feared the "gas and water"
socialists around the turn of the century, Plunkitt welcomed government takeovers as opening more jobs for his political appointees.

4. *Money To The People?* The growing disillusionment with civil
service bureaucracies and the lack of faith in half-and-half approaches,
like those adopted in the public transportation area, have lent impetus
to suggestions for market solutions. In the ultimate bypass of public
bureaucracies the taxpaying citizen has funds returned to him, or is
allocated vouchers, for the purchase of specific services—schooling for
his children, housing, possibly fire and police protection, or maybe trash
disposal. Private corporations and public agencies compete for consumer service expenditures. If the service is found to be unsatisfactory,
the consumer is free to change vendors. In the case of a municipal contract or neighborhood franchise, a new vendor can be hired when the
contract expires if the service proves unsatisfactory. This approach
would make available to the citizenry at large the options currently
available only to the wealthy who possess the resources to send their
children to private schools, to employ private security, and to buy other
replacements or supplements for public services considered deficient in
quality.

Obviously there are dangers in this approach. There will be foolish
choices on the part of consumers yielding to the blandishments of slick,
high-pressure companies that market valueless services much as they
peddle soft drinks, patent medicines, or cosmetics. There is also the
threat of increased bigotry and parochialism as narrow subcul-
tures—ethnic, racial, political, and religious groups—concentrate and
capture schools, police, and housing funds for indoctrination and
promotion of exclusivity. Since this latter danger is very real, it seems
apparent that careful regulations to guarantee some basic standard of
quality must be established.

There is a further consideration. With all their faults, it must not be
overlooked that public agencies have served as an important unifying

bond in a heterogeneous society. Civil strife over religious, linguistic, or racial differences can all too easily result from opting in favor of communalism instead of commonality. America's melting pot may not have completely fused, but we are not subject to the persisting internal religious or linguistic strife that characterizes many communal societies, including Lebanon, Canada, Belgium, and Northern Ireland. One Civil War is more than enough. For this reason mechanisms like voucher systems must be used with care. At the very least there should be a genuine accreditation system, careful monitoring, and quick withdrawal of support from bully-boy private police firms, from secessionist, exclusionary schools (for example, the lily-white southern alternatives to integrated public schools), and generally from vendors who fail to meet acceptable standards of quality and behavior.

There is no reason to believe that any of this will be easy, although there is ample precedent in the support for higher education through the veterans' G.I. Bill to suggest that this approach can be made feasible. It is worth pursuing because it offers an alternative to unresponsive public bureaucracies.

5. *Supplementary Action.* Proposals for redirection should not preclude steps toward internal reform. Fresh air would be helpful. More ombudsmen to guard against public and private abuses of power, more public interest law firms, more advocacy planners to fashion technically sound alternatives to official policy, more crusading reporters and courageous newspaper and book publishers, and more citizen review boards are needed if public and private bureaucracy is to be made accountable, reasonably honest, and at least moderately efficient. But, while publicity and pressure can be a valuable corrective, as is often reiterated in this book, if the staff and administrative structure is defective no amount of prodding, cajoling, or exposure will have much impact on moribund agencies. It is for this reason that in many cases drastic measures may be the only hope of correction.

Conclusion

This chapter has identified some of the reasons for recommending substantive action to change the pattern and trend of urban bureaucracy, despite the political risks of alienating a key constituency of the traditional Democratic party coalition—the public employees. For example, Republicans can make a considerable stir with appeals to selected, favored employee groups, most notably the police. Nevertheless there is a need to make a start on miniaturization, to fragment appropriate basic services like the schools, police, and trash removal into units small enough to comprehend and control, even at some risk. There is every reason for mounting carefully monitored voucher programs to serve as yardsticks on public agency performance and quite possibly to point the way toward more freedom of choice for the citizen consumer. And in instances where breakup or vouchers are not feasible, as in the case of public or private transportation and utility systems such as the telephone company, multiple exposure through ombudsmen, newspapers, etc. should be encouraged.

Obviously none of these approaches by itself is the answer. But in combination they offer a fighting chance that the slide to bureaucratic suffocation can be contained. And perhaps modest progress can be made in pulling backward from the brink. If the objective is to humanize the cities, government must be uncongealed. It must offer to frustrated city people the kind of closeness, human scale, and government responsiveness many suburban residents enjoy, but central city residents can now secure only by physical relocation.

Summary

Lack of public confidence in municipal government has grown in recent years, as a result of escalating taxes and increasingly poorer services. These high taxes, rent control, and deteriorating services have all accelerated the flight of middle-income people from the cities. But it seems almost impossible to increase the output of municipal agencies, because for many types of civil service jobs, such as teaching or police work, it is difficult to measure performance accurately. Moreoever, civil service tenure and municipal unions are powerful blocks to effecting any significant changes.

Although the financial difficulties of the cities are widely publicized, lack of money is not the basic problem. The real problem of the cities is their inability to control their bureaucracies. These bureaucracies suffer from stifling inertia, caused by the lack of competition, the tenure of civil servants, and the difficulty of measuring agency and bureaucrat performance.

Another reason for lack of public confidence in city government is inequity—the lower quality services received by the poor and the unfair employment practices in municipal government. Poverty programs and model cities programs of the 1960s designed to correct some of these inequities failed, with the exception of legal aid services. There have been other attempts to improve the position of the urban poor through legal attacks on municipal government, ombudsmen, little city halls, and political pressure.

Although internal reform of municipal bureaucracies is badly needed, it is almost impossible, partly because government employees, as one-sixth of the labor force in the country, have considerable political power. It seems more feasible to create bypass mechanisms, such as providing individuals chits for purchasing education, security protection, etc., rather than concentrating efforts on achieving reforms.

Recommendations

- Assuming a healthy national economy, use larger scale revenue sharing or redistribute fiscal responsibility to solve urban financial problems.

- Use bypass mechanisms around municipal bureaucracies, such as contracting with private firms to provide services, or giving individuals chits to purchase services.

- Establish genuine accreditation and a careful monitoring system for private firms offering services to citizens with chits.

- Practice fiscal brinkmanship in municipal government in order to effect reforms and cutbacks.

- Establish temporary task forces that can be disassembled after the job is completed, rather than permanent agencies.

- Decentralize such government functions as police systems and recreation departments to create manageable, responsive units.

- Take steps toward internal reform of bureaucracies through ombudsmen, public interest law firms, advocacy planners, and citizen review boards.

- By taking timely action, avoid such public takeovers of private disasters as AMTRAK's inheritance of mismanaged, rundown railroads.

Notes

1. Public Services Laboratory, Staffing Services to People in the Cities, no. 9, *Do Productivity Measures Pay Off for Employee Performance?* (Washington, D.C.: Georgetown University, 1975), p. 1.

2. "April New York Times/CBS News Poll," *The New York Times,* 23 April 1976, p. 16. The Democrats did *not* agree (43 percent vs. 47 percent), but Independents were in agreement (47 percent vs. 45 percent) and Republicans very much so, with 50 percent vs. 39 percent.

3. For an excellent review of the problems of urban bureaucracies see Michael P. Smith, "Alienation and Bureaucracy: The Role of Participatory Administration," *Public Administration Review* 21, no. 6 (November/December 1971), pp. 658 - 664.

4. Eric A. Nordlinger, *Decentralizing the City: Boston's Little City Halls* (Boston: The Boston Urban Observatory, 1972).

5. Alan Altshuler, *Community Control* (Indianapolis: Pegasus Press, 1970); Milton Kotler, *Neighborhood Government* (Indianapolis: Bobbs-Merrill, 1969).

6. Peter Marris and Martin Rein, *The Dilemmas of Social Reform: Poverty and Community Action in the United States* (New York: Atherton Press, 1969), pp. 177, 187.

7. Alexis de Tocqueville, *Democracy in America,* vol. 1, (New York: Vintage Books-Knopf, 1954), pp. 216 - 219.

8. William L. Riordan, *Plunkitt of Tammany Hall* (New York: Alfred A. Knopf, 1948), pp. 22 - 27.

9. Marilyn Gittell, *Participants and Participation* (New York: Praeger, 1967); David Rogers, *110 Livingston Street* (New York: Random House, 1968); George L. LaNoue and Bruce L. R. Smith, *The Politics of Decentralization* (Lexington, Mass.: Lexington Books, 1973), pp. 153 - 224. New York City's public education bureaucracy is notorious for its labyrinthine character. LaNoue and Smith (p. 159) cite a statement made by the president of the board of education in 1967 concerning John J. Ferris, the budget director: "Only two people know where the money goes—God and Ferris, and when Ferris dies, God will know a great deal more than he does now."

10.   The phrase is Arthur Schlesinger's, describing one of the reasons for frustration in the Kennedy administration in his *A Thousand Days: John F. Kennedy in the White House* (Boston: Houghton Mifflin, 1965, p. 683)

11.   See Dan Cordtz, "City Hall Discovers Productivity," *Fortune*, October 1971, p. 128.

12.   Melvin R. Levin, *Community and Regional Planning: Issues in Public Policy* (New York: Praeger, 1972), pp. 39 - 63.

13.   For conflicting evaluations of New York's More Effective Schools Program see *The Urban Review*, 2, no. 6 (May 1968), pp. 13 - 34.

14.   An excellent discussion of government fragmentation in metropolitan areas and alternative remedial approaches can be found in Allen D. Manvel, *Metropolitan Growth and Governmental Fragmentation,* Commission on Population Growth and the American Future, (Washington, D.C.: Government Printing Office), vol. 4, pp. 177 - 216.

15.   For 1973 figures on revenue sharing and local revenues see U.S. Department of Commerce, *Statistical Abstract of the United States, 1973* (Washington, D.C.: Government Printing Office, 1973).

16.   Advisory Commission on Intergovernmental Relations, *City Financial Emergencies* (Washington, D.C.: Government Printing Office, July 1973), p. 4.

17.   Neal R. Pierce, "Pension Crisis Threatens Taxpayers and Workers Alike," *Sunday Times Advertiser*, Trenton, N.J., 6 July 1975. p. 10.

18.   For vintage Republican rhetoric see Arthur M. Schlesinger, Jr., *The Politics of Upheaval* (Boston: Houghton Mifflin, 1960), p. 543 - 545.

19.   Ibid, pp. 516 - 625.

20.   In 1970 city, state, and federal employees numbered over 12 million out of some 76 million employed persons in the country. Using a crude but conservative multiplier of two, nearly 25 million votes might be mobilized against enemies of this group's interests. U.S. Department of Commerce, *United States Summary*, II, part 1 of *Characteristics of the Population, 1970 Census of Population* (Washington, D.C.: Government Printing Office, 1973), pp. 749 - 760. Similar figures are obtainable for most metropolitan areas. In greater New York City over 760,000 of the 4,500,000 employment total work for a government. In metropolitan Columbus, Ohio, 71,000 of a work force of 370,000 are government employees. Commerce Department, *New York*, II, part 34 of *1970 Census*, pp. 1180 - 1185; and *Ohio*, II, part 37 of *1970 Census*, pp. 1502 - 1509.

21.   U.S. Department of Commerce, *United States Summary*, part 1 of *Characteristics of the Population, 1950 Census of Population* (Washington, D.C.: Government Printing Office, 1950), pp. 288 - 289.

22.   Eric F. Goldman, *The Crucial Decade—and After* (New York: Vintage Books, 1965), pp. 240 - 243, 279 - 283.

23.   "Congressional Budget Office, New York City's Fiscal Problem," Background Paper no. 1., Washington, D.C., 10 October 1975, table 7, p. 17.

24.   Frances Fox Piven, "Militant Civil Servants in New York City," *Transaction* 7, no. 1 (November 1969), pp. 24 - 28, 55.

25.   Levin, *Community and Regional Planning*, p. 274.

26.   Ibid., p. 273. "Pyramidal mass" is Smith Simpson's vivid phrase. See his *Anatomy of the State Department* (Boston: Houghton Mifflin, 1967).

27.   Robert C. Wood, *1400 Governments* (Cambridge, Mass.: Harvard University Press, 1961), pp. 44. Reviewing the operations of Port Authority of New York, he cites its unwillingness to coordinate its efforts with the region's deficit-ridden commuter railroads, much less assume their operation. Wood concludes: "The outlook is for piece-meal development of physical facilities with no simultaneous consideration of the consequences of highway construction on other modes of transit."

28.   Walter Shapiro, "The Intractables," *The Washington Monthly* 8, no. 3, (May 1976) p. 18.

29.   See James A. Riedel, "Citizen Participation: Myths and Realities," *Public Administration Review* 33, no. 3 (May/June 1972), pp. 211 - 219.

30.   See "Making Mass Transit Work," *Business Week*, 16 February 1974, pp. 74 - 84.

31.   J. R. Daughen and Peter Binzen, *The Wreck of the Penn Central* (Boston: Little, Brown, 1971).

9

AFTERWORD

The central premise of this work is that there are important gains to be made in solving or alleviating problems of urban Americans by devising, adapting, and plagiarizing programs. I suggest that we can do a lot better than we have in the past, and that there is not only a role for government leadership, but an urgent need for it, specifically for federal intervention.

When the "sick sixties" were still the "soaring sixties," these observations would have seemed the most banal of commonplaces. But by the mid-1970s a profound change had taken place in American perceptions of the cities and of activist government. Unlike candidates in previous postwar presidential campaigns, neither of the 1976 candiates was issuing clarion calls to rebuild the slums, wipe out poverty, and create an urban environment better than any foreign model. Instead, the cities were apparently among the tertiary issues; the campaigns focused on claims and allegations of trust and mistrust, lying and truth telling, the sins of big government, and other issues with little direct relevance to cities.

In some respects this froth did have some bearing on the future of the cities. That is, it exploited and exacerbated a widely held suspicion that politicians are chronic liars and sometime thieves, and that government bureaucrats are arrogant bumblers whose misguided efforts make everything they touch worse—and at great expense. Insofar as there was a view of the cities in this campaign, it was as a kind of domestic Vietnam, a sinkhole capable of absorbing infinite amounts of money without discernible improvement, each new investment yielding a fresh dividend of loud-mouthed ingrates and congenital whiners.

It can be argued that the 1970s is a decade of exhaustion. The 1976 campaign echoed the familiar ambivalent demand for a blend of assertive leadership with a maximum of "leave us alone" privatism, reflecting the confusion and disillusionment that surfaces whenever government comes to be regarded with contempt and suspicion.

The obvious question that comes to mind is, why the fundamental change in attitudes from the optimism of the 1960s to the querulous pessimism of the 1970s? It would be tempting to blame it all on the gap between low levels of funding and inflated rhetoric—to say that the war on poverty was financed like a skirmish because the hot war in Vietnam siphoned away the necessary resources. Similarly, a connection can be drawn between lingering bigotry and urban neglect. As Carl Holman, president of the Urban Coalition, sees it, cities are neglected

because in the sixties, when there were the riots, cities became a metaphor
for blacks. . . . Some urban experts suggest that the blacks who were
salvageable were swept up and out into the suburbs—into decent jobs, and
all that. And they were acceptable, because they do not frighten people with
their differentness. So the ones who are left behind are locked in a life style
that the rest of America finds repugnant, and they are considered un-
salvageable, you see, and it is considered a waste to spend time and money
on them and worry about them. As the cities of the Northeast have become
more and more the preserves of blacks and Latinos, they have come to be
seen as expendable.[1]

In one of his more memorable epigrams, Oscar Wilde posed the two
tragedies in life: (1) not getting what you want, and (2) getting what you
want. Surely one of the prime reasons for the sour suspicions of government of the mid-1970s is that the liberal critics of the 1940s and 1950s
had their wishes come true in the 1960s. The fairy godfather was Lyn-
don Johnson. After decades of exasperated carping at the blindness and
callousness of highway agencies and manpower agencies and public
school systems and housing agencies and mortgage bankers, they had
their chance. Along came The Great Society with poverty programs,
model cities, etc.

The results were disappointing, demonstrating yet one more time
that armchair philosophizing and criticism is easier than accomplish-
ment. And this was not simply a matter of asking for a bit more to
finish a job well begun, like a highway that costs a million dollars per
mile halted halfway short of its goal for want of funds. The social efforts of the sixties were mostly people programs, huge experiments
designed to give some measure of control over their destinties to the
poor and to restructure and humanize urban governments that had displayed a comfortable tolerance for the miseries of slum people. Federal
leadership was weak and fragmented, the thinking was confused, the
state of the art primitive (despite all the confident claims), and the people who were to be helped proved more complicated and their problems
more obdurate than was thought possible.

As has been suggested in this book, the process of disenchantment
was much assisted by a growing band of righteous academic
Savonarolas who picked out and picked off vulnerable government
programs with as much enthusiasm as earlier generations of intellectuals had shown in exposing the evils of big business. One consequence
of this concerted barrage was to set in concrete the notion that govern-

ment is by definition foolish and incompetent. In its ultimate form, this attitude was crystallized by the Ronald Reagan campaign: "Government doesn't solve problems; government is the problem." And with softer variations of this line, other 1976 candidates—all of whom had extensive government experience—were busy running against a government of faceless, inept bureaucrats who—in President Ford's elegant campaign phrase—"couldn't produce a six-pack of beer for under $50."

What does all this betoken for the cities? In the first place, the mood is cyclical. We have passed this way before only to discover, again and again, that cities and their problems simply cannot do without government intervention. Furthermore, the winning Democratic presidential candidate and the congressional Democrats have not run up the white flag; on the 1977 agenda are comprehensive health insurance and a full employment bill (regrettably geared to prevailing wages rather than to unemployment compensation levels, as recommended in this volume). There is reason to suppose that expensive, incomplete delivery of health care and on-and-off joblessness are among the genuine problems that the Democratic majority in Congress (and the author and the voting public) would like to see alleviated; such alleviation would also be of enormous help to the cities.

This work is in fact based on the fundamental assumption that government has a duty to confront such problems, and moreover that it can do a creditable job when it takes up such unfinished business. True, this volume calls for humility: make modest promises but keep them. As one sage political observer recommended to a big city mayor, "Start by cleaning the streets." In contrast to the traditional meaningless political IOU's for reducing neighborhood crime rates and upgrading the public schools, this was a promise any mayor should be able to keep. (But he didn't.)

Experience suggests that we, like other nations, can provide comprehensive health care and employment programs with reasonable efficiency. But scale is important; if there is any lesson we should have learned from the sixties, it is the absolutely vital role of innumerable small, successful actions as opposed to the grand-scale, overnight reform.

An analogy can be drawn between household upkeep and guerilla warfare—both entail continuous, minor battles with traps for the unwary. In the absence of daily attention and maintenance, dwellings quickly deteriorate, and decaying structures can spread and multiply into slums and dying neighborhoods. Blight is a consequence of enervation, a quality not traditional in the United States. Tocqueville was struck by the special character of American enterprise in the early nineteenth century, when this nation was always building and rebuilding, its restless energies unleashed by local initiatives on innumerable small undertakings. He commented that these were not always well done or always completed, but they were indicative of vitality and they provided a broad base of practical experience for the electorate. It was this kind of confidence, founded on personal, local achievement, that gave rise to the uniquely American belief that the nation's only unsolved problems were those to which it had not yet turned its attention. A far cry, this buoyant attitude, from the cautionary mood of the 1970s—"Don't fiddle with it, you'll only make it worse."

People in urban areas can be told that they never had it so good, or that we overlook contented communities because we give too much attention to the troubled big cities where only 20 percent of our population live, as if the smaller Newarks, Camdens, Hamtramcks, and El Pasos were some sort of folksy Edens. And we are told that crime and poverty are inescapable miseries, the fruits of bad parents who raise malnourished, sometimes imbecilic, problem-prone children. We are informed that we simply have to learn to accept the fact that people do abuse their bodies with poor food, too much alcohol and drugs, and too little exercise. True enough—this book has identified limits for intervention, reflecting the author's conviction that promises to cure many social afflictions are futile, naive, and hypocritical. But realism is no counsel of despair. Reconstructing the broken slum family is beyond our powers, but this does not imply a supine acceptance of existing patterns and trends. Least of all does it justify the almost gleeful anticipation of an urban America which writes off older cities as irredeemable, obsolescent, and ungovernable morasses of vice.

Where do we go from here? We do not need to be hopelessly utopian. There are models of attractive housing, public transportation, community building, and environmental quality all available right now for copying and adaptation. Equally important, there are good working models for social programs. In a time when birth rates are down and population is stabilizing, we should do a better job of cherishing our people with improved medical attention and good day care. And is there any valid reason for any modern nation to permit the massive waste of manpower resources and low morale inherent in chronic large-scale unemployment?

With a modicum of common sense we need not face the awful dilemma

of the nineteenth-century patient forced to choose between two an-
tithetic schools of medical ignorance: the homeopath with his minuscule
doses which permitted the patient to die of his disease, and the allopath,
the traditional physician, who bled and injected mercury, killing the
patient with his drastic cures. If the 1960s were a time for social allo-
paths (for example, urban renewal) the 1970s so far seem to be reserved
for political homeopathy—social tokenism and uplifting rhetoric.

There are times, in cities as in medicine, when a placebo rather than
massive, expensive treatment is indicated. Patients frequently recover
on their own with no more than benign confident reassurance. So indeed
is the terrible spectre of an overpopulated America quickly fading, no
thanks to national policy, but to a myriad of individual decisions to use
the new contraceptive technology and the available low-cost abortions.

But contrary to some conservative claims, not all problems disappear by themselves if only we watch them long enough and do not in-
terfere with private initiative. From any reasonable standpoint
America's urban areas are much, much uglier than they have any right
to be, largely because many private businesses with no taste were permitted to make critical decisions. But there is indeed a cautionary
lesson from the sixties. To return to a medical analogy, there is almost a
triage moral in the costly frustrating efforts to focus on multiproblem
people in hardcore slums. (Triage is the medical practice of establishing
emergency room priorities—treating patients with a good chance to
recover, and pacifying but not treating hopeless cases.) Such efforts fly
in the face of deep-rooted social and economic trends rather than focusing on manageable objectives—conserving stable people in stable
neighborhoods and exploiting opportunities for growth.

This is not a prescription for bidding a fond farewell to the central
city slums, to the welfare mother with six children—two delinquent and
one pregnant—who lives without hope and without prospects in any of a
hundred cities. It does recognize that no political leader is going to
achieve office or stay in office by waving the flag for any of the dependent poor, with the possible exception of the senior citizen. Further, as
we have learned to our sorrow, even in wealthy America funds are not
limitless. It is all very well to point to Vietnam—$150 billion down the
drain—but the practicing politician is not likely to see much utility in
substituting one rathole for another.

One answer to the reformer's dilemma is to make progress by
minimizing costs and maximizing benefits. Neighborhood conservation
is the urban equivalent of preventive medicine. Another answer is di-

recting and channeling investment and expenditures *which would be made in any event* into newer and more desirable forms—an intelligent, attractive method of making reform relatively painless. In the course of the coming decades tens of billions of dollars will be spent for new housing, new highways, new sewers, and new water facilities. This book suggests some of the ways in which these funds can be expended with prudence and lasting benefit.

In a vast and diversified nation it makes a good deal of sense to encourage individual, local, and state initiatives. Many urban problems are complicated and locally particularized. No one pot is big enough to cook the great whale. That task requires many small pots, many sharp knives and much effort. Some of our troubles come from our failure to find a large enough cooking vessel through federal programs; others come from throwing up our hands in awe at the size of the monster, concluding that nothing can be done.

Holman's comments on the neglect of the cities in the mid-1970s offer an essential key for design of effective urban programs: cities have come to be viewed as places where only a fraction of Americans live and where lavish expenditures will yield meager results from ungrateful people. In short, core city programs, if they are labelled as such, are no longer saleable. What is the answer? By implication if not design, the 1976 Democratic campaigners have spelled it out in a fashion similar to this book: *devise broad programs, attractive and applicable on a nationwide basis (especially in manpower and health), but also critically important in the troubled cities.* The viable approach then is *not* to adopt the urban equivalent of affirmative action on behalf of the cities. It lies instead in a program package applicable to cities, to distressed rural and mining areas, to depressed outlying factory communities—and to the urbanized suburbs.

None of this is meant to suggest that there should be no federal role in coping with local problems like crime, land use, and municipal government. There is ample room for fiscal help in welfare and other areas to ensure that the cities will not go broke. And federal leadership and monitoring is vital to stimulate laggards and mediocrities and rein in spendthrifts.

This is no small agenda. And just over the horizon there may be tougher choices—income redistribution, national economic planning, controls over land use and natural resources, new immigration policies. But sufficient unto the day. There is much to be done. And we can do it, for this is a nation capable of improving on any useful idea developed anywhere else, and as capable of pioneering in new social and land use programs, when it has to, as it has been in science, technology, and business.

Notes

1. *The New Yorker*, 24 May 1976, p. 115.

INDEX